EMBRACING THE CALM...

It can take as little as a few seconds a day—
and it can change your life. By mastering
the simple breathing and relaxation techniques
outlined here, you can learn to eliminate
stress before it gains control of you—during
an argument with your spouse, when you're
stuck in traffic, or before an important
presentation. This proven drug-free approach
combines biofeedback and stress-reduction
techniques with physical exercise, diet, and
nutrition to alleviate the crippling, sometimes
killing effects of stress. Illustrated with case
studies of patients who tell how they conquered
unhealthy stress, this is your comprehensive
guide to a healthier, happier, more relaxed
life.

**"STRAIGHTFORWARD, RATIONAL,
ACCESSIBLE."** —*Publishers Weekly*

KEITH SEDLACEK, M.D., is Medical
Director of the Stress Regulation Institute in
New York. He has served as a member of the
executive board of the Biofeedback Society
of America.

THE SEDLACEK TECHNIQUE

Finding the Calm Within You

Keith Sedlacek, M.D.

A SIGNET BOOK

NEW AMERICAN LIBRARY

A DIVISION OF PENGUIN BOOKS USA INC.

SIGNET TRADEMARK REG. U.S. PAT. OFF. AND FOREIGN COUNTRIES
REGISTERED TRADEMARK—MARCA REGISTRADA
HECHO EN DRESDEN, TN, U.S.A.

SIGNET, SIGNET CLASSIC, MENTOR, ONYX, PLUME, MERIDIAN
and NAL BOOKS are published by New American Library, a division of
Penguin Books USA Inc., 1633 Broadway, New York, New York 10019

First Signet Printing, March, 1990

1 2 3 4 5 6 7 8 9

PRINTED IN THE UNITED STATES OF AMERICA

For my parents, John and Vivian,
whose strength, integrity, attention,
and love have always supported
my work and well-being.

To my wife, Diane, whose intelligence,
love, and support have made life
and this book better.

CONTENTS

ACKNOWLEDGMENTS

I would like to acknowledge my parents, John and Vivian Sedlacek, for their help, encouragement, and support throughout my life. My wife, Diane, and my siblings Thomas, Jarold, and Mona have contributed greatly to my health and well-being. We all have discussed many of these stress topics throughout our family life.

I would also like to acknowledge and thank many of my teachers and professors. At Harvard College, Eric Erickson and Harry Reisman, and at Columbia University College of Physicians and Surgeons, Lawrence Kolb, Robert Michels, and Willard Gaylin were my mentors in psychiatry. At St. Luke's-Roosevelt Hospital Center, John Cotton, Paul Nassar, Arnold Rothstein, John Rosenberger, Cyrus Ayromlooi, Alex Caemmerer, and Stan Heller have been helpful colleagues and friends.

In terms of biofeedback, Charles Stroebel was one of my most important teachers who enabled me to start working in the biofeedback field with excellent protocols. He told me, "Always do the best you can."

Nationally, outstanding people like Neal Miller, Elmer Green, Mark S. Schwartz, Robert Freedman, Pat Norris, Ed Blanchard, Bernard Engel, John Basmajian, Wes Sime, Tom Budzynski, Johann Stoyva, Bob Kall, Karen Naifch, Steve Locke, Sonia Ancoli-Israel, David Jacobs, George Fuller von Bozzay, Francine Butler, Melvyn Werbach, and many others have contributed as friends and colleagues toward understanding the effects of stress on our health.

Grateful acknowledgment is made for permission to print the following material: "1983 Metropolitan Height and Weight Tables" from the Metropolitan Life Insurance Company; a portion of Eat Well, Be Well seafood delight recipes from the *Eat Well, Be Well Cookbook*, Metropolitan Life, Health and Safety Education Division,

New York; a portion of the *Biofeedback—A Practitioner's Guide*, Chapter 9, pages 192, 194–195, by Mark S. Schwartz and Associates, by permission of Guilford Press, copyright Guilford Press, 1987; a portion of "Journal of Psychosomatics Research," vol. 11, pages 213–218, T.H. Holmes and R.H. Rahe, "The Social Readjustment Rating Scale," copyright 1967, Pergamon Press, Ltd.

INTRODUCTION

My main purpose in writing this book is to provide you with the tools to retrain your nervous system so that stress is reduced in your everyday life.

The Sedlacek Technique will teach you how to produce the same nervous- and cardiovascular-system responses produced by making love, exercising, acupuncture, taking aspirin and morphine, and electrical stimulation for pain relief. However, you will be able to produce the response voluntarily, on your own, without the need for drugs, acupuncture needles, or electrical stimulation. You'll learn techniques so easy even monkeys have mastered them. These techniques include biofeedback and stress management.

Since medical school I have been studying the interactions of the mind and the body. My medical training was in psychiatry. In 1976 I was appointed Investigator in Biofeedback and Stress-Related Disorders in the psychiatry department at St. Luke's Hospital in New York. There I set up a biofeedback service to treat stroke, headache, and muscle disorders. Since then I have developed a program called the Sedlacek Technique for treating additional disorders such as headache, high blood pressure, colitis, angina, tension (muscle contraction causing pain), and anxiety.

Over the last 15 years I have condensed my treatments into four Positive Stress Response (PSR) exercises. As the name PSR suggests, these exercises train people to have a positive rather than a negative response to stress. They are described in Chapters Three, Five, Seven, and Ten. In addition to these exercises, my technique includes physical exercise, plus diet and nutrition. Taken together, these strategies will help your mind and body work together in a healthier fashion.

Rather than having the prehistoric "animal" parts of your brain and nervous system controlling you, you'll learn how to control them. Your fight-or-flight emergency-response system developed as part of the collection of prehistoric reactions stored in the "dinosaur" part of your brain (animal brain). With PSR you'll learn how to tame the beasts in your brain and start them helping you instead of hindering you. These techniques will enable you to improve your cardiovascular functioning and help you cope in a generally healthier, less stressful way in both social interactions and alone. If you are suffering from pain, whether it is chronic back pain, arthritis or migraine pain, or the sharp, shooting pains of a stubbed toe, a burned finger, or tight-fitting shoes, you'll be better able to cope with it.

With practice, PSR will help you to be more in command of, and in touch with, your body and mind than ever before. The PSR techniques start with simple exercises; then you work up to even simpler, shorter, and easier ones as your mind-body self-regulatory skills develop. There are 10- and 20-minute techniques for when you have the time. There are techniques that last just a few seconds. You can use them when you are stopped at a traffic light or preparing to answer the telephone after an upsetting argument with your mate. Chapter One has a short breathing exercise that is expanded upon in the first PSR exercise in Chapter Three. This breathing exercise, as well as the four basic PSR exercises, is also available on a McGraw-Hill audiocassette.

My staff and I use these exercises with patients and clients at the Stress Regulation Institute for dealing with a wide range of stress-related problems. Our patients and clients have come from corporations, hospitals, schools and colleges, and many different occupations.

You will meet some of these patients in the brief cases that open each chapter. I have changed their names and certain details to protect their privacy. Their real-life stories tell how they have overcome stress-related illnesses and disabilities.

The Sedlacek Technique can be added on to any medical treatment you are receiving. This book is not a replacement for consulting a doctor or continuing your medical treatment. Just like beginning physical exercise, for example, the accepted procedure should be followed: Consult your doctor before beginning a program.

I think you will find that the stress management techniques and skills described in this book will help you tap the unused potential of your mind and body and produce a healthier, happier you.

CHAPTER ONE

YOUR ANIMAL BRAIN AND STRESS*

Self-control may be developed in precisely the same manner as we tone up a weak muscle. By a little exercise each day.
—*W.G. Jordan*

Susan's Ski Trip

Exhilarated by the perfect schussing weather, Susan and seven of her friends had been warming up for an hour by skiing on the easier slopes. Laughing and chatting happily, they barely noticed the avalanche hazard warning signs that had just been posted following the fresh 8-inch snowfall. One by one they waited for each other as the chairlift left them at the mountaintop. The wait was easy, though, since they could take their time appreciating the view of the valley thousands of feet below them. When everyone was ready, they started down the steep expert trail. Almost before they knew it, the skiers had reached the bottom of the upper slope. They regrouped and together were starting down the second half of their run when sharp, crackling sounds suddenly broke the cold mountain silence. Startled, a few of them stopped, eyed each other, and looked around in alarm. "Quick! Let's get out of here," someone shouted.

In a moment the rushing avalanche reached them, spinning them over and over, burying them in a heavy

---

*This chapter was jointly written by Keith Sedlacek, M.D., and Robert Kall, M.ED.

1

white-gray mass. Then, as quickly as it had started, it stopped. Everything was silent.

Susan opened her eyes and began digging. Her heart was racing. She wondered about the condition of her friends. Would a ski patrol find them?

Already she began to feel cold under the deep snow. Unwanted thoughts and memories of tales told around the ski lodge fireplace came to her. People trapped by avalanches usually suffered exposure and severe frostbite of the hands and feet. Her face was beginning to feel icy cold. In the dim light filtering through the snow, she could see the outlines of her hands. She looked at them grimly and wondered, How long will it be before they lose their feeling and become numb and blue?

Blue! She pulled her head back and drew in a sharp breath as she looked at her hands, picturing them blue with cold. She had often seen her hands blue and had felt pain in them when she'd skied last year. Finally, she'd been forced to give up skiing for the season because invariably, after only a short time on the slopes, the pain from her cold, blue hands would become unbearable. Her physician had told her she was suffering from Raynaud's disease, which meant that if she became upset or exposed to the cold, her hands would turn blue, white, and sometimes red. Luckily, her doctor had given her hand-warming training to control her blood vessels so that she could increase the blood circulation to her hands and get healthy color into them whenever she wished.

At least I can keep my hands and feet warm, she thought, heartened, and maybe I can avoid frostbite. She closed her eyes and began to use the Positive Stress Response (PSR) strategies she'd learned with biofeedback to let blood flow into her hands and feet. Soon she felt warmth in her gloves and a warm tingling in the toes of her ski boots. Her mood lifted, and she shouted confidently into the snowbank, "Hold on, everybody. We can all make it." She heard muffled cries and shouts in reply.

Susan's optimistic self-reassurances proved accurate. About three hours later, the rescue team reached the avalanche site where the friends were buried. Within an hour the eight friends were at the ski resort's small emergency medical facility. They all suffered from exposure, and seven of them suffered from frostbite.

Susan was sitting in a chair listening to a young doctor. The physician was surprised that she alone had incurred no frostbite injuries and was suffering the least from exposure. He was very interested to hear Susan explain about learning "hand warming" for Raynaud's disease and how she'd increased the blood flow to her hands and feet while awaiting rescue.

"So you can warm your extremities. That skill must have protected your fingers! What was the worst part of being buried?" he asked. Now that the ordeal was over, she remembered for the first time what her plans for the day had been. She laughed and answered, "The worst part was that I had plans to meet my boyfriend for lunch and I missed the date."

The Positive Stress Response

Susan's case is a good example of how people learn to use Positive Stress Response (PSR) to function better during periods of pleasure and pain, stress and relaxation.

Self-control techniques and strategies have advanced considerably in the last decade. For thousands of years, Indian yoga practitioners and mystics have practiced self-regulation. But their approach takes years of full-time, devoted training to achieve mastery. We've built our approach both upon those age-old techniques and upon brand new discoveries that U.S. researchers serendipitously uncovered while doing more conventional research.

In 1966 at the Menninger Clinic in Topeka, Kansas, Elmer Green, Ph.D., and his colleagues were monitoring a patient by using a polygraph, recording her muscle tension, brain waves, finger temperature, and other measures of psychophysiological activity. All of a sudden they noticed that her finger temperature went up. "What happened there?" Dr. Green questioned.

"That's when my migraine headache went away," she replied. "How did you know that?"

What had happened was a surprise to both of them. But since then, Dr. Green's team and other researchers have found that it is easy to learn how to control peripheral blood flow. Some people learn in just two or three hours. It used to take a yogi years to learn what the average person can do with just a few days or weeks of training. Swami Rama, for example, was tested at the Menninger Clinic. They found he could cause two points just a trifle more than an inch apart on his hand to differ in temperature by more than 10 degrees F. Ed Taub, Ph.D., one of the first thermal biofeedback researchers, showed that people could do even more specific "mental gymnastics" to promote blood-flow control with just a few weeks of training.

Since the "early days" of the 1970s, peripheral blood-flow control techniques have been improved and simplified even more. A common misconception is that biofeedback requires the use of complicated, expensive electronic equipment. That's true for some problems, but you can learn peripheral-vascular blood-flow control without any feedback at all. Unfortunately, very few people realize this because blood-flow control training is almost always grouped together with the more complicated kinds of biofeedback that do require special expensive equipment.

Feedback does help, of course, but equipment does not have to be expensive. At the Menninger Clinic, they now use rather *nonexotic* thermometers that cost about 50 cents each. They're ordinary red-dyed alcohol in glass thermometers—the kind you can pick up at any corner grocery or drugstore. The Appendix also lists manufacturers that sell inexpensive thermometers or thermometers for over $1000 each; it even lists a supplier of a talking thermometer. In most cases you'll do just as well with the one you probably already have at home hanging on a wall or stowed away in a drawer somewhere.

Most of the thousands of people already trained in the new self-control techniques learned them to relieve a wide range of problems, including pain, headaches, stress-related disorders, or sexual dysfunction. If they'd learned self-control strategies in the first place, a majority of them would never have encountered such problems, or they would have had much milder symptoms.

The people who suffer from body breakdown disorders

like arthritis, atherosclerosis, and postsurgical chronic pain will find that the information in this book provides them with considerable relief. The results are sometimes astounding. Cripples with vascular problems in their legs can walk again. Doped-up hypertension and chronic-pain patients can frequently stop taking medications they've taken for years. Migrainers who have had daily or thrice-weekly headaches become headache-free and can stay that way (though the techniques are so new that even the oldest case dates only from about 20 years ago). Arthritics can halve their pain and significantly increase their joint strength and flexibility. Their sedimentation rate, a blood test used to measure the severity of rheumatoid arthritis, is lowered considerably (cut in half in one study). Chronic headaches, neck and shoulder spasms, and low back pain can be eased or stopped.

Even if you don't have any of the above-mentioned pains or problems with anxiety and stress, even if you are a high-flying winner, seemingly doing everything right in your life, getting high on success, you can benefit from this chapter perhaps even more than others. You have more to lose, and your success could very well be due in part to Type A, heart-attack-prone, behavior.

At one point, most of the ailing people described in the paragraphs above were healthy. All types of stress, including accidents, illness, life's pressures, living life to extremes, and normal aging processes, take their toll. We want to teach you how to take greater responsibility for your body's *homeostasis*. A word rarely recognized outside of medicine and family therapy, homeostasis (root: *homeo*—same, *stasis*—state) refers to the body's capacity to maintain a healthy balance among all its systems—a steady, healthy biological state. Family therapists use the term to describe the balance that exists in family systems. The body's homeostatic mechanisms are what keep the body working when it is stressed by injury, illness, or emotional changes. Up until the last dozen years, Western physicians believed that homeostasis was an automatic, involuntary process. We now know that *you* can take an important role in improving the functioning of your homeostatic behavior by using the full capacities of your brain.

The "Animal Brain"

We might almost say that the reason all the skiers but Susan suffered from frostbite was that they had a dinosaur stomping on their fingers and other frostbitten parts. "What?" you could reply. "It was an avalanche and the cold, not a dinosaur, that caused their frostbite."

But the real cause was the dinosaur brain inside of them, reacting to the avalanche. Everyone has a dinosaur in their nervous system. Our brain is built in layers, with higher layers representing higher points on the evolutionary scale.

When the blood vessels in Susan's hands started to narrow and squeeze shut, leaving her hands cold and blue, the lower part of her nervous system at the dinosaur, or reptilian, level was reacting to the danger she was experiencing in the way it knew how to react. It was reacting normally for the emergency situation she was in.

Now, reptiles can be very stupid. The only way they handle danger is with fight or flight. That's true of some humans too, even though their repertoire of responses is usually far greater. But all humans still have the fight-or-flight response wired into their nervous systems. The primitive animal brain connects directly and quickly to start this fight or flight response.

When your human emergency response system is activated, your heart speeds up, blood pressure increases, adrenaline levels go up, and blood is shunted away from the nonessential areas—like the extremities—and toward more essential areas like the brain, the central organs, and the muscles, to maximize fight-or-flight ability. Until very recently, this was believed to be a totally involuntary response. Many doctors still have not heard of the use of PSR training to voluntarily warm the limbs to reduce the effects of these fight-or-flight overresponses.

Even though you've got a bigger and better brain and more thinking power now, you've still got that old prehistoric brain underneath the smart, intellectual brain on top of your nervous system. It lumbers through your body like a dinosaur, upsetting the delicate balance that keeps you running at the finely tuned level you are accustomed to. It is stress, equally powerful in either positive or negative form, which causes your old brain to react, unless you've developed some other strategies to control or regulate it.

The dinosaur has good intentions. If you were in an accident, injured or unconscious, it would respond by making sure that the most important organs for keeping you alive would get blood first. It would clamp down on the vessels bringing blood to your hands and feet—you could do without them in a pinch—and keep the blood moving faster to the vital organs (heart, lungs, and brain).

What this all means is that your nervous system has been wired to react to danger with a collection of responses that assume that you cannot think when you are injured and unconscious. Yes, you need the response. But all too often the problem arises that you are awake and aware of what is going on, yet the antiquated dinosaur part of your nervous system overreacts. The intelligent, upper level of your nervous system that would normally assess and weigh the various components of a situation for their threat to you, determining whether you were in danger, is trampled by the untamed, emergency response. If either our upper or lower nervous system catches even a sniff of a threat, it can let loose the dinosaur by increasing the activation level of the whole nervous system, putting it on a "condition-red-alert" status. Using the specific physical and mental exercises of the Positive Stress Response, you can turn off the red alert and tame your dinosaur. You can then use your higher mental capacities in harmony with your dinosaur's protective strength and alertness.

You wouldn't need to tame your dinosaur if it only came out for avalanches and the like. Even though it could cost you a few frostbitten fingers, you would probably be better off having the beast around in a more restricted way rather than getting rid of it altogether. Our prehistoric friend is quite sociable and frequently with us. It peers over our shoulders like a thoroughly neurotic, nervous backseat driver, overreacting, heating things up whenever it perceives us being the least bit threatened. Unfortunately, it is so simpleminded that when it feels things getting hotter (even though its own actions made it so), it gets even more frightened and fries our nervous systems even more. All you have to do is think about something dangerous and your dinosaur will stupidly overreact, believing that it is saving you.

All it takes is the thought—of being in a car accident, losing someone important to you, or talking in front of a group—and your pulse will start to race, your palms will feel sweaty, and you may even faint. Your dinosaur stirs within.

The extreme signs of the primitive response are easily noticed. At the less obvious level, you may feel anxious, nervous, tense, upset, or have trouble sleeping. Any of your organ functions also may be affected via the "danger response," and without your being consciously aware that your own mind or nervous system is reacting.

So although you may hardly realize it, any part of your nervous system may be overactivated. This can cause problems in the head (migraine and tension headache, sinus problems, pain in the jaw or gums), chest, heart, lungs, and bowels, including heart attacks, arrhythmias (irregular heartbeat), asthma, ulcers, colitis, diarrhea, and constipation, or your limbs may be cool or exceedingly cold (Raynaud's disease, or so-called poor circulation).

That sneaky, half-turned-on emergency reaction can create muscle pain or spasm, anxiety, nervousness, and overreactions in all the organs—heart, lungs, bowels, sexual organs, skin—as well as in the immune system and the arteries. Even the pain from medical problems with clear-cut causes, like back injuries and rheumatoid arthritis, can be made worse when the nervous system is overexcited by the primitive part of the brain. This overreaction is like turning up the volume of a stereo. When you are dealing with pain, louder means more painful.

Fortunately, your involuntary nervous system is not involuntary. You can learn how to control your dinosaur. You can train it and begin to positively tap its energy and passion.

It's easy to learn how to sense your dinosaur's first stirrings and bring them under control before they get out of hand. We'll teach you how to use strategies that improve the connections between the different parts of your brain and the other systems in your body.

Our stress-emergency response system can sneak up on us, setting us up, so that only a slight increase in the environmental stress we are experiencing can set off a much worse reaction (proportionately). This is undesirable. A quick way to recognize this is to put your finger on a regular thermometer so you will get an approximation of your actual skin temperature. If your finger temperature is low, below 86 or 87 degrees, then you know your nervous system is getting overexcited and is reducing the blood flow to the fingers and probably to the other extremities. The dinosaur is itchy and rubbing its hide on your emergency reaction buttons.

If your finger temperature is low, then it is probably worthwhile to take the half minute or minute it will require to quiet down your dinosaur by using blood-flow control. You can turn your nervous system's response pattern around and set yourself in a more relaxed direction by detaching yourself momentarily, going inward, and quieting yourself down. Then you can get things rolling on the right track again, rather than letting that old dinosaur start lumbering along, pushing things into its goofy old anxiety-stress-body-tension momentum rut.

Cold Hands—A Sign of Arousal

The vessels in the skin of the hands and feet act as a kind of reservoir for storing blood. When the sympathetic nervous system is activated under stressful conditions, the vessels squeeze down, making the extra blood available to the organs and the skeletal muscles—the muscles we use to move ourselves, to change body position, to fight, or to escape from danger. If you were running from a hungry saber-toothed tiger, or if you were chasing your dinner prey through the primeval forest, the extra blood made available to your organs and muscles would be an obvious asset.

But in today's world such a response is maladaptive. Your breathing changes from slow, deep, relaxed stomach breathing, called *diaphragmatic breathing,* to short, shallow chest and shoulder breathing, called *thoracic breathing*. The bottoms of your lungs don't fill with air. The replacement of the blood's carbon dioxide with oxygen is less efficient. Less blood gets oxygenated with each breath. The heart has to pump faster to get the same amount of oxygen to the cells of your body.

In addition to reacting to the fight-or-flight situations, the peripheral vascular system also acts as a cooling system for your body, like the radiator in a car. If your body gets too hot, blood, heated at the core, is sent to the skin—the surface of the extremities—to allow heat to be dispersed into the cooler air around the body. The warmer you are, the more wide open your peripheral vasculature will be. Conversely, when you are cold or when it is cold outside, the peripheral vasculature closes down, preventing excess surface heat loss. The cold acts as a stressor on the system. On top of that, other stressors can exaggerate the response to cold, even to air-conditioning.

Summing up, the emergency response tenses the peripheral blood vessel muscles in order to supply more blood to the tensing skeletal muscles and essential organs. Breathing changes from deep diaphragmatic breathing to shallow thoracic breathing. The shoulder, chest, and neck muscles get tense from this breathing pattern. Digestive tract muscle rhythms are disrupted. Heart rate and blood pressure climb.

The common factor is muscle. Even the heart, which begins to race when the dinosaur response goads it on, is one big muscle system. At a higher level, all of these body systems are monitored by the brain. Nerves in the skeletal muscles send messages through the spinal cord to the brain, telling it that things are tense down there. To the brain, this means that the muscles need more energy, more oxygen, more help with getting rid of waste compounds used up in the burning of energy—that is, the muscles need more blood. To fulfill that need, the brain sends a message out to the peripheral vasculature, ordering it to tighten down, making more blood rapidly available to the muscles. This is part of the fight-or-flight response reaction. It can be a small reaction, or it may continue to increase.

Once the brain is activated, it's a circular pattern. Any body activity characteristic of an increase in the level of sympathetic nervous system arousal—faster heart rate, higher blood pressure, tensed muscles, faster breathing, cold hands—will start the dinosaur part of your brain preparing for danger. Even thinking dangerous or stressful thoughts can set it off.

The way out is to change a link in the circle. You have voluntary control over your muscles. You can relax them. Though your respiratory system works fine while you are asleep—that is, when you are not paying attention to it—you can learn to shift voluntarily from fast, shallow thoracic to slow, paced diaphragmatic breathing. This is why the first brief breathing exercise and the first PSR exercise are so helpful. With them you can begin to learn to relax the muscles in your peripheral vasculature and warm your hands voluntarily.

When you do any of these behaviors, the higher brain sends a different message: that the lungs, the muscles, or the peripheral vasculature can be calm and quiet, safe, without the need for emergency succor. It's kind of like voice voting. Whoever shouts the loudest wins. Naturally, if you can relax your muscles, breathe slowly and diaphragmatically, and warm your hands, you'll win the vote, convincing your brain that things are relaxed and quiet. Then the brain will actually help. That doesn't mean you have to go to sleep, either.

For instance, when you make love, you're excited. Your heart races and certain muscles are quite active. But your hands are warm. You shouldn't feel uncomfortable. You should feel good. If you don't, it may be that you have overreacted and become generally emergency-aroused. Once you've got control of your physiological voting blocs, you can determine how much, when, and the way you get aroused or excited. A little adrenaline can make an ordinary experience fantastic, just as a pinch of pepper can season a meal to perfection. But drop a whole shaker of pepper on your plate or pump too much adrenaline into a situation and the result can be unpleasantly hot. The trick is to stay in control of the systems that affect you.

The PSR doesn't take hard work—only practice, like physical exercise. It is very simple. It is a passive process of letting go. Some people find this extremely difficult and even frightening. Although actually you are increasing your self-control, it can feel at first that you are relinquishing it. If you keep your mind focused and busy, at a higher level of activation, then you can feel in control. Letting go of muscle tension and excess sympathetic activity is accomplished by discipline and practice. The initial fear comes from inexperience and lack of information.

When you are getting started there are some sensations of deep relaxation that can scare you if you don't understand them. You may experience some of them in your first and second PSR exercises in Chapters Three and Five. They may include dream-like imagery, not unlike what you've experienced when falling asleep or waking up. At first it can seem so real that you may feel excited or scared, but this is definite evidence that you've quieted your nervous system. These experiences are so close to sleep level that you may experience occasional muscle twitches or short dreams in color or black-and-white. As you relax deeply, your muscles will occasionally discharge excess tension that has built up. It's a good sign when you have those twitches, but since they can sneak up on you, they can be disconcerting.

You may also feel temporary sensations of tingling, pulsing, vibration, heaviness, or floating of your body parts. These are experienced because you are paying much more attention than usual to your internal body processes. These experiences are hardly ever anything to worry about, and they are worth exploring and experimenting with. You can use them as your teachers to gain more insights about your body's and mind's interactions.

Since you already have some experience with breathing and controlling your skeletal muscles, they are a good place to start your self-regulatory program. Try to recall how you learned to control your bowels, to write, to play a sport, or to develop any other physical skill. Or watch a child learning to walk. Keep in mind that it takes time and practice to get the skills right. First we'll start with a short breathing exercise. We'll also suggest a breathing exercise in Chapter Three, followed by a longer specific muscle relaxation exercise in Chapter Five. These two exercises will have you ready for the blood-flow self-regulation exercises in Chapter Seven.

A Short Breathing-Awareness Exercise

Smooth, even, regular breathing sends a relaxed message to the brain. So sit yourself in a comfortable chair or lie on a rug. Take a nice deep breath and let it out slowly and evenly. Let your diaphragm do the work, like a bellows, pulling air into the lungs.

Keep your shoulders and chest relaxed and loose. You don't need to use them to breathe. Tensing and raising them to fill your upper lungs can send warning messages to the brain. The message is translated as preparation for fight or flight. The brain responds by revving up the rest of the body in preparation for the ordeal the tensed-up breathing pattern has falsely warned of.

When you breathe with your diaphragm, your stomach pushes out when you inhale. It is amazing how many people try to inhale and suck in their guts at the same time. It doesn't work. We've seen patients and workshop participants get very frustrated because they were trying to breathe this way. It's easier to master this skill if you put one hand on your stomach. When you inhale, your stomach should move your hand out and when you exhale, push your stomach gently in. You may fight it a few times until you get coordinated, but eventually you'll get it right.

As you take that deep breath, keep your inhalation even. When you start feeling full of air, gradually let the diaphragm relax and let the air out just as evenly. Keep the transitions smooth from inhaling to exhaling to inhaling, not abrupt.

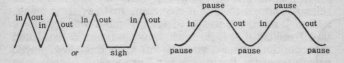

SHARP, ABRUPT TRANSITIONS   SMOOTH, PACED, EVEN TRANSITIONS

Sit quietly, breathing this way for 1 to 2 minutes, while at the same time allowing your muscles to stay relaxed, loose, and limp. Don't work at the breathing. Let it come slowly and easily, smoothly and naturally. Don't push for the deep breaths. Let your breath flow in and out easily. But keep your mind passively focused on it to make sure the respirations don't begin responding to messages impulsively sent by your nervous dinosaur. Even a few minutes of this peaceful breathing will send a calming message to your brain, telling it to tone down increased nervous system activation throughout the rest of your body.

Notice that we have repeatedly used relaxing words, such as "let" and "allow." The PSR training to calm your nervous system begins as a passive process. It consists of deactivating or decreasing the activity levels of unnecessarily active behaviors. There is no hard work, no trying, no extra energy involved. The whole process is relaxing. Even the mental exercises and imagery techniques you'll be learning are designed to distract you and refocus your attention at a more relaxed level.

It is very simple but not always easy to let go. While doing the breathing exercise, you probably found your mind wandering a few times. Most people starting out can't keep their minds focused for even 2 minutes. They start thinking about things they did earlier or things they have to do later in the day. They enter a kind of daydreaming mental state.

Don't worry or get upset if that happens to you. Actually, it's a good sign. It means you freed up your attention long enough to allow some other lurking thought to pop into your awareness. At least temporarily, you quieted part of your mind.

When you realize your mind has wandered, give yourself a mental pat on the back. After all, you had to be relaxed enough to give it free rein. Just say to yourself, "Aha. I relaxed enough to let my mind wander. Now that I realize it, I'll go back to what I was doing," and then continue where you left off with this slow, paced breathing of the Positive Stress Response.

When you relax your muscles or consciously regulate your breathing so that it's diaphragmatic, smooth, and even, you send a powerful quieting message to your brain. Some people can deeply relax their muscles and begin quiet, passive breathing in just a few seconds. Initially, it may take you longer. It's like any other acquired skill, such as piano playing, tennis, or bridge. You get better with practice. Even if you don't practice, these techniques can be helpful. But regular practice will make you more proficient at the skill of relaxation. Stress-prone and hard-driving people have a difficult time allowing themselves 2 minutes, much less 10 or 20 minutes, once or twice a day, to relax. But the investment of that time brings a very worthwhile return, especially when you first begin using these techniques. In tennis or piano playing, after a certain amount of practice, awkward sequences of movement become automatic. You don't have to think through each note of your chord or each step in your serve. The motion flows naturally through you. The same is true of learning a calming breathing pattern, which is the first step to learning PSR. Once you get the response nailed down with practice, you can turn it on much more easily when you need it. By that time, though, you may find you like the indulgent luxury of taking a short relaxation break to ease the hectic pace of your day. Your dividend will come in the form of increased efficiency and effectiveness that will more than make up for the time you've spent practicing this first breathing exercise. Try this slow, paced breathing pattern before you go on to read about the development of the Positive Stress Response in Chapter Two.

CHAPTER TWO

STRESS AND THE POSITIVE STRESS RESPONSE

> The mind, as it was fit, then this most excellent and superior faculty alone, the gods have placed in our power.
>
> —*Epictetus*

Ed and Rose's Boat Trip

It was a beautiful day for sailing. The sky was bright blue, the sun warmed the water, the boat, and the couple. A nice breeze was blowing about 10 to 12 knots, and Ed decided to treat his wife to one of her favorite summer pastimes. Rose liked to be pulled on a rope behind the sailboat where she could bounce gently through the 2-foot waves. This was exciting, and they would take turns being pulled by the sailboat. Ed dropped his wife over the side of the sailboat and gave her the rope. She tied the rope around her waist, and her husband playfully sailed through the ocean. Suddenly there was a strong, gusty wind, and the sailboat rapidly picked up speed. Rose screamed as she was pulled under and through the big waves that began to build. Ed turned and saw her swallowing water and being pulled under by the waves. His first reaction was to dive in to save her. However, he quickly remembered his stress training at the Stress Regulation Institute and realized he could save her by letting the sails go slack. Quickly he released the mainsail instead of diving into the water. With the boat no longer at a high speed, he dived in, loosened the rope from around Rose's waist, and pulled her aboard. Though she was shocked and had swallowed some water, Rose was feeling much better in about 5 minutes. The only side effects were some nausea and diarrhea later in the day from all the salt water she had swallowed.

In recounting the story of a beautiful summer afternoon which almost turned into a tragedy, Ed told me that before his Positive Stress Response training, in an immediate reaction to this kind of emergency, he would have dived in to save his wife, since this is traditionally what people are taught to do—to save a loved one. But because of his PSR training, which taught him to think about the real problem—the speed of the boat caused by the wind, he thought of the *best* emergency reaction. He recognized that in panicking and diving in to save his wife, he might have lost not only her life but perhaps his own as well. If he had missed either her or the rope, he would have been left in the ocean and she would have been almost assuredly pulled to her death by the boat. If by chance the winds had quickly stopped, she might have been able to recover, but he realized that there was certainly no better than a 50/50 chance of that.

The foregoing is one example of Positive Stress Response (PSR) training and how it can help people in times of emergencies to *do* what is best and *not do* what is most commonplace. Ed and Rose were very thankful. Now, if they pull each other behind the boat, they both wear life vests, and they keep a knife next to the rope in case they need to cut it loose. This is why it is so important for people to train the nervous system, so that the brain will direct the body to do what is best in a difficult or emergency situation. The PSR training will also help in the many hassles that people undergo every day. This is just like any other physical or mental training; if you do not train regularly, you may react with an old pattern when there is an emergency or a unique situation. The old pattern may not be the healthiest or best way to cope with a new situation. That is why in making decisions in business or finance, people are more likely to make a good decision if they stay calm and alert. In many cases, they become overemotional, lack emotion, or overintellectualize when making decisions.

The Nervous System

To understand the PSR process you must know something about the nervous system. Consider that there is an "intellectual mind," the cortex, which thinks and runs our creative processes. Physically sitting below the cortex is the "primitive mind." It runs the emotions and the physical functions of the body, such as those governed by the heart, sexual organs, intestines, and skin temperature. This primitive part—the limbic system and the hypothalamus—acts more like the ancient dinosaur, or like a wild animal. The animal reactions are strong, full of emotion, and are at the basis of most of our thinking and reacting, both mentally and physically. Both the intellectual functions and the animal physical-emotional functions can be overreactions which can drive people into patterns that are unhealthy and often destructive for them and those around them. Alcoholism, obesity, excessive drug use, and womanizing (Don Juan complex) are examples of this. Additionally, in women the reactions may take the form of being subservient or tolerating abuse. People may use sexuality by being promiscuous, or they may use sex to make a living as prostitutes. Hypersexuality and overeating can be addictions similar to alcoholism and may need to be treated.

How do we learn to react with these primitive responses? One of the ways happens in the beginning of childhood. If you think about how children observe this world, you will see that from the very beginning they have startle responses and react quickly to sounds and noises. These startle reactions are the beginning of emergency reactions which often become overreactions. If not retrained, they can lead to maladaptive reactions. Then the reactions tend to continue or to become worse. This is one of the reasons many people make mistakes in their lives and repeat the same physical or emotional problems. This is also one of the reasons why people are accident-prone or feel they are trapped and cannot change their life situations. One of the purposes of this book and the accompanying tapes is to help you retrain these patterns. PSR training will help you overcome these overreactions and develop a healthier and more vital you.

With PSR training, we can get people to balance their intellectual mind and their animal-emotional mind by retraining them. This balance is the key to healthy mental and physical coping in life. When learning to play the piano, football, golf, or tennis, you need to practice many repetitions of the skill before you improve. This is true for your mental and physical patterns in everyday life.

The statement "Life is a struggle" can be used either optimistically or pessimistically. You can usually evaluate people by how they respond to such a statement. Life is stressful, and you can react positively or negatively. Another way of stating this is that life is a struggle, therefore our experiences will be stressful. But our attitudes about life and our coping abilities make a tremendous difference in how well we do both physically and mentally. One's being under stress does not determine the outcome unless the stresses are overwhelming. In a war, for example, people have to do whatever they can to survive. People vary in the ways they react to war. This can be important to their survival as well as to their mental and physical health. As I describe the mental and physical reactions and overreactions, remember that you will be looking at both your intellectual and your animal mind. By reviewing the stresses and patterns of your life, you can use PSR training to develop healthier responses. In fact, you can be more creative and cope better with whatever situations you face. The sailing incident I described shows how the use of PSR produced a better reaction and saved a loved one. Remember, in each stressful situation there is not only a challenge but an opportunity to be stronger and develop more coping skills. That is why I do not recommend that people try to avoid all stresses but rather take them step by step in little pieces they can learn to handle. Then they will grow stronger and more able to handle bigger pieces of stress in life.

The Fight-or-Flight Response

The *first rule* of the nervous system is a very primitive *fight-or-flight response*. This means that with any change in environment—a sound, a noise, a telephone ringing, or a thought—the *brain triggers arousal* in the whole nervous system. This can be a large emergency-alarm reaction, such as the fight-or-flight response when there is a fire in a building or you are driving down a road and see a car suddenly pull in front of you. Your whole system races, adrenaline makes the heart beat faster, and your blood pressure goes higher. The arousal can also be less intense, where there is just a slight increase in heart rate or blood pressure, a tightening of the muscles, or sweating. These smaller arousal signs happen 20 to 50 times a day and even during sleep. While some of these responses are helpful in an emergency situation, like meeting a bear when walking in the woods, they are not helpful for these 20 to 50 other minor stresses during the day.

Because of the racing of the nervous system in the arousal reaction, we can see how having nervous reactions triggered 20 to 50 times a day can lead to stress-related problems such as high blood pressure, headaches, backaches, sleep disturbances, eating disorders, colitis, diarrhea, constipation, general tension, and anxiety. All of these warning signs are signals that the system is operating at a higher and faster level than is necessary or healthy. If too many stresses continue, the nervous system races even more. One example of this buildup of stress is where people jump at the sound of a telephone ringing. These signals of high arousal, if continued, can become symptoms. As the nervous system becomes habituated, or locked into a pattern of high arousal, these symptoms can worsen rapidly. Once the symptoms "lock in" people begin getting headaches once or twice a week rather than once a month.

This is why I want people to use the techniques of PSR training in a preventative way when they experience warning signs and signals. Once the nervous system locks in at a higher activation level, they will need not only the PSR training but also additional medical treatment, such as biofeedback or medication. Instead of the general stress management model of 8 to 12 training sessions, 15 to 40 medical treatments may be needed to change habituated (locked-in) stress patterns.

The written exercises in Chapters Three, Five, Seven, and Ten, and those in the audiocassettes, will give you the basic elements of the PSR training. These exercises will be very helpful in the first two stages of prevention and dampening down of the stress signals. This may not be sufficient if you are in the third stage, where the system is already locked in, and you have symptoms, illness, or disease. Then you probably will need medical treatment in addition to the PSR skills. In my work with people in corporations, schools, universities, and hospitals, I have found that approximately one-third of them can use the PSR techniques in preventative ways so as to be healthier and to maximize their work potential and energy. Another third need to change their systems by using PSR skills to reduce the warning signs and signals of stress problems. The remaining third need medical treatment in addition to the PSR to correct and alleviate the locked-in disorders or diseases. I estimate that only 3 to 5 percent of the population is healthy and able to naturally handle the stresses of life. The rest of us will profit from PSR training.

The Speed of the Nervous System and Stress Response

The Indianapolis 500 provides a good analogy about stress. This race, held every year in Indianapolis, is 500 miles in length. To this event come the best-equipped teams of drivers and mechanics. They bring the best equipment available. Their cars are well tuned, and they usually bring two cars because there are mechanical breakdowns. These drivers race their cars at extremely high speeds, above 200 mph on a short track. Thus, the wear and tear on both machines and drivers is incredible. Each year only approximately 50 percent of the cars that start the course are likely to finish. The others burn out, fall apart, or have a problem that knocks them out of the race. Even with the best cars, best drivers, and best maintenance teams, driving at extremely high speeds in a very competitive race causes about half of them to break down. Similarly, if you drive your system too hard, too long, or at too high a speed, you greatly increase the risk of having an illness or other serious problem. Thus, while we can replace an engine or tires in a car, it is difficult to replace a heart. The recent mechanical heart replacements show how poorly this works. As of October 1986, all five men given heart replacements had died, and they had had a limited sense of well-being while they lived. In May 1987 the U.S. government decided to stop funding this type of heart replacement because of the poor results. In 1988, because of pressure from some senators, partial funding was restored. So remember, it is important when considering stress to look at the speed of your life and remember the Indianapolis 500 analogy.

Animal Wishes versus the Domesticated Mind

In thinking about the brain and the body and how we react to different situations, it is useful to realize how domesticated we have become. For "domesticated" you might substitute the word "civilized." We are asked to interact with other people and to attempt to share goals like productive work, a family life, and enjoyment. When children are given a choice or are allowed to speak their minds, they will say something like, "I want that ice cream cone now!" As they get older, they learn to ask for the ice cream cone. They learn to say thank you when they get one, and later in life they learn to pay for the ice cream cone with money. The primary feeling and thought is still "I want the ice cream cone now." You can see this in adult behavior with overeating, when people not only have their ice cream cone but finish off the whole quart. If they are binge-type personalities, they will have 1 or 2 half-gallons. For anorexics, the inner demand of "I want it now" becomes disguised as the statement "I don't want that food now; I will starve myself instead."

These wishes and desires of human beings are very primitive and strong emotions. This type of reaction pattern is more subtle in adults than in children. Adults learn that they are supposed to ask for some things and not ask for other things. For example, in a recent case in New York City, a house of prostitution was run by the "Mayflower Madam." She said she was providing a service for men and wanted to provide the very best service. Here the natural wish for sex is changed to sex provided on demand. In visiting prostitutes, men want sex with little mental and emotional connection to it, only monetary. Perhaps sex is not exactly like an ice cream cone, but it shows a similar childlike wish.

To use another example, consider pets. Pets have been domesticated much as people have been domesticated. Your cat or dog is very much attuned to your wishes and to what you have taught it, yet maintains its own wishes. For example, I have two cats. One day I brought home half of a broiled chicken and put it on the kitchen table. Then the phone rang and I talked with a friend for 4 or 5 minutes. I went to the bathroom to wash up and came back to find no chicken. All I found was a ripped-up bag on the kitchen floor and two very contented cats in the living room licking their paws. My two cats, although they had already been fed, made quick work of half a bird. In thinking it over, I realized that that was their animal wish—they smelled chicken, saw it, knocked it on the floor, ripped open the bag, and ate it. They had not done anything wrong, except I did not approve of it because I had not eaten. From their viewpoint, they were just having an after-dinner snack—a bird dessert.

Think about the difference between a domesticated dog as "man's best friend" and a wild, dangerous wolf. People have very different images of these animals. The domesticated brain is like the dog and the primitive brain (animal brain) is like the wolf. Each of us has both levels of wishes, feelings, and drives going on in our brain. When thinking of yourself and other people under stressful conditions, keep this image in mind: the primitive animal brain and the "new brain" (cortex), which developed as people became civilized, are always functioning together. This accounts for many arousal situations where people do not want to be aware of these wishes or try to avoid bringing this conflict of the two brain levels into their conscious thinking. An example would be people who say they want a stable, loving relationship and then stay in an affair with a married person. These people do not want to be aware of their conflicting wishes. Another example would be patients who do not want to be aware of some of the benefits of being in the "sick role," such as being taken care of. Many types of anxiety or painful behavior have to do with this conflict between the old, primitive brain and the new, domesticated brain. A better balancing of these parts of the brain is possible by training with PSR.

What You Need to Know about Stress

Many people have an uncomplicated view of stress. The most common opinion is that stress is negative. This is untrue. A job advancement or the birth of a baby is stressful. Many good events can trigger an overreaction to stress. Even though the stress is pleasant and exciting, it can cause problems. For example, the stress of having a baby, while very positive, depends to a great degree on the number of stressful events experienced by the individual and her spouse. A mother who has time to relax and take it easy the last trimester will be much more comfortable handling the stresses of having a baby than one who has had emergencies or had to move or is malnourished.

Think about stress as anything that activates the nervous system (the brain and the body). This can be a thought or a memory or an anticipated event. It can be an immediate stress, such as a cold day. For Raynaud's patients and headache patients, stress can cause an attack within a few minutes or seconds.

There are also other types of stress that can build up to trigger a headache in 24 to 48 hours. Some of the buildup is due to food and other substances. I call these "stress foods." They are listed in Chapter Six.

Keep in mind that stress is anything that activates the

nervous system, and the stronger it is, the more it activates the fight-or-flight response. Just thinking about having been in a stressful situation in the past may trigger a large or small reaction today. One example is seeing a fire and remembering you were once threatened by a fire or almost burned. Another example is seeing a car accident and slamming on the brakes just in time to avoid it. Your nervous system rushes adrenaline to the body and you might experience a pounding heart and shaky knees, or you might get a headache or throw up. If at another time you heard the screech of tires on the street, you would almost instinctively react with a tightening of muscles and quickly look toward the source of the sound.

A simpler example of physical stress is when you start an exercise program. The first couple of days after you start walking or exercising on a bicycle or in an aerobics class, your muscles will feel tired and sore. After the first two or three workouts, as you strengthen the muscles and the cardiovascular system, the discomfort will ease. Knowing this, people can move through a graduated exercise program and maintain it. The key here is that the stressors at first appear more difficult or powerful to the body because the body has been inactive. As the muscles and the cardiovascular system become more active, they handle exercise more comfortably. You begin to enjoy the exercise and get the benefits of more vigor and of a sense of physical and mental well-being.

One of the key factors in dealing with stress is to realize that you cannot escape it. You have to deal with stress. As you learn to deal with it, your coping abilities allow you to do so more comfortably. In other words, you can have a healthy adaptation to stress by using the knowledge and techniques described in this book. There is evidence that some people who are not exposed to moderate stress do not increase their coping ability and in fact become more uncomfortable with everyday stresses.

Not only are major life changes and events stressful, such as those of moving, getting married, buying a new house, going to jail, or having a business setback, but there are also a whole series of minor stresses and hassles that can add up to make your day difficult and cause headaches and pain. As I've said, some stresses trigger headaches or other problems within a few seconds or minutes, while some cause these discomforts to develop later on. One clear example of the latter would be if normally you do not chop wood and one day you do. Later that night or the next morning, your back, shoulders, neck, and arms are sore and tender. This pain can be eased by taking a hot shower or hot bath before going to bed that night and by stretching or exercising the back and arm muscles you have used. If you then repeat this exercise the next morning, you will reduce the muscle pain and soreness. Being aware of factors like this can often ease many of the negative consequences of stress. The key here is that the pain and muscle tightness does not always come right after the activity but may occur 3, 6, or 14 to 24 hours later.

People often say they do not believe stress has anything to do with the way they are feeling mentally or physically. They do not see a connection between stress and their sleep problems or difficulties such as constipation, diarrhea, gas, ulcers, or spastic colon. You can almost be certain that stress has been a factor in developing or aggravating these conditions. The difficulty is that people's minds are trying their best to deal with the daily or weekly stresses. If the brain cannot do anything about these stresses, it tends to say to itself, "I am doing the best I can." It will block out or deny that stresses have activated the nervous system to cause these problems or worsen them. Thus, the nervous system may inadvertently increase the symptoms or difficulties. If you ask people if they have noticed that thinking about problems or planning the next day's events before they go to sleep upsets them, they will tell you, "Yes, sometimes." If the brain is thinking and repeating a thought or worry about a problem five or ten times, the body is kept awake and it is difficult to fall asleep. The skills of PSR help the brain to realize that thinking it over once or twice is enough. Repetition of the thought or problem does not help and in fact may hurt. To change these unhealthy patterns, one has to be aware of these factors and practice physical exercise, good diet and sleep habits, and PSR. In Chapters Three, Five, Seven, and Ten, I will describe the techniques that help people to relax physically and mentally so that your brain can run the body even when thinking about a problem.

If you think about your life, you will note some specific stresses that have been building up to a point where they trigger overreactions in the nervous system. This can happen in as little as 2 to 3 months or as much as 12 to 18 months. Looking back over the past 1 to 2 years, you will often see an increase in the number of events or stressors that have changed your health. Not only the number of stresses but often the key ones, such as a person losing a parent, may trigger a problem or illness. Another important stress may be if a close friend is ill, or if one has to deal with several severe stresses for months. I have found that most often you can go back and identify these major stresses. This helps you realize that the stresses have added up to cause the nervous system to race so much that it locks in at the higher speeds. The nervous system has become less able to successfully deal with daily problems.

One of the other major problems in talking with people about their stress overreactions is that they think if they are reacting to stress, they are weak or have some mental problem. The truth is that everyone reacts to stress.

Everyone!

When people experience a certain number of stresses and overreactions, they can learn to change them or dampen them and use the PSR skills to cope better. This does not mean they will not react; the nervous system always reacts. What it means is the system won't overreact and lock into a higher level of activity that is exhausting and often triggers stress-related disorders or diseases. Many benefits result from practicing the PSR skills and using them. They are very much like learning to write, whereby you learn to communicate with written words and letters. Without this skill, communication is limited to your voice. Applying this analogy to your nervous system and PSR skills, you will increase your ability to communicate between your mind and your body and with the outside world. In other words, you will allow yourself to react and adjust to stress so it is less likely to become an overreaction. In addition, you can watch others, wait for their reaction and/or overreaction, and then modify your reactions toward them. This allows them an opportunity to do the same toward you.

As you think about your body and mind reactions, realize that any time you undergo major stresses, such as those involved in an exam, childbirth, or a promotion, your mind accelerates the body and triggers certain over-reactions. These overreactions can cause headaches, back-aches, bowel problems, irritability, or sleep problems. Most people have two, three, four, or sometimes five areas of their mental/physical nervous system that will overreact. As you read and think about these reactions in some of my patients, do not be surprised if you notice one, two, or three areas of mental/physical reaction in which you have experienced your body or mind over-reacting. As you use the exercises and techniques in this book, you will be able to work through many over-reactions, uncovering layers of relaxed concentration where you feel calm and peaceful. You will begin to notice more energy and a calmer way of using your mental and physical energy.

Why You Need the Positive Stress Response

In the 20 years since I started my medical training, there has been a great change in our understanding of nutrition, health, and stress responses. Early in the 1920s, Dr. W. B. Cannon described the emergency or fight-or-flight response that was the beginning of our understanding of the output of the nervous system and the high arousal pattern. In 1936 Dr. Hans Selye defined stress as a "non-specific response of the body to external demands." These responses included discharges of arousal chemicals such as epinephrine (adrenaline), norepinephrine, adrenocorti-cotrophic hormone (ACTH), glucocorticoids, and other hormones.

More recent work shows that the nervous system produces a series of responses that can be quite different in individuals. One of the major discoveries is that there seem to be two types of nervous system reactions—a positive or a negative response. The positive response is manifested in the person's appropriately coping, or trying to cope successfully. The negative pattern influences the person if the coping response is unavailable (or thought to be unavailable). The fight-or-flight response (which can be modified by PSR) includes an increase in muscle activity, more blood flow to the skeletal muscles, and an increase in heart rate, cardiac output, and blood pressure. It is an attempt to cope. However, if a person is under stress and does not think of or have a coping response, then the organism can have a negative or defensive stress response. This involves an increased vigilance, increased blood pressure, increased peripheral resistance (cool fingers), and decreased skeletal movement. Often this negative stress reaction has a negative mental attitude of helplessness attached to the coping attempt. If these activities or patterns continue, they can become locked in and produce high blood pressure, muscle spasms, or many other stress-related responses, such as anxiety, depression, irritability, and sleep problems. They may even reduce your immune system's ability to fight off colds, infections, and cancerous growths.

These patterns are well described in *Stress and Coping* by Field, McCabe, and Schneiderman. They define stress as a "change or a threat of change demanding adaptation by an organism." The stimulus for this change is called a stressor, and the adaptation they describe is behavior (e.g., fight or flight) and physiochemical responses (e.g., increased cardiac output and/or secretion of norepinephrine and other chemicals). This definition of stress reveals that many patterns of reaction can occur. The work by Dr. M. Frankenhaeuser shows that when effort is associated with distress, both the catecholamines and the cortisol secretions increase. If there is an effort without distress, there is an increase in catecholamines and a decrease in cortisol production. Supporting this theory is Glass's work stating that moderate effort without distress, such as walking upstairs, releases norepinephrine, whereas effort associated with psychological stress, including self-consciousness or harassment, may lead to more release of epinephrine. This ratio of norepinephrine and epinephrine may dramatically affect the body and mind. So there is chemical and other physical evidence in the body and mind reactions that shows whether or not we are reacting in a positive way and attempting to cope. This coping helps us get the task done or the stress over with in a healthier way. The negative stress response seems to lock the muscles and blood pressure into a more tense situation that can create serious mental and physical problems.

These physiological changes are the basis for recommending positive thinking. It has been suggested that people who are optimistic rather than pessimistic toward themselves and life do better.

Recent work in research on the way people explain what happens to them in life is very revealing. In general, pessimistic people tend to give a negative explanation as to why they failed an exam, or why they did not get a desired job, bonus, or raise. They generalize this into a feeling that they will have more setbacks, and therefore they do less, or they do not exert themselves to achieve more for themselves.

Optimistic people will try to learn from the situation and change their behavior to influence others so they can get more of what they want. This has been demonstrated by George Valliant, M.D., of Dartmouth Medical School, who followed up on some Harvard men who graduated from 1939 to 1944. He found that the optimistic men in college were healthier in later life than the pessimistic people. After age 45, the pessimists' health began to worsen more quickly. Their attitudes very much affected their mental and physical condition 30 and 40 years later. One explanation is that the pessimists may neglect taking care of their health and therefore experience more health problems. An additional explanation is that their pessimistic outlook on life becomes a self-fulfilling prophecy. While everyone has a mix of some optimistic and pessimistic thoughts, your personal attitude very much determines how you experience life's ups and downs.

Work has also been done showing that if you feel helpless or have a pessimistic attitude, it influences your immune system and reduces your resistance to infections such as colds and even to tumors (cancers). A pessimistic or negative attitude can lead people to experience depression, other illnesses, and less satisfaction and enjoyment. Having a new skill like the PSR develops a more positive attitude toward life and allows people to learn from their mistakes. You can then persevere and overcome many of the inevitable disappointments, frustrations, and problems in life.

It is my belief and the belief of others that these arousal patterns are in place by the first or second year of school. Some tests show that one's attitude as early as the second or third grade can be predictive of a person's attitude for the rest of one's life. Perseverance and motivation is very important when a person gets a C on an exam rather than the B or A that was desired or expected. By making use of a simple cognitive restructuring technique, you can be fairer to yourself both physically and mentally. By this I mean the following: When you have a negative thought if something is fearful or upsetting, replace it with a neutral thought, such as "I got a C on this paper; I will be able to pass the course," rather than "I got a C on this exam and that means I may not pass the course." The third thought should be positive and optimistic, such as, "I got a C on this paper this time. Perhaps by studying more or writing a better paper next time I might get a B or a B+." By introducing the neutral and positive statement to balance the negative thought, you rebalance your mental anticipation of the future. This type of positive restructuring supports you in ascertaining what steps you might take to improve your score on the next exam or paper. This positive restructuring exercise can be used for almost every situation you face.

The physical exercises and techniques that I will describe allow you to restructure yourself both physically and mentally, building a healthier and more positive optimistic mental attitude. This feedback principle of mind and body working together will stack the odds in your favor. As you see from the example above, thinking one neutral and one positive thought in your favor will balance the negative thought. Many people think negatively and this starts a negative thinking process and a negative physical arousal process, meaning that you stack the odds against yourself two to one. By using the PSR and this cognitive restructuring exercise, you support healthy mental and physical patterns in your thinking and feeling.

Let me diagram the different results from the same stress (an argument) when you use the Positive Stress Response (see Table 2-1).

In my work with patients, they come to understand the physiological arousal that comes with the fight-or-flight response and learn to alter the mental and chemical changes that cause overreactions. This allows them to reverse the physical and mental patterns that cause self-defeating behavior and illness. In this way you can change the odds to two to one in your favor when dealing with stressful situations.

TABLE 2-1 The Stress of "An Argument"

	Negative Stress Response	*Positive Stress Response*
First Minute:	Overreaction (anger, fear, yelling, headaches, bowel problems, poor communication)	Strong reaction (anger, fear, yelling, communication is tension-filled)
First Hour:	Escalated overreaction (walking out, fighting, "blinding headache," "back slips out," sick with constipation, diarrhea, "cold shoulder," goes to bed)	De-escalated reaction (calmer, no headache, can relax, sleep and bowel problems do not develop, communication remains open)
1–4 Weeks:	Escalates further (heart attack, stroke, hospitalized for "exhaustion" or operation) *or* Days later (irritable, angry, fearful, headaches, bowel and sleep problems continue to worsen)	Physically healthy, enjoys work and has time to play and be happy
3–6 Months:	Continues medical treatment (or death) *or* Problem continues for months or years *or* Begins medical treatment	

Increased Stress Experienced in the Modern World

One of the reasons people are having more stress-related problems is the tremendous increase in stimuli that are bombarding us each day. The generation since World War II has had to face the possibility of a nuclear holocaust. The Japanese suffered two cities destroyed, many thousands dead, and many others scarred and damaged from the atom bombs, as well as the scar that was left on the whole world. Everyone who can read or listen to the radio or watch TV is aware that large parts of the world, perhaps the whole world, could be destroyed in a nuclear war. Fear of nuclear war has been inculcated in American children. We have been trained since childhood what to do if there is an atomic bomb attack. Not only adults but children particularly are aware of this possibility. This has been shown in such films as *Dr. Strangelove,* and more recently in the *China Syndrome*. The recent accidents at Three Mile Island in Pennsylvania and Chernobyl in the USSR remind us of this worldwide threat. The whole world has been affected by this fear of a nuclear accident or war.

Another major change has been the growth of communication—radio, telephone, and TV—which has made the world into a "global village." Broadcasts from Vietnam sent back scenes of suffering and death on nightly TV. In addition, films like *Apocalypse Now* and *Platoon* showed some of the effects of war on individuals, and other war films, such as *Rambo,* showed the effect on people returning from the war. Thus, children of many nations now see and understand the message of films and TV and hear musicians who speak and sing of the threat of war and nuclear holocaust.

As with most stresses, there is a positive aspect to the global village. Communications technology allows people to be aware of other countries' plights. This benefit has been shown by musicians raising funds for the starving, starting with George Harrison for Bangladesh, and more recently with the "We Are the World" concerts and recording done in 1985. Global communication has both heightened fears and allowed possibilities of changing people's attitudes and actions. Perhaps one of the major factors of change is the TV, records, films, and novels that now are circulated worldwide. For example, *Dallas* reruns are watched in Europe and Africa as well as in South America. Films and TV shows have become a valuable American export and have an effect on values and people. The global village both stimulates fears and allows us to confront some of them.

Another example of stresses are the terrible events where children are kidnapped and/or killed. For many months in Atlanta, for example, children were murdered by a serial killer. Parents have to teach their children not only to refuse food and candy from strangers but also to be afraid and to stay away from people. This fear of kidnapping was not as pervasive just 20 years ago. Then it was a rare event. Now we see these pictures of missing children on our milk cartons. This brings fear to children as well as to parents. Violence and the threat of violence add considerably to the constant arousal of our nervous system.

Another type of stressor involves stores that remain open 24 hours a day, often 7 days a week. In New York City you can shop for food and certain alcoholic beverages at any time of the day or night. This is one example of how people can be on the go 24 hours a day. In earlier times, in rural communities and even in cities, people were usually home by 10:00 p.m. getting ready for bed. Now so many activities are possible that people have to make choices and are often overscheduled. This adds to their stress burden. In many cases, I recommend to people that they try to stay home one night a week and relax, exercise, or do nothing. This can be a valuable de-stressor.

Stress Created by New Technology

One of my patients told me that her headaches and menstrual cramps increased a great deal when she worked on a large project. This was even more true when her secretaries shifted from typewriters to word processors.

Now they do twice as much work and my patient must do more work as well. This example clearly illustrates the important fact that while technology is helpful, it has its drawbacks: she can produce twice as much, but it puts an increasing stress and strain on her mind and body.

We can become more productive, therefore, but it is like the factories that work 24 hours a day. People who were used to working 9:00 to 5:00 had to change to the 8:00 to 4:00, 4:00 to 12:00, or 12:00 to 8:00 (graveyard) shift. Mental and physical changes create great demands on our bodies and nervous systems. New technology is increasing these stresses and will continue to do so. We can have phones in our cars and airplanes, and walk around with phones in our pockets. Thus the capacity to make more phone calls creates an increased demand on our nervous systems.

The Habituation of Stress Patterns and Creative Energy

People often have the mistaken idea from their early childhood training that faster is better. The nervous system tends to go into faster, higher arousal states or an emergency fight-or-flight response, and this is one of the basic reasons for the belief that faster is better. When people are nervous or thinking about something, they tend to get physically active and mentally hyperactive. This tendency to speed up causes much of the frenetic behavior you see in the workplace and at home. People become irritable and angry, and have sleep problems. All of us have felt like this at times. We have seen other people who will jump at the sound of a telephone ringing or who walk around smoking cigarette after cigarette. This pattern becomes habituated so the person can no longer readjust to a calmer and quieter state. A calmer state is necessary for creative thinking or for dealing with people who are not at hyperspeed or excessively driven. Research has shown that this "racing" is a major factor in the Type A personality. Racing, and a feeling of anger that one has never accomplished enough, can lead to serious consequences, such as heart attacks and strokes.

Another example of the racing nervous system is found in many people who lecture or speak to large audiences. This is demonstrated by the fact that it is commonly accepted procedure to have water for the speaker. The water is provided not because a speaker cannot talk for an hour or two. It is because the crowd and the anticipated anxiety of speaking tends to race the nervous system and cause a decrease in saliva so that the speaker gets a dry mouth. In private conversations people can talk or dictate for an hour or two and not get a dry mouth.

Negative Stress Pattern

Recently more people have become conscious of good health habits, although many people still do not know what these good health practices are. For example, they never thought about such basics as having three small to medium-size meals every day. They may have been brought up with parents who had a cup of coffee every morning and rushed out to work, and then grabbed something at lunch. Then they had a big meal at six or seven o'clock. Or even worse, they may have been in a family where people ate at eight, nine, or ten o'clock, then went to bed on a relatively full stomach an hour later. These habits are not as healthful as having a light breakfast, a moderate lunch, and a moderate dinner early in the evening, around six or seven o'clock.

Another common problem is that people are brought up to be so active that they try to cram too much into a day. Many people have a "superman" or "superwoman" fantasy. They overschedule themselves, or plan 13 little tasks that they'll do after work or on the weekend when only 8 or 9 can be done. They'll often worry about it or stay up late and then be tired or exhausted the next day.

This behavior can be described as burning the candle at both ends. An example of this is the person who, because of excessive drive or competitiveness or need to achieve, may become exhausted or develop a heart attack or stroke. Some of the warning signs are light-headedness, dizziness, or faint feelings. That's why it is important to try to define your stress pattern. Some are mild problems and can be easily corrected by using a stress management technique such as going on vacation. At the next level, stress patterns can become more per-sistent and cause you to be irritable, less efficient at work, and prone to errors, owing to poor concentration or poor judgment. The next level is where people actu-ally get physically or mentally ill and need medical treat-ment. Problems such as overeating or undereating are often stress-related. Persons thus afflicted are trying to get away and avoid some of the stresses. They eat too little and become skinny or even anorexic, yet they have a powerful conviction that they're still attractive and healthy. The brain can be so powerful as to hold this view against virtually everyone else's opinion. About 10 percent of anorexics actually kill themselves by starvation. On the other end of the spectrum are people who overeat and underexercise so that they become obese. Their obesity protects them from certain fears or concerns. There are very few happy fat people. Through using PSR tech-niques, dieting, and other new techniques, many people regain their healthy weight. By using PSR skills, they continue to maintain their weight loss or weight gain.

People often push too hard and are affected by stress but are not aware of it. They can actually do more or achieve more in the same time by retraining their ner-vous systems. People who learn to use the PSR get more work done in 24 hours and stay more relaxed and rested. They can make quick adjustments if they need to change their schedules or their physical or emotional patterns. That's why it is useful to jot down the pattern of mental and physical stresses and see how they affect you. Simply listing the colds, accidents, operations, dental work, or any other kind of mental or physical pattern in the last year is useful in identifying some of your own particular patterns. You will be quite pleased as you do these PSR exercises because you can adjust your eating habits and sleeping cycle so that your energy will stabilize or increase.

Relaxation

The major reason that relaxation techniques, in general, have not been especially helpful in stress management is that they are not powerful enough. They cannot change the emergency arousal or fight-or-flight response that is wired into the old animal brain. When people get excited, frightened, or angry, the whole system goes on red alert and overrides the general relaxation effect of such techniques as meditation, power of positive thinking, relaxation response, psychotherapy, or analysis. Modern scientific stress management techniques combine the old relaxation techniques, such as yoga, physical exercise, meditation, and psychotherapy with biofeedback, with the recent knowledge of how the brain works to develop a new skill that helps the new brain and the old brain dampen down this arousal mechanism. Common to all arousing situations, including athletic events and other high-performance situations, is that the nervous system tends to continue to run at a high level.

These new skills are learned in the same way you have learned other skills, such as writing or playing the piano. When learning to play the piano, you have to practice the scales and then practice simple songs like "Mary Had a Little Lamb." Then you begin to play more complex songs. In a similar way, when you learn the PSR, you first learn the basic scales of the nervous system and how to go up and down those scales. Then you can use these simple exercises at home twice a day for 15 minutes. As the new skills develop, you can start applying them to the everyday situations of stress. The analogy with the piano would be that you learn to play songs and then you can sight-read new music and play pretty well the first time. You can go to a friend's party and play songs you have memorized on other pianos in different circumstances. You can even play quite well with lots of other people around you singing and dancing. At first, under these changing conditions, you would not have been able to play well. By training step by step, you can.

What has been missing in the other relaxation techniques is not only the actual learning of new skills but, even more important, the spreading of those skills into everyday situations. As I describe the use of the PSR in the treatment of stress-related problems, keep in mind these key steps: first, learning to relax, learning the PSR skills, and then practicing them so that you can apply them to everyday stressful situations. This takes from 1 to 2 months, and the skills will continue to develop for an additional 8 to 10 months.

While these PSR skills are very good for the signs and symptoms, they are not always sufficient for the medical problems that sometimes develop from stressful situations. If you have a medical problem or are under treatment by a physician, you should speak with him or her about how to use the PSR skills. They are not a medical treatment. You need a physician to supervise you if you are going to use them for a medical condition. Usually the physician will have to teach you additional skills or add medication or other medical treatments.

Stress and Successful People

In talking about stress, many people think only of the negative aspects of stress or that stress affects only sick people. Stress is pervasive and affects all people throughout their lives. There are key times or key stresses over a period of time that cause specific problems to develop.

When I talk about stress I am talking about external and internal factors that influence everyone. This was made clear to me when I did a PSR training for a large corporation whose headquarters were in New York City. The group consisted of 18 men, aged 28 to 32, who were the "cream of the crop" and would be advancing to be vice presidents and the chief executive officer (CEO) of this corporation. After examining and testing them, I found that all of them were Type A personalities, and two-thirds of them already had stress-related symptoms and diseases. These men, while very successful, had problems such as low back pain, alcoholism, skin problems, ulcers, colitis, diarrhea, constipation, hypertension, insomnia, and lack of concentration (being easily distracted at work). This group of executives exemplified the finding that from 60 to 80 percent of successful people have stress-related symptoms, illnesses, diseases, or disorders.

By using PSR training, these men were able to reduce their Type A behavior and other symptoms. The more they practiced, the more they were able to concentrate and be efficient at work. They also reported feeling more relaxed and less irritable with their families. The work with these executives points out how symptoms can develop in 25- to 35-year-old people that can dramatically offset their health and job performance. More companies are encouraging or providing stress courses for their employees. AT&T, Johnson and Johnson, and Coors are just some of the corporations that have instituted large fitness and stress management programs.

Remember, a warning signal is when the symptoms start occurring more frequently. A chronic problem could be the development of low back pain every day, instead of once or twice a year. Or instead of having one or two headaches a year, you might begin to have one or two a month or one or two a week. This is when the symptoms begin to interfere with one's well-being and livelihood. A good example of this is the great basketball player Kareem Abdul-Jabar, who off and on in his career, particularly in 1983–1984, had to miss several basketball games or play with a pounding migraine headache. He probably learned how to handle stress better and in the 1984–1985 season he had very few of them and the Lakers won the championship. John F. Kennedy and his brother Ted both had chronic back problems aggravated by injuries and assorted stresses in their private and political lives. JFK was reported to have received many treatments for this problem, and it may have affected his presidency. One of the best things you can do for back problems is daily stretching exercises. Often they will ease and reduce the pain. With the PSR training, you can add exercise and biofeedback, which often reduces or stops much of the pain.

These are just some examples of how a stress can build up until it becomes a serious illness or a disease with life-threatening consequences. If it goes too far, medical treatment may be required. It is important to recognize that the PSR techniques can be used in addition to medical treatment for illness but are better used early on when the early warning signs of stress are just beginning to build. Unless successful people practice stress management they are just as likely to operate at a "hyper" level which causes fatigue, burnout, or more serious symptoms. Stress may limit the potential present in your nervous system. By use of PSR techniques and exercises, you will be able to head off many stress problems and continue to be successful.

Summary

In looking at the stress in your life, realize that it comes in many forms and from many directions. You react with either a negative stress reaction or a positive stress reaction. If you are feeling hopeless, helpless, or negative about the stressors in your life, then you are probably experiencing the negative stress response. If you are somewhat optimistic and looking for lines of action that you can take or awaiting developments, then you are probably handling stress in a positive way. As I have mentioned in this chapter, it is very important to develop positive stress reactions. If you are inactive or into a negative cycle, the negative stress reactions will continue and probably worsen. This can lead to serious changes in your moods and can cause irritability, depression, or other negative states of physical or mental illness.

The PSR allows you to be steeled by the stresses so you can enjoy more of them and be stronger and better prepared for future stresses. People are often not aware of having these reactions, but having gone through this chapter, you are better able to identify your particular stressors. You also can begin to see what additional stresses might be coming up for you. Your health will vary depending on your mental and physical reactions to the number of stresses you experience and how you react to specific stresses. In the next few chapters, I will give you more exercises for breathing, muscle tensing, and relaxing, as well as exercises for your internal organs. I will also review your nutrition and exercise program and make suggestions for improvement so you can further your ability to use the PSR. You will get the best results by following the chapters in succession, step by step. Practice each of the PSR exercise chapters for about 7 to 10 days before moving onto the next one. Thus, if you want to skip ahead, make sure you take the stress test in Chapter Four and follow the book's exercises, which are explained in Chapters Three, Five, Seven, and Ten. These exercises are repeated in my voice on the audiocassettes.

CHAPTER THREE

THE FIRST POSITIVE STRESS RESPONSE EXERCISE: BREATHING, TENSING, AND RELAXING

No genius can recite a ballad at first reading as well as a mediocrity at the fifteenth or twentieth reading.

—*Ralph Waldo Emerson*

Sam's Anxiety Attacks

At first, Sam noticed that he was beginning to experience light-headedness and a fast-beating heart while he was working very hard on some key papers for his company. This did not bother him too much, and his doctor suggested he try relaxing a bit. Sam had quite a bit of work to do the rest of that month, so at the end of the month he relaxed and thought he felt a little better. After working extremely hard for over 60 hours the previous week, however, he noticed some dizziness on the weekend, a fast heartbeat, and trouble catching his breath. His doctor tested him for hypoglycemia with a glucose tolerance test and for heart problems with an EKG. These tests were negative. Baffled, his doctor asked Sam if he was under stress. Sam said, "No, not anything unusual. I've been working 60 hours a week and on the weekends. Some nights I take work home, but that's my usual work load." His doctor suggested taking it easier at work and told him to call if he had more symptoms.

The following month while going to work, Sam noticed that his heart was pounding. He started to sweat and felt frightened. It felt "as if I were going to die." His breath was shallow and fast—like a dog panting in the heat. He rushed back to his doctor, and the doctor again checked him out, with an EKG for his heart and additional blood tests. The tests turned out normal, and his doctor prescribed some Valium. The Valium helped for a few days. Three weeks later, however, when he was preparing to fly out for a business trip on a Sunday night, he had another attack. His heart was pounding, sweat was pouring off his head, and he was frightened he might be dying. He was taken to a local hospital, where he was diagnosed as suffering from hyperventilation and an anxiety attack. An injection calmed him.

His doctor then referred him to me because it was clear that the anxiety attacks with hyperventilation were to a large degree due to stresses over the last 3 to 6 months. When I saw Sam it was obvious that he was worried and nervous about these attacks. He told me it seemed as if his body was "threatening" him. He understood he was not dying, but he often feared he was going to die. His theory was that he had a brain tumor or some other life-threatening illness. Since he was worried about a tumor and he had some headaches in the last few months, a CAT scan was ordered. It was normal. I proceeded with Positive Stress Response (PSR) training. I saw him twice a week and gave him breathing exercises. After 3 weeks, he no longer experienced the rapid heartbeat and could slow down his short, fast breaths. By practicing twice a day for about 15 minutes, he was able to pace his breathing to 10 to 12 breaths per minute. Previously he often held his breath or was breathing 18 to 25 times per minute. Now he rarely hyperventilated or broke out in sweats. By the second week, Sam was able to go back to work and to take his business trip. He did have a little sweatiness on the trip, and his heart speeded up twice while he was away from home. Coming back on the plane, he used the breathing exercises and the home tapes that I had given him. He found that plane trips are a good time to practice these exercises because you can easily devote 15 or 20 minutes to them.

When I saw Sam in the fourth week he was much more confident that he could get through the anxiety attacks. Now he rarely had light-headedness at work. By the fifth week we were working on the fourth exercise. Now he could use the 5-minute exercise to relax his breathing and his muscles. He had virtually no light-headedness by the sixth week and had had no anxiety attacks or palpitations for over 2 weeks. After the sixth week and ten treatments, I needed to see him only once a month for the next 6 months. He continued to do well and had only one anxiety attack, which lasted for 1 to 2 minutes, in the following 6 months. He told me he had been doing just one exercise per day during that week because "he was so busy." I told him that people need to practice the exercises 15 to 20 minutes twice a day for 12 to 18 months. Then he might be able to reduce to once a day, with many short breathing checks of three to five breath cycles throughout the day when he was stressed. Some people need to practice these exercises twice a day every day for the rest of their lives. Others, after 12 to 18 months of practice, can use a variation of one or two exercises per day as their stresses increase or decrease. Sam could now self-regulate and control his breathing, which meant his heart did not race (palpitations), and he did not break out in a sweat (hyperhidrosis). After 12 months of home practice, Sam usually had to do only one practice of 15 minutes per day as well as "breathing checks" of 20 to 40 seconds throughout the day.

Sam's case is an example of how you can use these breathing exercises to learn to manage stressful situations. These types of overreactions—fast heartbeat, headaches, bowel problems, sweaty palms, and light-headedness—are often exaggerated fight-or-flight responses. If Sam had not received treatment and had continued taking medication, some of the symptoms might have been kept in check. However, he may have needed a higher dosage or several medications to control the symptoms chemically. Medication like Valium, Librium, and sleeping pills should be used only for 1 or 2 months. Otherwise they tend to cover up symptoms. It is much healthier to learn new skills to reduce the symptoms and use medication only as a backup once a week or once a month as needed.

Sam now saw that he did not have to be totally in control of himself when he faced stress. He could regulate his body and nervous system better with his PSR exercises. He also came to realize that working 50 to 60 hours every week, plus working at night and sometimes on weekends, was not healthy. He had not been doing physical exercise, so I helped him start a physical exercise program, which I will describe in Chapter Eight. He now works out three times a week and continues to do his 5 to 15 minutes of stress exercises once or twice a day.

It has been over 2 years since I first saw Sam, and I was able to have him vary his 5-minute exercises of breathing with one of the tapes once a day. He does his breathing checks every day as needed. If he gets into a more stressful situation at work or home, he can increase his sessions to two or three times a day. This is one example of how the PSR training can work in as short a time as 3 to 4 weeks. It may take 8 to 10 weeks, or 12 to 20 weeks in very difficult cases. People continue to improve for as much as 9 to 12 months. After a year they usually have maximized the stress skills. At this time they become more or less automatic. As happened in the sailboat story in Chapter Two, a person can think and react in new ways. You can have new, healthier automatic patterns as well as react in new, creative ways.

One of the most important functions of the nervous system is to regulate breathing. That is why there is so much focus on breathing in disciplines such as meditation, weight lifting, and childbirth, where specific breathing patterns are recommended. This is because the nervous system can use the breathing cycle as one of the ways to regulate and calm itself. If you are breathing short and fast, you are going to accelerate the nervous system. This can bring on a headache, giddiness, dizziness, faintness, light-headedness, vertigo, numbness, palpitations, chest discomfort, and pain. Hold your breath or take big gasps of air, and this irregular breathing will cause an increase in the activity in the nervous system and the body, requiring more oxygen. My mentor, Dr. Charles Stroebel, at the Hartford Institute for Living, taught me that breath is at the very center of our existence, beginning with our first breath as newborns and ending with our last breath at the end of life.

From childbirth on, you have a strong tendency to use emergency fight-or-flight responses which are expressed through your breathing patterns. The first emergency experience is being born. Your nervous system puts out a lot of norepinephrine (an arousal hormone) at birth. This helps you survive the decrease in oxygen experienced while passing through the vaginal canal in the birthing process. A group at Duke University led by Theodore Slotkin has demonstrated with rats and humans that this first surge of norepinephrine helps direct the blood flow to the brain, heart, and lungs, so the infant can survive on less oxygen while being born. Later in adult life, emergency breathing patterns become more complex and are connected to thoughts, fears, rushing around, planning to do things, and excitement. In all these situations, the main survival function is to get blood to the brain and heart and lungs. This is called "the crucial triangle" of the heart, lungs, and brain because these organs are absolutely necessary for us to function.

When you are excited or afraid, your breath is either held or it is fast and shallow. This increases arousal in the nervous system and keeps the emergency fight-or-flight response going. Excited breathing is often done in the upper chest, with very little breathing done by the diaphragm. You are using the diaphragm when the abdomen comes out on the "in breath." The abdomen should pull in as the diaphragm goes up on the "out breath." People who hyperventilate may be breathing so fast that they go into muscle spasms severe enough to shake the whole body. One way to change this breathing pattern is to have the person breathe into a paper bag. This shift in the ratio of oxygen (O_2) and carbon dioxide (CO_2), effectively forces a change in the breathing pattern since the person is inhaling a different mixture of oxygen and carbon dioxide. A better way is to practice the PSR breathing two to three times per day. Then you will have a healthier breathing pattern available to apply in a stressful situation.

When people are tense or excited, they often hold

their breath. The phone rings and they jump or gasp. People also gasp if they are frightened or upset about something. This very much goes along with the fight-or-flight response. People also mouth-breathe when in surprise or shock or fear rather then nose-breathe, which is healthier. This gasping or holding the breath continues to fire up the nervous system so that a person feels more tense, more excited, or more fearful. As you read this page, observe how you are breathing. Are you breathing in the upper chest, the middle chest, or with the abdomen (diaphragm)?

To check your breathing, simply put your left hand on your upper chest so your thumb is sticking in the notch of your collarbones; spread the hand down on the upper chest—your left hand will cover your upper chest. Then put the palm of your right hand directly over your navel. Now breathe again for two or three breaths and notice which hand moves and how much. Does your upper hand (the left hand) move more than the lower (right) hand? If the answer is yes, then you are breathing with the upper chest. If the lower hand moves more than the upper hand, then you are breathing more with the abdomen. The most restful, calming, and energizing breathing method is to breathe down into the diaphragm—the bottom of the lung cavity. The diaphragm moves down slightly and the abdomen comes out on the in breath, and you may even feel some motion to the right and left side of the abdomen. Then, as you breathe out, the abdomen will gently come in an inch or two as the air goes out (exhalation). What you would like to do is have the lower hand move outward more on the inhalation, and then pause. To exhale, gently pull in the abdominal wall so that your hand moves toward the spine, and then pause again. After about a week of practice, you should be able to breathe only with the abdomen and the diaphragm. Notice the pattern of your breathing during the day. You will be surprised at how often you breathe in the upper chest. I want you to train yourself to breathe down in the abdominal area. The abdominal wall should come out a little bit on each inhalation. Breathe at a calm, easy pace, about 10 to 12 breaths per minute. If you are breathing above 18 or 20 breaths per minute, the nervous system will race and you will have a tendency toward hyperventilation.

Try for 1 to 2 minutes to notice how to breathe with the abdomen (diaphragm). Calmly breathe in and out through your nose. Breathe in for a count of three or four. Then pause and breathe out for a count of three or four and pause before the next inhalation. As you practice this breathing exercise over the next week, you should be able to bring the breathing rate down into the range of 8 to 12 breaths per minute. This is best done in a quiet room where you have a few minutes by yourself, sitting comfortably in a chair that supports your head, arms, and legs. The slow, paced breathing, if diagramed, would look like this:

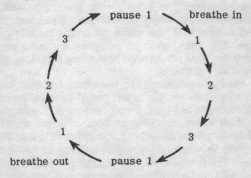

During the first few weeks of practice you should count out your breaths as illustrated in the diagram. The breathing exercise is basically to take the breath in through the nose to the count of three or four, and then pause for a count of one (gently hold your breath for one count). Then after the pause, gently exhale to a count of three or four. Pause for a count of one and then repeat this breathing cycle. To time yourself in your breathing, just say, "one thousand one, one thousand two, one thousand three, one thousand four." This will be about 4 seconds. This pattern of breathing in for three or four, and then pausing, and then out for three or four, and then pausing, will come to be a very calming and relaxed breathing pattern.

At first you may find that this breathing pattern seems unusual or forced. Try this new breathing pattern twice a day for 1 week, and you will see that you are able to use it comfortably. In a week you will be able to start using it in stressful conditions to calm your nervous system. Keep practicing, and more and more you will be able to say to yourself, "Be calm, breathe, and relax." You will think more clearly and be more relaxed in stressful conditions. You will be able to concentrate better in many different situations.

Some of the other calming statements you might use are (1) "Gee, this is not an emergency. I will just breathe and relax." (2) "I can deal with this by breathing and relaxing. Then I can figure out what to do next." As you do the breathing exercises and add the muscle-tension-relaxation exercises I will be giving you next, you will relax during the day. Many people use these exercises to fall asleep at night. If you wake up in the middle of the night, you can often go back to sleep by relaxing and tensing different muscle groups and using this slow, calm, paced breathing pattern.

After you have practiced the breathing for 6 or 7 days, I would like you to try this calm, paced breathing pattern in real-life situations. Practice when you are riding in an elevator. Just rehearse three or four of these breathing cycles of slow, paced breathing. Or practice when you're at a stoplight in your car or while walking or on the bus or subway. Try it when you are thinking about making a telephone call or when you receive a telephone call. Think about the person you are going to call, then do three or four of these slow, paced breathing cycles as you're starting to dial the telephone number. This way you will be relaxing and calming yourself while preparing to talk.

When you receive a phone call, try three or four slow, calm, paced breaths as you answer the phone. By the time you pick up the phone, you will be into your first or second cycle of paced breathing. When you say hello, you will be into your second or third breathing cycle. Once you are ready to talk, you will find you have used the PSR breathing to be more relaxed, calmer, and more alert. This breathing cycle is also an excellent way to prepare for a meeting with someone. Use these breathing patterns to go into very important meetings in a relaxed, calm way. You can also use this breathing check when you are in a meeting, to relax and calm yourself so you can think clearly and do your best.

As you continue practicing these PSR breathing skills, you will find that your breathing will become a good friend that will calm and relax you. Practice these skills at home in a calm and relaxed way so you have them available when you are in a stressful situation. That is why regular practice is necessary; otherwise you have nothing to call upon when you try to do these exercises in a real-life stressful situation. Try to do them in two to three different situations so you will continue to develop and improve the skills. The first time you try them in a stressful situation will be the most difficult. If you try a second or third time in a similar situation, you will notice an improvement. After practicing these breathing exercises people notice how often they hold their breath and how tense it makes them feel. They are able to recognize holding their breath only as they practice this slow, paced breathing. The brain had ignored the fact that they were holding their breath or tightening up. I believe this is because the brain cannot change the breathing pattern without regular practice, so it ignores the tense breathing pattern. Do not be surprised if you notice many of these different patterns when you practice the PSR exercises. The more you practice these exercises, the more skillful you will become at identifying stresses, breathing calmly, and thinking on your feet.

People ask why the specific written or taped exercises are useful. There are several reasons. When you first start using the exercises the tendency is to speed things up. You are often unaware of how the mind will race through exercises. So I have included the pacing and speed that is best to start with on these PSR exercises. They are also on audiocassettes so that you don't have to read them as you do them. Do not memorize them. Read them to yourself and go through them step by step.

A second reason is that as you continue doing the exercises, you will pick up more from each reading (or listening) and from the repetitions. Not only will you be repeating them and practicing the skill, but your mind will think about the exercises and learn from them even after many, many repetitions. Patients have told me that they started noticing some of the key elements that they did not hear the first month or two. As you repeat the exercises, some of the phrases, words, and images will have additional meaning as you acquire more skills and put them to use.

As I have said, it is best to begin the exercises in a quiet room where you will not be disturbed. Use a comfortable chair that supports your head, body, arms, and legs. Or, as you learn the exercises, you can stretch out on a rug or an exercise mat. Lie on your back and put a pillow under the back of your knees. This supports the thighs and relaxes the lower back so that they do not tighten up. You might use a thin feather pillow so your head does not roll to the right or left when you relax. Do not use a thick pillow, which pushes the head and neck far forward. Put your hands out about 6 to 10 inches from your hips with the palms facing up. You can do these exercises outside; however, I would recommend you wait for at least a month or two until you have practiced and become more skillful. Although doing them outside is often very comfortable, it is initially a little more arousing than being indoors.

I prefer that you not do the exercises after a full meal because the sounds of digestion and movements of gas in the stomach and bowels may be distracting. The best time to do the exercises is in the morning before breakfast, before lunch, at the end of the workday, in the middle of the evening, or just before bed. Do not do them on a bed or on a couch because these locations are associated with resting or sleeping. You can use the exercises for sleep, but acquire the skill first. Many people also tell me that they enjoy using the exercises on tape because this lets their minds focus on my voice and on the specific instructions.

First, read through these instructions so you have the general idea of the exercises; then read them again and do them step by step.

Sit in a chair or lie on a rug or exercise mat. Now I want you to take a deep breath and hold it as you tighten your right fist. Maintain that tension for about 6 to 8 seconds. Feel the tension, hold it, and then breathe out.

Let go completely and breathe again, easily and calmly, for two or three breath cycles. Let the relaxation spread into your wrists and fingers.

Good. Now take another deep, slow breath. Hold the breath and make the left fist into a tight fist— tighter, tighter, tighter. Hold that tension in the left fist for 6 to 8 seconds. Now breathe out and let go.

Let your breath become easy now. Let the relaxation spread into the hand, wrist, and fingers as you breathe for two or three breath cycles.

Good. Now take another slow, deep breath. Hold the breath and tense both fists, tighter and tighter. Feel that tension now in both fists. Hold that tension for 10 seconds. Now breathe out and let go.

Let the muscles of the hand and forearm become loose and limp and relaxed as your breathing becomes slow, regular, and calm. Pace your breathing in for three or four counts, pausing for a count, and then exhaling for a count of three or four. Then pause for a count and repeat.

Good. Breathe for two to three breath cycles.

Now take another deep, slow breath, tighten up the whole forehead, and clamp down your jaw muscles as if you were biting on something. Feel that tension in the forehead, face, and jaw. Hold the tension; hold it for 6 to 8 seconds. Now breathe out and let go.

Let your forehead, nose, face, and jaw muscles relax. Let your neck relax as you go back to the slow, calm, paced breathing for two to three breath cycles.

Fine. Now take another deep breath and tighten up your legs. Pull your toes up toward your face and feel that tension from the buttocks right down into the toes. Feel the tension right down the calves and down to the heels. Hold that tension. Tense from your buttocks right down to your toes for 6 to 8 seconds.

Now breathe out and let go. Let your breathing become slow, easy, calm, and paced. Breathe for two to three breath cycles.

Good. Now, as you take another deep breath, I want you to tense all the body parts that you can. Tense the fists, forehead, shoulders, back, and legs. Hold that tension all over the whole body. Feel that tension for 8 to 10 seconds. Let some muscles tremble if they want to. Now breathe out and let go.

Let all those muscles relax—the head, arms, chest, back, stomach, and legs. Breathe for two breath cycles.

Let's repeat that tensing. Take another deep, slow breath and tense the whole body. Tense all the muscles while you hold the breath for 8 to 10 seconds. Hold that tension; *hold it*. Now breathe out and let go.

Let the muscles become loose and limp and relaxed. Use the slow, calm, paced pattern of breathing in for three or four counts, pause and breathe out for three or four counts, and pause. Continue using this slow, calm, paced breathing and think about relaxing even more. Relax from the top of your head to your shoulders, into your chest and stomach region, and down to the back and buttocks, right into the thighs, knees, calves, ankles, feet, and toes. The whole body is now relaxed, calm, and peaceful.

Good! Now take the next 2 minutes and use the slow, paced breathing pattern to relax as deeply as you can.

Take another six to eight breath cycles and let yourself relax even more.

To end the exercises, say to yourself, "I feel calm and relaxed." Then count one, two, three, and slowly let your eyes drift open. Yawn and stretch your arms and legs. Let yourself get up feeling relaxed and refreshed.

As you do these exercises, I want you to notice the difference between tension and relaxation. At first you may feel tired or even exhausted. You will become aware of how tough the day or week has been. As you go on practicing the PSR exercises, this weariness will decrease. Start and end your day calmly by doing these exercises. Notice the difference between tension and relaxation. As you learn the PSR skills, your heart rate will slow and blood pressure decrease. Usually this change takes place gradually over 10 to 20 weeks. However, if you were to jump up during the PSR exercises or at the end without counting one, two, three, and stretching your arms and legs, you might feel dizzy or light-headed. So always count one, two, three, and stretch and yawn. Remember, the PSR exercises are often as powerful as many meditations.

These exercises should not cause any pain. If you do have pain or other side effects, check with your physician.

After you have practiced these exercises for a few days, you will often feel calm and relaxed not only for 10 to 15 minutes after the exercises but for an hour or two. As you get used to the exercises and slow, paced breathing, you can use your breath as a "breathing check." This means that you observe how you breathe and then breathe in and out in a slow, paced manner. Use the abdominal breathing pattern for a count of three or four, pause, and then breathe out for a count of three or four and pause. As you do the exercises, you may wish to increase the count to four or five, with a pause between the in breath and the out breath. You can use these breathing checks many times during the day, anytime you are under stress or have a worry or concern.

People who have problems with diarrhea, constipation, or passing gas can use these breathing exercises when they begin feeling some abdominal cramping, gas, or pain. People also find it useful to do a breathing check as they think about going to the bathroom, or while walking into the bathroom. Many times bowel problems increase when people think about or anticipate going to the bathroom or where they will find a bathroom. By immediately using a breathing check or using the PSR exercise, you can de-stress yourself. You can think of going to the bathroom in a more relaxed, calm way.

Another good time to practice is when you are walking, or if you are driving and come to a stoplight. Using a breathing check for three to four breath cycles can be very helpful. While you are driving a car, tense the left foot, if you are not using it to drive, for one or two breath cycles, and then relax the foot. Then tense the right fist on the wheel, and hold it for a count of two to three before relaxing it. Breathe an abdominal breath, and then tense the left fist and relax it and breathe in a relaxed, paced manner. By using these breathing exercises and putting them into different stressful situations, you will decrease the stress you feel and will do better. The calm, paced breathing, coupled with the phrases "Relax, there is no emergency" or "I can relax and figure out what to do" will be very helpful.

Summary

Do not underestimate the effectiveness of practicing these techniques. Over the next 4 to 5 weeks, you will find that using the PSR exercises will enable you to be calmer and more energetic in many stressful situations. If you are excited or waiting for some pleasurable event, you will be able to enjoy the pleasure even more. I will discuss this in Chapter Nine when I write about the effects of stress on sex. So enjoy the exercises and do them once or twice a day and three times on the weekends. Add the breathing checks, and you will be able to transfer these stress skills into your everyday situations. Remember to breathe and say to yourself, "Relax." Practice calm abdominal breathing, and let a little smile come to your face as you think about handling the stressful and exciting situations in your life even better. Use these exercises before going to bed or when you are in a pleasurable situation so that you can increase the pleasure and maintain it longer.

Just as in learning to write, play the piano, or ride a bicycle, you need regular practice. So use these exercises every day. The PSR breathing will be a major help to you in handling the 10 to 20 little hassles, aggravations, disappointments, and angry events of the day.

CHAPTER FOUR

STRESS AND ITS CONSEQUENCES

We want ups and downs in life. And the difficulties we encounter in the course of it arouse our energies and augment our pleasure.
—*Molière*

Paul's Skin

I had experienced episodes of allergic eczema on my arms since childhood. In adolescence this condition worsened and at times in winter covered my entire trunk. Thereafter it abated somewhat, and I was not much bothered in my latter years in college and graduate school.

This condition was at its worst during cold weather months, and I associated healthy skin with summer, sunlight, and salt water. Thus, it seemed logical that in the years following school when I joined the Peace Corps and lived in the Far East and central Africa, I was relatively unbothered by the condition.

I returned to America in 1979 at the age of 27. I tried to start a small business on the west coast, and within a year I was living in New York working for a film company. The company failed 6 months later, and once again I was searching for work. This experience, coupled with the increased pressures of living in New York—pressures on time, on money, and on the nature of human contact—led to a gradual worsening of the old condition.

However, it now manifested itself in new forms. I began to experience a red rash on my face, and this spread to my neck and arms. For the first time, the rash did not respond to summer weather. I found work, and in fact in 1982 gained an excellent position in a well-run publishing company, but this too caused stress. I had to confront the fact that I needed additional financial skills to progress in my job, and I began to concentrate on the development of those skills. This was helpful, but it meant that I could not pursue my primary pursuit outside work—writing.

A final creator of stress was the failure of a romantic involvement, which dragged out painfully over a period of months.

The result of all these events was a distinct worsening of the condition, until the rash had spread over my entire body. I scratched constantly, suffered allergic attacks, migraines, insomnia, palpitations, a constantly racing mind, and extreme anxiety.

I managed to deny most of these symptoms until June 1983 when my doctor, to whom I had gone for an ear infection, asked, "Why is your face all broken out?"

"It's not broken out."

"It is broken out, and you should do something."

"Like what?"

"Get thee to a dermatologist."

"Who?"

"Well, Dr. X does interesting work. Dr. Y does interesting work. And then for really weird cases, there's Al Grokoest."

"Exactly what is the precise medical definition of 'really weird'?"

"Someone like you who has no reason to be all broken out."

Gentle persuasion having thus made its mark, I spent 6 months intermittently seeing Dr. Grokoest. He attempted to direct me toward seeing for myself the correlation between stressful situations and outbreaks of dermatitis, and he also stressed the importance of early childhood connections. I resisted this interpretation for some time. I could not quite see it, but, near Thanksgiving of that year, the death of a close family friend was the cause of a severe episode, and at last I recognized the linkage.

At this point, I was introduced to Dr. Sedlacek and biofeedback. We began in December of 1983 with a general review of my case. I began the treatment and home relaxation sessions immediately (PSR). At first there was little improvement. I had difficulty in concentration and often drifted off to sleep in mid-session.

As I progressed, however, I began to improve my relaxation and circulation skills and hit a first crest within about 5 weeks. Skin rash was down, surface temperature up. More important, the principles of regulation that Dr. Sedlacek emphasizes became real rather than mere abstractions. I began to be able to make my body and brain work together, whereas before, the latter drove the former 24 hours a day, at work and at play.

Some results?

I began going out far less, staying home at night to read instead. I felt rested for the first time in years, and often slept straight through the night, also for the first time in years. Anxiety disappeared, and my work became more productive. Finally, I began to write seriously again and was able to finish a novel I had left undone for some time.

The benefits accrued throughout the winter, and by 6 months into the treatment my physical condition was 90 percent improved. At this point, it was Dr. Grokoest's suggestion that I see a psychiatrist. I did so and was advised that it was unnecessary to undergo psychotherapy. "Come back if you think you need to."

Throughout the summer and mild fall my condition continued to improve and with it my sense of well-being and enjoyment of life. At Christmas I decided to further regulate my regimen by reducing my alcohol intake to less than half of its previous level. This adjustment, though only a month old, seems to have yielded clarity, more positive thinking, better endurance. I had been ignoring a chronic disc problem and now have addressed that condition, so far with favorable results.

On my last follow-up session with Dr. Sedlacek I was disappointed to see that my temperature-raising skills had eroded. True, it was a cold day, but this is an area to improve. Other goals must be formulated as well. In general, however, the treatment has been gentle and therapeutic. It has made a profound change in my life, fostering a relaxed and healthy state of mind as opposed to the anxious and tense condition that preceded it.

Paul's case shows how we can use Positive Stress Response (PSR) for skin problems, low back pain, anxiety, sleep problems, palpitations, and use of alcohol. His worry and racing mind tended to activate all of these symptoms. In many cases, patients have tried numerous potions and medications without really getting to the heart of the problem, which is the speeded-up nervous system. As I used PSR and biofeedback with Paul, he began not only to relax but to calm his whole nervous system. He was able to reevaluate his life and put in new, calmer, mental/physical patterns. He now has more positive thinking, better endurance, better skin, and less pain. He also points out the important fact that if patients do not continue to practice regularly, when they come back in for follow-up they will often have slightly increased signs of arousal. By using a regular practice schedule, people can continue to use PSR and live healthier lives.

The Stress Test

Now that we have discussed some of the key factors about the nervous system, its arousal pattern, and the number of stresses, I suggest you use the Stress Regulation Institute Health and Stress Scale (Table 4-1). As you see, there are seven items for you to score. We have used the seven-item test at the Stress Regulation Institute for training individuals from corporations, hospitals, and schools. In the seven items, you will see some of the key elements of health of your daily life: sleep, weight, exercise, relaxation techniques, humor and play, smoking, and the Holmes-Rahe Life Events Scale (Table 4-2). This stress scale is called a health and stress scale because it focuses on the health factors that you can improve in your life. I will briefly discuss each of these points, and then I would like you to add up your Life Events Scale and score yourself on the seven items. I will outline the scoring and what it means in terms of the research and clinical work we have done in the last 14 years.

Stress Test

1. Sleeping from 6 to 8 hours a night is probably ideal. Thus I have asked people who sleep 6 to 8 hours at least 6 nights per week to give themselves 1 point on the health scale. Give yourself zero (0) points if you are sleeping less or more than 6 to 8 hours. This is a warning sign that you are getting too little or too much sleep.

2. If you are within 10 to 15 lbs. of your ideal weight, give yourself 1 point. You are staying at a healthy level. If you are more than 20 percent over your ideal weight, you are putting yourself at a higher risk for many diseases and disorders.

3. You need to exercise at least 15 to 30 minutes three times a week. This will be explained in Chapter Eight.

4. A good relaxation, biofeedback, or meditation program can help your nervous system. Positive Stress Response (PSR) training will help even more, but give yourself 1 or 2 points if you are already practicing a "calming" technique.

5. Give yourself a point if you have a few minutes of laughing four times a week, preferably a belly laugh. In Norman Cousins's book *The Anatomy of an Illness* he suggested that by looking at humorous films and laughing and enjoying them, you are keeping yourself in a positive mental and physical framework. The mechanism you are strengthening is your immune system, which can help you recover from illness.

6. In general, if you do not smoke at all or if you smoke less than five cigarettes a day, you get a point on the health scale because this shows you are treating your lungs and your nervous system very well. If you smoke a pipe or cigars, give yourself zero (0) points. If you are smoking more than five cigarettes a day, you are starting to increase the risks, so give yourself zero (0) points. If you are smoking more than one pack of cigarettes a day, give yourself a minus 1 (—1), since you are actively asking for lung cancer and a decrease in your life expectancy of from 5 to 20 years.

TABLE 4-1   Stress Regulation Institute Health and Stress Scale

_____ 1. If you get 6–8 hours of sleep at least 6 nights per week, give yourself 1 point, 0 if less or more than 6–8 hours.

_____ 2. If you are within 10–15 lbs. of your ideal weight, give yourself 1 point; if you are not within 10–15 lbs. of your ideal weight, give yourself 0 points.

_____ 3. If you exercise for more than 15–20 minutes steadily and increase your heart rate 70–80% from your resting heart rate twice or three times per week, give yourself 1 point. If you exercise four or more times a week, give yourself 2 points.

_____ 4. If you practice a relaxation technique such as meditation, relaxation response, or biofeedback for 15–30 minutes at least five times a week, give yourself 1 point; if you practice these techniques ten or more times per week, give yourself 2 points.

_____ 5. If you smile, laugh, or are pleased for 2–3 minutes four or more times a week, give yourself 1 point. If you only have a good "belly laugh," enjoy playing with a pet, child, or friend three or fewer times a week, give yourself 0 points.

_____ 6. If you do not smoke cigarettes, or smoke fewer than five per day, and if you also do not smoke cigars or a pipe, give yourself 1 point. If you smoke between five cigarettes and one pack per day, give yourself 0 points. If you smoke over one pack of cigarettes a day, give yourself minus 1 point.

_____ 7. Use the Life Events Scale to score yourself. If your Life Events Scale is below 125, give yourself 2 points. If your Life Events Scale is below 250, give yourself 1 point. If your Life Events Scale is above 250, give yourself 0 points.

_____   Total Points

TABLE 4-2   Holmes-Rahe Life Events Scale

If any of the following events have occurred to you within the last 12 months, place the Mean Value of the event under the column marked Your Score. Then total the Mean Values that are in the column marked Your Score.

Rank	Life Event	Mean Value	Your Score
1.	Death of spouse	100	
2.	Divorce	73	
3.	Marital separation	65	
4.	Jail term	63	
5.	Death of close family member	63	
6.	Personal injury or illness	53	
7.	Marriage	50	
8.	Fired at work	47	
9.	Marital reconciliation	45	
10.	Retirement	45	
		Subtotal ____	
11.	Change in health of family member	44	
12.	Pregnancy	40	
13.	Sex difficulties	39	
14.	Gain of new family member	39	
15.	Business readjustment	39	
16.	Change in financial status	38	
17.	Death of close friend	37	
18.	Change to different line of work	36	
19.	Change in number of arguments with spouse	35	
20.	Mortgage over $10,000	31	
		Subtotal ____	
21.	Foreclosure of mortgage or loan	30	

TABLE 4-2 *(Continued)*

Rank	Life Event	Mean Value	Your Score
22.	Change in responsibilities at work	29	
23.	Son or daughter leaving home	29	
24.	Trouble with in-laws	29	
25.	Outstanding personal achievement	28	
26.	Spouse begins or stops work	26	
27.	Begin or end school	26	
28.	Change in living conditions	25	
29.	Revision of personal habits	24	
30.	Trouble with boss	23	
		Subtotal _____	
31.	Change in work hours or conditions	20	
32.	Change in residence	20	
33.	Change in schools	20	
34.	Change in recreation	19	
35.	Change in church activities	19	
36.	Change in social activities	18	
37.	Mortgage or loan less than $10,000	17	
38.	Change in sleeping habits	16	
39.	Change in number of family get-togethers	15	
40.	Change in eating habits	15	
41.	Vacation	13	
42.	Christmas	12	
43.	Minor violations of the law	11	
		Subtotal _____	
		Total _____	

   Since this is a positive Health and Stress Scale, smoking is the only negative point included. Smoking is such a terrible risk factor for cancer, heart attacks, and strokes that if you smoke, you are not caring for yourself.

7. Look at the Holmes-Rahe Life Events Scale, and list the number of your stresses by checking them off and adding them up. If your total is less than 125, you have not had a very stressful year. Give yourself 2 points because your chances of not having an accident or illness are more than 50/50 according to the Life Events Scale. If your score is less than 250, you are in the middle range. On this scale your chances are 50/50 that you may have an accident or illness. Give yourself 1 point. If you total over 250 points, you should give yourself a zero (0). This amount of stress indicates that you are at a high risk. Approximately 75 percent of people with more than 250 points may experience an accident or become ill within the next year. As you look at the key stress factors, you can see some of the things you can do to improve your health. Exercise, relaxation, biofeedback, and positive stress management can help you.

Understanding Your Score on the Health and Stress Scale

There are 10 possible points. If you scored 1 point or less on this stress test, then you have failed. This indicates that you are doing little or nothing for your health. In fact, you are doing negative activities to score less than 2 points. Give yourself an "F."

If your score is 2 or 3, then you have a poor approach in terms of healthful factors to reduce stress and turn it into positive stress. Give yourself a mark of "D."

If your score is 4 or 5, you get a good rating because you are doing several things to help yourself throughout the week. Give yourself a "C."

If your score is 6 or 7, give yourself a very good or a "B." You are doing most things quite well.

Eight points and above is an excellent health program. You should give yourself an "A." You are doing a great deal for your health. By adding the PSR techniques in this book, you can get into the "A+" range.

Item 7, the Life Events Scale, is a large variable. In some years you may have a great deal of stress that is not under your control. If this is the case, be sure to use all your PSR techniques.

Stress Problems and Your Own History

A useful exercise is to review the type of problems, diseases, or disorders that have occurred in your immediate family. Consider the health pattern of both sets of grandparents, your mother and father, brothers and sisters, as well as your aunts and uncles on both sides of the family. In my family, for example, there are several diseases and disorders—diabetes, arthritis, ulcers, phlebitis, colitis, and heart attacks. By reviewing your own history you can assess possible future risks. For example, if your grandmother and grandfather had diabetes and your mother or father had diabetes, then you have a 30 to 50 percent risk of diabetes later in life. If there is a history of heart disease in your family, then you should use the PSR training so you can reduce your risks. If people don't retrain their nervous systems, they are likely to perpetuate their family history of health problems.

Many sports activities, such as football, baseball, basketball, or soccer, entail risks—broken bones, bruises, aches, and pains. However, with high-risk activities like mountain climbing, serious accidents such as falls, frostbite, and even death can occur. For example, since 1953, about 150 men and women have successfully scaled Mount Everest in the Himalayas. Sir Edmund Hillary and Tenzing Norgay were the first to scale Everest in 1953. Since then, approximately 65 people have died trying to climb it. So, if your goal is to climb Mount Everest successfully, you can see from these figures that approximately one in three people attempting to reach the top will die. A 30 percent death rate is a high rate of risk for climbing a mountain. In some competitions you risk your life.

Usually in sports, work, or daily life the risks are not this high. However, because of negative stress reactions many people pay a high price for their attempts to succeed by pushing their bodies and minds too hard, too far, too fast, or too high.

Reviewing the accidents and injuries you have experienced, together with your family history, will give you a good picture of your physical and mental background for stress problems. If you have had a series of injuries or accidents, then you know you will have to be a little more careful of those parts of your body and those activities. Stress may affect you by increasing the number of injuries or accidents you may have.

In this book, I will discuss ways you can change old habits and add healthy new habits. You cannot change your genes, so you cannot do much about your height. However, you can affect your weight and other risk factors by changing your nervous system. You cannot do too much about your IQ, but you can adapt and use your brain better through the use of PSR.

A Real Emergency—"Fire!"

Symptoms tend to build up during very stressful periods. Then the stress will change or ease off over time, but the mental system will continue to act as if the stress is still there. The nervous system is locked in (habituated) at a higher level, and until it is unlocked, the symptoms will continue or worsen. Stress overreactions are very complex. We need to look at what starts the habituation, what maintains it, and the fact that the nervous system tends to keep this habituation going at a higher level even though the stresses are reduced.

One example of this from my life was when I was at the Fairmont Hotel in San Francisco to give a lecture on stress for the leaders of the 500 top corporations in the United States. The night before my lecture, there was a fire. An arsonist had started a fire on the fifteenth floor. I was asleep on the fourteenth floor when the fire alarm went off at 1:00 a.m. I went to the door and put my hand on it. It was cool, so I decided to look outside. The hallway was filled with smoke. Usually a hotel room has a diagram that shows the location of the fire escape, but there was no sign on the door. It is quite scary to be awakened in the middle of the night and not know whether you should go right or left in a smoked-filled hallway. One way could mean escape and the other way being burned. I called the operator and she said, "Just wait in your room." I knew that the hotel personnel knew there was a fire and that help would be coming. But how long would it take? I rushed to the window and opened it. It was 14 flights down with no ledge or any way to walk or crawl away. I thought about soaking myself in the bathtub or shower with my clothes on so I could run through the hallway if necessary. The worst thing was that I felt trapped. My chances were 50/50 of either running into the fire or running away to safety.

By using PSR, I was able to slow down my heart rate. I again checked the door to feel if it was warm so I would know if the fire was closer. Then I heard someone yell in the hall. I looked out the door and saw a flashlight moving up and down to the left. So I ran quickly down the hall in bare feet with only pants and a shirt on. Out of the next room to my left came a middle-aged couple with their two sons. One was about 14 and the other about 12. The children came out dressed only in their underwear. They started to run down the hall. Their parents were fully dressed and had prepared because they came out carrying two handbags. They probably had their property and valuables with them. I remember thinking they looked like German or Swiss tourists. We all rushed down the hall to the flashing light where the fire escape was located. We started down the stairs. With each floor I went down, I felt more comfortable. When I reached the first floor and was away from the flames and smoke, I sat down. My heart was still pounding, but now with relief. I looked around the first floor of the Fairmont Hotel. People were walking around as if there had been no emergency. Some were dressed in black tuxedos, having come from the nightclub, and were heading back to their rooms.

There were the five of us in the lobby. I was barefoot,

the children in white underwear, and their parents dressed and carrying their bags. After the fire was put out, the Fairmont desk personnel wanted me to go back to the fourteenth-floor room. I said no. I wanted a different room someplace on the third floor or lower. They were fully booked and sent me to another hotel. I gave my stress lecture the next day with renewed excitement about the fight-or-flight response. I vowed always to look to make sure I knew where the fire escape was even if there was a map on my hotel door. More recently, in August 1986, I was invited to give a lecture on the cost-effectiveness of biofeedback, in Washington, D.C. The night before my lecture I was staying at the Washington Sheraton, and I had gone to bed early. About half an hour later, I heard an emergency alarm go "beep, beep" and a recorded voice saying, "Please go immediately to the fire exits." I put on my shirt and pants and grabbed shoes, slides, and notes for the lecture. I ran to the fire escape, which I knew was just to my right, having already looked at my map on the door. I was down to the second flight of stairs when I heard the second automatic voice announce, "This has been a false alarm. Please return to your room. There is no fire." At this point, there were 30 or 40 people in the fire escape. We all returned to our rooms in different stages of dress or undress.

Even though this time there was no smoke or fire, my heart was still pounding. My nervous system reacted with the fight-or-flight reaction, just as in the incident in San Francisco! This is an example of how the brain recalls or remembers a threatening situation and pumps adrenaline through the body. It shows how the thought of fire or a fire alarm can trigger reactions from a whole series of past events. This is not just a mental reaction, however, but a very strong physical one as well. When people think of old events, emotions, upsets, or traumas, therefore, they often retrigger them. They have virtually the same type of reaction or overreaction as happened before with the real threat (fire, anger, loss of a loved one). This is why it is so important to retrain the mental and physiological reactions so the retriggering mechanism does not trigger all the old traumas as strongly. Psychotherapy and psychoanalysis and other techniques are also useful in retraining the brain's overreactions.

In all emergencies or overreactions there are physical signs of anxiety, such as increased heart rate, sweating, bowel problems, or high blood pressure, and it is very helpful to retrain the nervous system. When you retrain the physical system and reconnect these new coping skills through the PSR, you get a much better result. An example of this is the treatment of Raynaud's patients where stress often triggers attacks. While relaxation may help approximately 30 percent of these patients, if 20 to 30 treatment sessions of PSR with biofeedback are done, over 90 percent of these patients will get a good to excellent result. With the PSR training and biofeedback, they will be able to reduce the blanching, color changes, or pain that the fingertips and toes undergo. This has been demonstrated by Dr. Robert Freedman and in my work. Similar results happen with classic migraine headaches. Using the PSR training and hand warming with home temperature equipment, people become quite adept at slowing or reducing the symptoms. As many as 60 to 80 percent of patients with migraine headache can be helped by these techniques of PSR plus biofeedback.

Other Common Stress Signs

Some stress signs are often so involved or so enmeshed in our society and culture that they are not easily recognized as stresses. For example, if you listen to Madison Avenue ad campaigns, you are made aware of some of these stress reactions. Millions of dollars are spent advertising products to fight bad odors. We get sales pitches on the use of deodorants, perfumes, mouthwashes, and breath sprays. One of the many ads says to put your hands up "if you can." Their meaning is that if you are under stress, you will sweat more, and people often sweat under the arms and stain their shirt or blouse. The ad warns people to be fearful or embarrassed to raise their arms.

Among my other favorite ads are those for foot deodorants. Some people's feet sweat and no one at work knows. When these people go home and powder their feet, their spouses or other family members know because their feet smell bad. This is a more subtle sign of stress. Remember, the heart rate goes up, sweating increases, and your heart pounds just as if you were frightened by a bear or were in a near car accident or fire.

Other ads that relate to stress are those promoting antacids for upset stomach and gas. A recent one shows Dave Johnson, manager of the New York Mets, reaching for a tablet for his "nervous stomach" when making a coaching decision. When there is increased arousal of the nervous system, more acid is produced. In some cases this can become an ulcer, and it can bleed. Prescription drugs for ulcers are used to reduce the acid output. Although they are supposed to be used for only 1 to 2 months, they are now being overused in the same way as Valium. Initially people were taking Valium once every day; then many increased their intake to three times a day. People are supposed to take the drug for 2 to 3 months, but more often they continue for 3 to 6 months or for years.

Another example of stress was shown in the 1980 World Series involving the Kansas City Royals. The pressure of being a "star" acted on George Brett's nerves and he developed hemorrhoids. He had to receive treatment between games 2 and 3 to enable him to play effectively. I believe hemorrhoids can be caused when people tighten down the buttocks and anus as part of their stress reaction. This irritates the skin and the blood vessels around the anus. It becomes inflamed and is very painful. Hemorrhoid medication can reduce the pain and irritation. However, PSR could offer a better alternative.

These are some examples of other stress reactions for which people spend millions and millions of dollars. PSR training can help people have better health and spend their money on better food, exercise equipment, or other endeavors that support health. In other words, money spent for these perfumes, deodorants, and antacids could be better spent on other items that support your health.

The Timing of Stresses

People often think of stress as a particular tragedy in life. What is more common is that there are several stresses and hassles that occur 20 to 40 times a day. One of the most common is the tension, anxiety, and stress people feel late on Sunday afternoon and in the evening as they anticipate going to work or dealing with particular problems the next day. Many people have a restless night's sleep and come into work tired on Monday morning. This may affect the rest of the week. I have often said that one of the reasons people suffer from sleeplessness is "worry stress." I believe these people are at higher risk for heart attacks and strokes. While many of us in the stress field have mentioned this, it was not until recently that there was more hard evidence of this phenomenon.

These data come from recent research demonstrating that heart attacks tend to occur at a particular time during the day. James Muller of the Harvard Medical School found that not only heart attacks but strokes, angina, and sudden death from heart disease all tend to occur around 9:00 a.m. This finding was based on work by the Multicenter Investigation for the Limitation of Infarct Size, which was sponsored by the National Heart and Blood Institute. The study was designed to see if two different drugs, propranolol or hyaluronidase, could reduce damage from heart attacks. With 847 patients, as well as data from 2000 others, they found that these patients tended to have heart attacks around 9:00 a.m. The most infrequent time for heart attacks was about 11:00 p.m. People are three times more likely to have a heart attack in the morning than at 11:00 at night. These researchers knew the reported time of the attack, and they could study an objective measure of the attacks, the variance of the enzyme creatine kinase. Creatine kinase is released in the bloodstream after a heart attack begins. By double checking the blood levels of creatine kinase, it was clear that the timing of 9:00 a.m. was correct. Dr. Muller then wanted to see if perhaps this was true for strokes. By checking with the stroke data of over 1200 patients at the National Institutes of Health, he found that there was a greater likelihood that strokes would occur between 8:00 and 9:00 a.m. As I have discussed in relation to the emergency fight-or-flight response, one of the reasons for these heart attacks is a surge of the plasma catecholamine that occurs in the morning and causes coronary vessel spasm. The catecholamine surge may also burst a blood vessel and cause a stroke. Since people are getting up and preparing to go during the day, this combination of a need for blood and a spasm or a vasoconstriction of crucial blood vessels could explain why heart attacks occur in the morning.

These studies of over 3000 people with heart attacks and strokes suggest that stress management exercises before going to bed, and particularly upon getting up in the morning, would be helpful. The additional use of PSR skills that are described in Chapter Seven could be a great help. Another option is for patients who are on medication to take it upon rising. Knowing when to use your stress management skills may help you to decrease your chances for a heart attack or stroke.

Personal Cost of Stress

An example of the cost of stress is the recent career of Dick Vermeil, the former coach of the Philadelphia Eagles football team. After having played at UCLA and coaching college football, he went on to have a fantastic career coaching the Philadelphia Eagles. He was not asked to resign but decided to leave after 5 years. His explanation was that the stress was so much for him that he was "burned out." He felt he had to leave this high-paying and very active job. The Philadelphia Eagles not only had become a respected team but had challenged for the Super Bowl title. At the top of his career, he left the Eagles because he said he was spending every night preparing for the next week's game. He often would sleep at the office and watch game films. His intensity helped him as a player and as a college and professional coach, but it caused such a high level of stress that he had to stop what he loved doing.

This is an example of how stress can burn out a successful person, or possibly ruin a healthy life. In Vermeil's case, he was smart enough to recognize the warning signs of stress and decided his only choice was to leave the Eagles. He stayed in football by becoming a sports announcer, a "color man" who comments on the football games. Thus, he can still be close to the game, but he no longer has to put in long stressful hours as a head coach.

He has maintained his health and has more time for himself and his family. If Dick Vermeil had PSR training, he might have had an alternative. He could have continued coaching for a few more years rather than just dropping out.

Another example is Len Bias, the young Maryland basketball player who was drafted by the Boston Celtics in 1986. Sometimes positive happenings or excitement can create deadly stresses. In the case of Len Bias, his excitement about being drafted as one of the top picks caused him to celebrate at a party. Either he was slipped some cocaine or he had inadvertently taken too much, and the drug caused his death.

One of the options people have by doing the PSR is that they are able to handle more stress more calmly and be more efficient with less wear and tear on their bodies and minds. Different individuals can tolerate and enjoy different amounts of stress. What is fascinating is that we have more potential in our nervous systems than many of us think. We can train to increase our stress tolerance and use our minds and bodies better. By using the PSR techniques and exercises you can use more of the potential that is available in your nervous system. The brain has billions of cells that can be trained or retrained and then used in everyday life. It is like learning to ride a bicycle. If you do not learn how to ride, you miss the enjoyment of riding with friends. So, as with learning to ride a bike, there is a great deal more you can get out of your nervous system, but if you do not train and use the new skills, they are not available and the potential will not be used for your benefit and enjoyment.

Financial Cost of Stress

An indication of how much stress-related problems cost financially comes from a review of health costs for 1986. In that year, the total spending for health care rose by 9 percent. These costs continued to go up twice as fast as other prices. Health costs took 10.9 percent of the gross national product in 1986. In 1987, health care costs were estimated to be 11%. The total cost in 1985 for health care expenditures in the United States was $458 billion. That comes to an average of $1856 per person per year. Because of changes in insurance policies and government policy, people are paying more out of their own pockets.

A total of $30.6 billion was spent on drugs and sundries (meaning eyeglasses, other appliances, and supplies). Approximately half of this amount, or about $15 billion, was spent on prescription drugs. Health officials say that stress-related disability claims have doubled over the last 5 years. By using PSR techniques, cost of disability and medication can often be reduced by as much as 30 to 50 percent. It is quite possible that 30 to 40% of these drug costs, or approximately $5 to $6 billion, can be saved by using PSR techniques. Preventative and prophylactic retraining of people's nervous systems will enable all of us to experience better health and lower health costs.

Control

The brain is interested in control, in controlling our bodies and the environment around us and the result of what happens to us. From childhood on we are taught to be in control of ourselves. We are told to "take charge of your life." By this people generally mean that you should try to influence events. Yet there are some events you cannot influence or control. For example, you cannot influence the sun's rising or setting. As the old saying goes, "Time and tide wait for no man" (or woman). While there are some things not within our control, there are many others we can influence. That is why, as you do the PSR training, you will learn to control events when possible. In other situations you just want to try to cope, to adjust quickly and in the best possible way. In the sailing story in Chapter Two, the husband had no opportunity to control the wind. What he could do was adjust the sails to prevent a tragedy. While thinking and looking toward controlling situations, your brain can be happy with regulating, adjusting, or readjusting in various situations. In fact, when people attempt to control things or attempt to overcontrol, they may get a negative or an opposite result of what they are hoping for.

Often you will want to exert, as President John Kennedy used to say, a "proper amount of power." He used this expression in terms of dealing with people and with crises. You can use it when dealing with stressful situations. Focus on the things you can influence, and do not worry and spend a lot of energy on things you cannot control or influence. The brain gets smarter by using the body and mind's energy on issues and situations where results are possible.

The PSR training allows you to wait more calmly or comfortably for events to change or to gather steam. When your brain immediately says, "Control the situation," try to think about the situation to see if there are other options. This will give your brain two or three options to consider rather than going in only one direction.

My patients have found that instead of saying to themselves, "Control yourself" or "I've got to control the situation," they say, "I've got to regulate or adjust myself" or "I'll regulate or adjust to the situation." This allows the brain to focus on doing the best in the situation and not having fantasies of control, which often waste your energy and your purpose.

Taking Charge

Think about activities in a calm way and then choose a course of action. What you want to guard against is choosing in a fast, tense way. You can choose in a calm yet fast way with a relaxed nervous system. Much of the research with Type A individuals shows that it is not bad to want to get things done and achieve things. The problem is if you drive yourself too much and race the whole system and are exceedingly demanding of yourself. This makes you less efficient. Thus, you want to work but in a calm, active mode. Practice gearing up and then easing off. For example, if you work for 4 to 5 hours on the weekend, take a half hour off after 2 hours before going back to your work. It is this "pacing," being able to speed up and slow down while holding your concentration and creative abilities, that you want to keep working toward by using the PSR training. Remember that faster is not always better.

Freeze Response

We have discussed the fight-or-flight response when there is a real threat or danger to you. Your brain orders your body into an emergency alert action and pumps powerful hormones through your body to prepare you to fight or flee. This arousal can have many subtle effects. Not only does it occur when you are ready to fight or run if you meet a bear while walking in Yellowstone National Park, but it can also affect your thinking and concentration. We call thinking an intellectual function. While you can either fight or flee, the third reaction that people experience intellectually and emotionally may be called the "freeze response." Examples of this might be when you are thinking of someone's name and you cannot recall it even though you know that you know it, or you are in a situation where there is some stress and you cannot remember something. Another example would be if you are talking with people and you cannot react to them. You freeze up, or, as one of my patients said, your "tongue gets locked up." These are examples of the subtle type of fight-or-flight response that can affect our thinking and feelings. I call it the "freeze" response.

Another emotional pattern of the freeze response is a kind of aloofness or distancing from other people when they are talking about strong emotions. The activation of the fight-or-flight response may cause people to think they are in such a fearful situation that they will say nothing even though their business partner, spouse, friend, or lover requires or expects a response. By not saying anything, responding defensively, or acting confused, you can lead the other people into believing you have nothing to say about the topic. They may get angry at you because you have not said anything, or they may interpret the lack of response as a negative response. Actually, you may have a positive response that you have not been able to communicate because of stress. It may be so positive a thought or response that you are frightened into silence by a negative stress response. Even if it is a negative response, you should say it. This gives an opportunity for communicating. No response gives no opportunity for responding or communicating. These fight-or-flight responses are not always big emergency situations but can be complex interactions between people.

Another area that may be affected is called creative thinking. When people are tense or anxious over a deadline or a decision, they will often become exhausted. This may lead to being mentally tied up or to having a creative block. Just like a swimmer or a runner, if they try too hard their muscles will tighten up or go into spasm. They will not have the fast time in the race that they could have had.

We reflect this mental and physical process in trying to describe emotions and creative thoughts or actions—that is, "I just flew by the seat of my pants" or "The name is on the tip of my tongue." People get tied up intellectually and can no longer think creatively, on their feet, or by the seat of their pants. Notice how many of the phrases that people use are physical ones: "tied up," "fly by the seat of my pants," "bound up." I think the term "fight-or-flight response" needs to be expanded to include these intellectual and emotional reactions and be called the "fight, flight, or freeze response."

PSR training can help you relax and not "freeze up" physically, emotionally, and mentally. Remember the sailboating emergency—"freezing up" or the wrong emergency reaction could have caused the death of a loved one.

What about Meditation?

One of the most frequent questions that people ask me is "Doesn't meditation help people?" I reply that meditation can be helpful. Dr. H. Benson, in his book *The Relaxation Response*, states that people with hypertension can reduce their blood pressure 4 to 5 points systolic and 2 to 3 points diastolic with meditation. This is a statistically significant change, but it is not a clinically effective change. A clinically effective change is a reduction of 10 to 15 points.

I suggest to my patients that meditation can be helpful for self-growth, awareness, and as a healthy daily practice. Meditation is not specific, however, in providing new skills that are immediately available to people. What do I mean by this? It is not specific in that meditation can take several months or a year or two to change physiological patterns. Let's compare Dr. Benson's work with some research I did at St. Luke's Hospital in New York City. I used the PSR training with the temperature biofeedback equipment and tapes described in this book. Jonathan Cohen, Ph.D., and I showed that people who use these techniques and practiced for as little as 10 weeks averaged a reduction of approximately 14 points systolic and 12 points diastolic. These people all had had histories of hypertension for over 2 years, and 27 out of 30 were on medication for high blood pressure. We not only reduced the blood pressures by 14/12 points, from 144/95 to 130/83, but three out of the seven people in the PSR and biofeedback group were able to reduce 50 percent or more of their medications. These blood pressures were taken as they would be normally when you come into the office or the hospital for treatment. They were even lower after the patients did the biofeedback and PSR training. Since physicians use this entering pressure to determine the amount of medication to use, I have reported this blood pressure.

Another example that makes it even clearer is that of learning to play the piano or ride a bicycle. If you think about it or meditate, you are still not riding a bicycle or playing a piano. What is needed is a skill-acquisition period. This means practicing how to balance on a bicycle or learning how to play the scales on a piano. As you get your balance, you can start moving forward without falling down. On a piano you can start playing "Mary Had a Little Lamb" and then advance to other songs.

There is a step-by-step acquisition of skills that is made available to people who use a retraining program. This is generally not available with meditation. Thus, meditation, in my view, is a helpful preparation for growth of skills but does not teach specific skills. This is why I recommend a specific 8-week training program. You can use PSR training and practice these skills until they are developed, and you can use them every day. Then they are available to the brain, and the brain can use them when dealing with stressful situations.

You will develop a concept of being able to steel yourself or to inoculate yourself against stress. You become stronger by learning to handle stress in a positive way. The brain can also generalize these skills into other situations. Thus, in a new stressful situation, such as the one I recounted at the start of the book with the sailboating accident, you can use your brain to create new and healthier solutions. When you learn to play some songs on the piano, you can sight-read and play new music fairly well. You are confident and willing to try out new music. Or, using the bicycle analogy, when your friends suggest riding up the hill and across a narrow bridge, you can be confident that you can do it after you have practiced the skills of riding.

Corporate Stress Management

I have worked with hundreds of executives from corporations such as Penney's, Mobil, and Celanese, as well as from hospitals and schools. I have found that stress management skills are helpful not only for the individual's health and well-being but also in helping the corporate managers and executives work better with other people. Jim Manuso, Ph.D., worked at Equitable Insurance, where he treated headache and stress clients. He showed that the corporation obtained approximately $2 in return for every dollar they put into their stress management program. He also told me that they did not have an accurate estimate of the real cost of employees who had muscle contraction headaches (a dull ache in the forehead, neck, and/or shoulder areas). Many of these hardworking people would come into work with a headache. They used aspirin and other pain medications. Not only did their work suffer, but these headaches also created problems with people working around them. They would complain about noises, were irritable and obviously in pain. From 60 to 70 percent of the patients who took Dr. Manuso's program got better, and he referred the other patients for medical *stepped care* to an expert in headache treatment. Stepped care means adding additional treatments to obtain a successful treatment. With PSR training, biofeedback, and medication for some, many of these unsuccessful patients were able to reduce their headaches.

One of the other major problems that people face in business is they push and drive themselves to be successful, either to become millionaires or to obtain leadership of a business or company. When they succeed, they often find that success is rather empty. In many cases, these people have vague feelings of dissatisfaction. Others feel depressed and are not able to sleep or eat well, or they are restless and irritable. They may develop headaches or bowel problems or alternate between a series of these symptoms. This has been well described in *The Success Syndrome,* a book by Steve Berglass, Ph.D. As many people recognize, to lead a good life you need more than money. Success can be stressful. It can cause problems mentally as well as physically.

Stepped Care with PSR Training

Stepped care means starting with the mildest drug and the smallest dosage to reduce symptoms such as high blood pressure. This used to mean starting with a diuretic, like hydrochlorothiazide. If this did not reduce the blood pressure to the normal range, then the doctor "stepped up" the strength of the treatment by adding a second drug, usually a more powerful one. If this did not work, a third drug would be added. One class of these newer drugs are the "beta-blockers." These drugs block the betareceptors of the heart and affect the brain, arteries, and blood volume to reduce blood pressure. They also have many negative side effects, such as tiredness, increased urination, weakness, headaches, impotence, or even hallucinations.

Psychologists such as Edward Blanchard showed that they could reduce blood pressure with progressive muscle relaxation (PMR) and stress management technique. However, by using only PMR and stress management, just a few patients could reduce the two or three different drugs to one or two. With 18 sessions of stress management combined with biofeedback treatment, many people step down a whole class of drugs. They can remove one of their two or three types of drugs. They go from two different drugs three times a day to one drug three times a day. This of course reduces the side effects as well as the amount and cost of medication. Each level of drug use can cost from $100 to $1000 per year. As I mentioned earlier in this book, this could amount to billions of dollars of savings.

Some of the best use of the stepped-care treatment approach has been employed by Bernard Engel, Ph.D., at the National Institutes of Health in Washington, D.C. In studying people who are 60 or older, he found several negative side effects in treating their hypertension. He prescribed simple breathing exercises and self-monitoring of blood pressure. If necessary, he would then add the stress management techniques. For those whose blood pressure had not been reduced sufficiently, he would add (step in) the biofeedback treatment. By using a stepped-care treatment program, you are able to pull out the first group, who can use the simplest techniques for the lowest cost. Then you can go to the next group, who need more treatment or more extended treatment.

Dr. Engel and his associates have also shown that stepped care works very well in approaching common problems in the elderly, such as fecal incontinence and urinary incontinence. Urinary incontinence is often called "stress incontinence." When these people laugh, stand up, or do certain movements, the bladder and the urethra "spill urine." The more serious problem of urinary incontinence is when a complete voiding of the bladder is triggered. Dr. Engel stated that the stepped approach of stress management plus the addition of biofeedback as needed helps anywhere from 60 to 90 percent of these people to become continent again. This makes a tremendous difference in their feelings about themselves and is a major help with their health. Instead of being institutionalized, they can remain at home with people who love them and are used to caring for them.

In stepped care, PSR training can be accomplished in about 6 to 8 weeks if you are healthy. If you have symptoms or anxiety problems, it may take 12 to 15 weeks, and you may require additional training with biofeedback. If this treatment does not work, then you have to use PSR training and biofeedback and then add medication or other specific training programs such as psychotherapy, analysis, or assertiveness training. In general, this is necessary only for people who have two or more serious diseases or disorders.

You must always discuss a stress management program, physical exercise program, or diet with your medical doctor. Your doctor may need to do additional testing or change your medications as you become involved in changing your nervous system. Your doctor may also want to advise you on which foods, vitamins, or exercises you should take or not take. Remember that this stepped-care approach provides for cooperation in helping you develop healthier skills as fast as possible or for additional treatment as needed.

PSR Training and Biofeedback in Treating Airsickness

Airsickness is a continual problem for astronauts, pilots, navigators, the military, and their students. In many cases, they have to be grounded. Airsickness symptoms consist of pallor, cold sweating or warm flushes, malaise, nausea, and/or vomiting. The problem also occurs with astronauts who are blasted into space and with people riding in cars, planes, boats, and trains. Anywhere from 50 to 80% of astronauts can be out of commission for two or three days, then the airsickness eases off. In many cases, sufferers have tried using amphetamines (Dexedrine), Scopolamine, or other medications. To treat severe airsickness, recently the military has used biofeedback and a stress management program of 12 to 16 hours. The patients are trained in spinning chairs or under severe acceleration. They are trained to respond to the stress response when they feel cold, flushed, weak, or nauseous. Training is done both before and during the time in the spinning chair or under acceleration. An earlier counseling program was supplemented with experience in the spinning chair. Only 48 percent of military pilots were able to return to flying when the training consisted only of counseling and using the spinning chair. But with stress training and biofeedback, more than 84 percent of these officers were able to return to active flying duty. Think about the number of hours that it takes to train pilots and astronauts. If they are disabled by illness or disease, they have to be replaced and new people have to be trained at a considerable cost and loss of time and efficiency. PSR training of pilots and astronauts has been exceedingly beneficial.

Summary

You have now had a chance to rate some of the stresses in your life and some of your possible risk factors. Are you doing healthful things? Do you get 6 to 8 hours of sleep, engage in regular exercise, eat a healthful diet, and practice a relaxation technique? I think you now have an understanding of the general effects of stress and how it can enliven your life or burn you out. Are you ready to enhance your physical and mental skills with the PSR training? In the next chapter, I will give you the second PSR exercise so you can continue retraining your nervous system.

CHAPTER FIVE

THE SECOND POSITIVE STRESS RESPONSE EXERCISE: MUSCLE TENSION AND RELAXATION

Correction does much, but encouragement does more.

—*Goethe*

Richard's Muscle Knots

I was involved in an automobile accident which resulted in multiple injuries, including broken ribs and damage to muscle and surrounding tissue. I did not engage in an active physical therapy program, and in subsequent years I began to experience muscle spasm and other discomfort in the affected area—rib cage, back, shoulder, and neck.

My physician suggested that I begin a physical therapy program. I saw the therapist periodically, whenever I would experience symptoms. Treatment consisted of deep heat, electrical stimulation, stretching, and strengthening exercises. When the symptoms persisted, my therapist suggested that some of them might be stress-related and recommended stress management therapy with the biofeedback technique.

My treatment with Dr. Sedlacek has been very beneficial. Discussions with the doctor during treatment sessions have enabled me to identify areas of my life that cause particular stress, especially these areas where the pressure is largely self-imposed, and to recognize patterns of behavior on my part which contribute to the stress cycle. With this knowledge, it is possible to greatly reduce the self-imposed pressure and to respond appropriately and calmly when the pressure is real.

Equally important is the biofeedback technique itself. It focuses on proper breathing technique and on the contrast between muscle tension and relaxation. By monitoring my breathing and the muscular tension throughout my body, I have seen how the perception of stress or pressure causes involuntary muscle tension. With this knowledge and with the use of a series of warmth and relaxation tapes, I have found it possible to create a feeling of physical warmth and emotional calm that breaks the stress cycle by controlling the negative physical response. This procedure is useful throughout the day. Even during an activity which requires as much physical and mental concentration as driving a car, I am able to reach a state of deep relaxation merely by breathing deeply and regularly and clenching and releasing various muscle groups.

A third area of treatment has involved a program of increased physical activity, including brisk walking, cycling, rowing, and a range of stretching exercises. These three areas of treatment, along with periodic massage therapy, have greatly reduced my physical symptoms and generally improved my outlook.

At one point after I had begun treatment, I went through a period of great stress and neglected my program for lack of time. The symptoms for which I had consulted Dr. Sedlacek returned immediately. When I put things in a different perspective and resumed my program, the symptoms were again brought under control. I have learned the importance of regular practice of all of the principles of the biofeedback technique.

This is a typical story about a patient with severe muscle spasms and pain. The medical term for this condition is "fibrositis" or "fibromyalgia." Often there is a slight or major trauma that the patient experiences, and a few months later there will be chronic muscle spasms. This is often worsened by arthritis, or in some cases it may be similar to arthritis pain in the neck and shoulders. When I examine the patient I find small tight knots. These are muscle spasms the size of a pea or even larger, like the size of a small plum. Instead of being soft, however, they are almost rock-hard. That is why they are called knots, like a knot in wood. These feel more like the knuckle of your finger rather than the muscles on the shoulder or bicep. Muscle fibers run in bundles, so they should be long and loose, not hard and tight.

Other patients have reported that their chronic muscle pain developed slowly over the years. They may not have a specific injury, as this patient did. In some cases, it is a chronic pain syndrome and may need medication or hospital treatment for 2 to 3 weeks. The brain can keep the muscles tightened up in knots, and these knots can persist for years or for a lifetime if not treated successfully. Although physical therapy helps some patients, many continue to have chronic pain. What is needed are specific exercises practiced for 2 months or longer. The pain slowly begins to ease off and the muscles relax. Then the patient begins to have a normal muscle pattern again. It is important for a successful result to use a combination of stress monitoring, physical exercises, biofeedback, and medication. In a severe case, once the pain has begun to ease off I start the patient on a physical exercise program. Between the physical exercise and stress management exercises, most chronic pain can be reduced. The muscles still may get tight or tense once in a while, but the chronic condition is stopped. The patient can recover full flexibility with this combined treatment.

Richard has been followed up for over 4 years and continues to lead a very active physical and social life. He also continues to be successful in his line of work. By doing his physical exercises every day and using the stress management exercises, he continues to have little or no pain and to lead an active, happy life.

The Second Positive Stress
Response Exercise

Before doing any exercise program, you should check with your physician. These exercises should not cause any pain. If you have any pain, check with a physician. When you exercise, pick a quiet room. Unless there is an emergency, you should not be disturbed while you are doing the Positive Stress Response (PSR) exercises. Use a comfortable chair to support your head and feet. You can also use a rug or an exercise mat. Lie on your back and put a pillow under the back of the knees. This supports the thighs and relaxes your lower back so that they do not tighten up. You can also just pull your knees up with your feet flat on the floor if you don't want to bother with a pillow. If you want to, use a thin feather pillow under your head so that the head does not tend to roll to the right or left. Do not use a thick pillow, which would push the head and neck too far forward. Put your hands out about 6 to 10 inches from your hips with the palms facing up toward the ceiling or sky. You can do these exercises outside; however, I would recommend that you wait for at least a month or two until you have practiced and become more skillful with the exercises. Doing them outside or at the beach, shore, or lakefront is very comfortable, but initially it is more arousing than being in a quiet room.

I prefer that you not do the exercises after a full meal because you might have a lot of bowel activity in the stomach and intestines. These sounds and movements of digestion may be distracting. I recommend that people do these exercises in the morning before breakfast, before lunch, at the end of the workday, in the middle of the evening, or just before bed.

I suggest that you do not use a bed or a couch because they are associated with resting or sleeping. You can use PSR exercises to sleep, but first acquire the skill and then you can use them in bed to help go to sleep or if you wake up at night. Many people tell me that they enjoy doing the exercises by listening to tapes because this lets them focus on my voice and the specific instructions. You will have a good sense of relaxation as you repeat these exercises in a calm manner.

To start the muscle tension exercise, I want you to begin with the easy, paced breathing pattern I described in Chapter Three. Breathe in for a count of three, pause for a count, and then breathe out for a count of three and pause for a count. As you continue to practice you may want to increase this count to four, five, or six over the next few weeks. Remember to let the abdomen come out as the diaphragm pulls the air in, pause and let the abdominal wall pull in as the diaphragm goes up, pushing the air out. Then pause and repeat the breath cycle. The instructions that follow will give you the length of time for each exercise. Remember to keep breathing with a calm, paced breathing pattern as you tense and relax different parts of your body unless I tell you to hold your breath. Breathe in and out through your nose.

> To start this exercise I would like you to begin with five or six of these slow, paced breaths (about 45 seconds).
>
> Now I want you to wrinkle up your forehead and frown. Feel the tension in the forehead and let the rest of the body relax. Use two or three slow, paced breaths (about 15 seconds).
>
> Relax the forehead and notice how the relaxation spreads across the forehead and into the scalp (about 10 seconds).
>
> Now, as you continue breathing in a slow, paced manner, I want you to tighten your eyes by squinting and pulling them together. Hold that tension.
>
> Use two or three slow breaths (about 15 seconds).
>
> Relax your eyes. You will notice that you can now relax the eyes and forehead even more.
>
> Use one or two slow breaths (about 10 seconds).
>
> As you continue the slow, paced breathing, I want you to tighten the jaw muscles and hold that tension as though you are biting down on something.
>
> Use three or four slow breaths (about 20 seconds).

Relax the jaw. Feel that relaxation in the jaw, the eyes, the forehead, and the scalp. Use one or two slow breaths (about 10 seconds).

Now I want you to tighten up the forehead, the eyes, and the jaw; feel the tension in the face and scalp and eyes. Hold that tension.

Use one or two slow breaths (about 10 seconds).

Relax the forehead and the whole face. Feel that relaxation flow into the scalp, the forehead, and around the eyes, nose, lips, and jaw, and right down into your neck. Enjoy the relaxation of the face and head.

Use two or three slow, paced breaths (about 15 seconds). Now lean your head forward gently and let the weight move your chin toward your chest. Feel this tension as you gently let the weight of the head pull the forehead down and forward, stretching the neck muscles. If you are lying down, hold the head up toward the chest. Hold that position.

Use one or two slow breaths (about 10 seconds).

Relax the neck and bring your head back to your normal upward position, against the back of the chair or flat against the floor.

Use one or two slow, paced breaths (about 10 seconds).

Now gently push your head back into the chair or floor for one or two slow breaths (about 10 seconds).

Relax your neck.

Use one or two slow breaths (about 10 seconds).

Now I want you to take a deep breath and pull the shoulders up toward your ears. Hold that tension.

Use two or three slow breaths (about 15 seconds).

Relax the shoulders and feel the relaxation spread into the shoulders and neck.

Good. Just notice now how relaxed the head, scalp, neck, and shoulders are becoming.

Use one or two slow breaths (about 10 seconds).

Now I want your brain to direct attention to your right arm. Tighten your right hand into a fist and feel the tension. Hold that tension in the right fist with relaxation in the rest of the body. Keep breathing in a slow, paced manner as you tense your fist.

Use two or three slow breaths (about 15 seconds).

Relax your fist. Let relaxation flow into your hand, forearm, elbow, and shoulder.

Use one or two slow breaths (about 10 seconds).

Now do the same with your left hand. Tighten the left hand into a fist and hold the tension. Feel that tension in the left arm and the relaxation in the rest of the body.

Use two or three slow breaths (about 15 seconds).

Relax the fist and notice the relaxation spreading from the fingers into the hand and up into the forearm, elbow, and shoulder.

Use one or two calm, paced breaths (about 10 seconds).

Now tighten both fists at the same time and feel the tension as you tighten both fists and hold that tension in both fists. Feel the tension in the fists and the relaxation in the rest of the body.

Use two or three slow breaths (about 15 seconds).

Relax both fists and feel that relaxation spread from the fingers into the hands, wrists, forearms, elbows, and up into the shoulders. Good!

Use two or three slow breaths (about 15 seconds).

Now I want you to tighten up both arms as if you are making a muscle by tightening the fist and pulling up and making your biceps tight in both arms. Feel that tension in both fists and arms and right up to the shoulders.

Use two or three slow, paced breaths (about 15 seconds).

Relax the arms and feel that tension just easing away. Notice the shoulders relaxing, biceps relaxing, forearms relaxing, wrists relaxing, and hands relaxing right down to the fingers. Enjoy that relaxation!

Use three or four slow breaths (about 20 seconds).

Now notice how you are beginning to feel more relaxed in the hands, arms, shoulders, face, neck, and scalp.

Use one or two slow breaths (about 10 seconds).

I want you to take a deep breath into the upper chest and hold that breath. Hold that breath! (about 8 seconds).

Breathe out and relax. Notice the relaxation in the upper chest.

Go back to the slow, paced breathing and feel how the chest, arms, shoulders, head, and neck are relaxing even further.

Use one or two slow breaths (about 10 seconds).

Good.

Now I want you to tighten up the abdominal wall and feel the tension in the abdomen. Pull in your stomach. Hold that tension there. Hold your breath! Hold it! (about 6 seconds).

Breathe out and relax the abdomen. As you use the calm, paced breathing, notice the relaxation in the abdomen, chest, arms, hands, neck, face, and scalp develop more and more.

Use two or three slow breaths (about 15 seconds).

Good.

Now I want you to gently tense your lower back by arching your back. Make a small arch forward by pushing the abdomen forward and arching the lower back forward. Keep the rest of the body relaxed. Notice that tension you now feel in the lower back.

Use one or two slow breaths (about 10 seconds).

Relax the lower back and enjoy that relaxation as the back returns to its normal position. Notice the relaxation in the spine, back, abdomen, chest, arms, hands, neck, face, and scalp.

Use one or two slow breaths (about 10 seconds).

Good.

Now I want you to tighten your buttocks as if you were pushing down on the chair or floor with your buttocks. Tightening them together and down. Feel that tension now in the buttocks and hips. Hold that tension.

Use one or two slow breaths (about 10 seconds).

Relax the buttocks. Feel that relaxation spread through the buttocks into the lower back and down into the thighs. Enjoy a couple of slow, paced breaths as you feel the relaxation from the buttocks up to the lower back, abdomen, chest, shoulders, arms, hands, neck, face, and scalp.

Use two or three slow breaths (about 15 seconds).

Good. Now feel the tension as you tighten the calves by pulling the toes gently toward your face. Feel that tension in the calves.

Use two or three slow breaths (about 15 seconds).

Now relax the calves. Feel that relaxation in the lower legs, thighs, buttocks, chest, back, shoulders, arms, neck, and face.

Use one or two slow breaths (about 10 seconds).

Good. Now feel the tension in the ankles and feet and toes by pushing the toes down into the floor or straight out if you are lying flat on the floor. Feel the tension now in the ankles, feet, and toes as you push the toes forward or down.

Use two or three slow breaths (about 15 seconds).

Relax the toes, feet, and ankles. Use your slow, calm, paced breaths as you notice the relaxation that flows into the toes and feet. You feel relaxed in the toes, feet, ankles, calves, knees, thighs, and buttocks. This relaxation is a good, warm, easy feeling as it spreads into the buttocks and hips, into the lower back, abdomen, chest, shoulders, arms, and hands. Relaxation spreads even further into the neck, jaw, eyes, forehead, and scalp. Enjoy the relaxation now as you do your slow, paced breathing. Feel this relaxation throughout the whole body.

Use three or four slow breaths (about 20 seconds).

Good. You may feel your heart beating in a slow and relaxed manner as it pumps good warmth into the muscles you are relaxing. Your scalp and face are relaxing. The relaxation spreads into the neck and shoulders and down to the hands and fingers. All of the parts of your body are relaxing. The upper chest, lower back, and abdomen down to the hips and buttocks are relaxing. The relaxation continues to spread into the thighs, knees, calves, ankles, feet, and right into the tips of your toes. Feel that relaxation as it spreads from your scalp down through the whole body to the tips of your toes. You may feel warm or loose or limp and relaxed, or drifty and calm as you use the slow, paced breathing.

Use three or four slow breaths (about 20 seconds).

Now just take another minute or two to relax even more as you use the slow, paced breathing for another 12 to 24 breath cycles. If you like, you can count each breath in and out. This will take 60 to 120 seconds.

Enjoy the calm, relaxed feeling in your muscles, head, chest and limbs.

Say to yourself, "I feel calm, relaxed, and alert." Now count to yourself, one, two, three, open your eyes, and stretch your arms and legs.

It is a good idea the first few times you do the exercises to count the breaths to yourself. You can count out approximately 4 seconds by saying, "one thousand one, one thousand two, one thousand three, one thousand four." Then, as you get better at it, you will become good at estimating 1 to 3 or 12 to 24 breaths. Twelve breaths will be about 1 minute, 24 breaths about 2 minutes. You will get better at the timing as you go along.

Rmember that because of our busy society and training, the brain tends to speed up your time sense. So it is a good idea always to count out the breaths for the first 8 weeks or so. Then once every week, count out your breathing to check yourself. This is a very healthy biofeedback check so that the mind does not use this tendency to speed up and to race through the exercises.

This exercise should be done at least once a day. For a second exercise of the day, do the first PSR exercise. As you see, this exercise hits the major areas of the body so you can think about tensing and relaxing them systematically. As you practice this exercise, you will get better at feeling relaxed and using the muscle or muscles you need for daily tasks. This will replace the old tense patterns. You will recognize that when you tighten the fist you may also tighten the neck and shoulders, or perhaps part of the face. Or you may tighten the abdomen as you tighten one or both fists. One of the physical goals of this exercise is for the brain to know each part of the body better and use only the minimal amount of muscle activity for the specific task. Thus, when you write you should use only the muscles in the hand and forearm, not those in the shoulder and neck or face.

Remember, I want you to observe the tension and the relaxation as you go through the major muscle groups in your body. You do not have to, nor do I want you to, give a 100 percent effort tensing your muscle groups. If you tighten 50 percent, 70 percent, or 80 percent, that is just as good as 100 percent. In fact, it is better if you vary the exercises by 5 to 10 percent each day. Then your brain will notice the differences more easily. This is particularly helpful after the first week, when your mind will notice a better connection with the various muscles and parts. I tell my patients to give it a good effort. You do not have to give a 100 percent effort each time. I certainly do not want you to think about giving it a "110 percent effort." A 110 percent effort is a fantasy. The most you can give is 100 percent. With these exercises a 50 to 100 percent effort of tensing will work fine.

As you are doing these exercises you will observe certain areas of mental and physical tension, mental and emotional patterns that you do not like or are surprised by. You will also notice some that you like and are pleasantly surprised by. With all of these observations or feelings I want your mind to take a calm, friendly, objective view of yourself and your body. Do not be judgmental or negative because this will only heighten your arousal mechanism and make it more difficult to observe yourself calmly. It is much better to relax; then you can develop these skills more rapidly.

I want you to adopt a friendly and caring attitude toward yourself, your nervous system, and your body just as you would do in teaching a child or a pet or some other person a task. In other words, be gentle and generous toward yourself. Many people, particularly Type A people, are demanding of themselves. They often tend to be fairer to other people than they are to themselves. So remember the two "G"s—generous and gentle to yourself with your observations. This is key to any self-awareness and self-regulation. This is an important pattern of observation because if you treat yourself well you will treat others well. As St. Francis de Sales said, "Be patient with everyone but above all with yourself."

As you practice this exercise your brain will begin to notice that it can use the same pattern mentally. That is, the brain can think about doing things and leave the body and the rest of the nervous system calmer or in an idling state. You will be alert and will react to people and events without overreacting. This exercise is useful both mentally and physically because it trains both the mind and the body to work efficiently and calmly in stressful situations. Do not be surprised if you notice one, two, or three areas that tighten up when you try to do specific parts of the exercise. Notice the patterns that have built up over the years. Then you can begin to separate them so you use the specific muscles that you need to and no more. People waste a lot of energy throughout the day by activating these tight muscle patterns. The most common areas of muscle tension or spasms are the forehead, jaw, neck, shoulder, and lower back region. Most people overuse one or two of these areas. This is one of the reasons there is so much jaw and shoulder pain. The jaw tends to bite down with the fight-or-flight response. Sometimes people wake up with pain in their teeth and gums because they are biting down at night. If this is severe you may even crack your teeth. This muscle condition is called bruxism. The exercises are helpful for this as well as for shoulder and back pain, but they need to be practiced every day to change the old patterns of muscle tightness. That is why it often takes 8 to 10 weeks to change some of the musculoskeletal patterns. The more practice sessions you do, the more quickly your tension and spasms will ease off. After alternating the first and second PSR exercises for a week, use the second PSR twice a day for 2 days in a row. On the third day, alternate the second PSR exercise with the first PSR exercise. After 2 weeks you will be ready to start the third PSR exercise (Chapter Seven).

These exercises are derived from a longer set of exercises called Progressive Relaxation. These were developed by Edmund Jacobson, M.D., the "father" of muscle relaxation. His book *You Must Relax* has additional details if you want to read more about the history of this muscle relaxation technique.

A useful way to increase your relaxation is to pay attention to your facial muscles. The facial muscles perform the job of reflecting your emotions—your pain, pleasure, anxiety, anger, love, passion, and peace of mind. Though the muscles are small compared with other body muscles, a disproportionately larger amount of your brain is devoted to monitoring and operating them. Even a little facial muscle tension is noticed by your animal brain. That's why, along with blood flow control training, forehead muscle relaxation training is one of the most common relaxation techniques used in biofeedback treatment and in stress management.

Facial muscle progressive relaxation can teach you a lot about how to relax, even without the forehead muscle biofeedback. Once you learn it, it's easy to use anytime, anywhere.

A Brief Muscle Awareness Exercise

Begin by squeezing your eyes shut as tight as you can, holding them shut for 7 seconds. Then let go. Let them totally relax so your lids droop and go limp. Focus, as in the previous exercise, on the tension and relaxation sensations and the differences.

Then squeeze your eyes shut only half as tightly as you did the first time. Hold for 7 seconds. Then let go. Focus and scan for increased awareness of tension.

Squeeze your eyes again, half as tightly as you did the last time, hold 7 seconds, and then relax. Keep halving the muscle tension you use to close your eyes until you have a hard time discerning tension differences. Back up a bit and repeat this exercise. This is a great way to learn how to sense the early onset of increased muscle tension before it gets painful, and how to deeply relax your eyes.

Next, use this same halving exercise on your forehead. You can tighten the muscles there two ways—raising your brow (tensing up) or knitting it (tensing down). You can use the halving approach with all of your muscles. But if you want to save time in moving along to the rest of the exercises, just try it with your facial muscles. The goal of muscle relaxation is to help you to learn how to recognize and then be able to voluntarily produce a deeply relaxed muscle state. After you've practiced these relaxation exercises awhile, you can practice the relaxation pause, allowing your muscles to go limp and loose two or three times every day. No one else will notice this exercise—only that you are more relaxed and calm, and look better.

Once you get the hang of it, this can be a very effective and fast way to loosen up. Even while riding in a bus or train or sitting in your car while stopped at a red light, you can let your eyes tense and then go totally loose. Many brief relaxation sessions during the day will complement your two daily practice sessions, which take 10 to 15 minutes.

At the Stress Regulation Institute, I monitor different muscle groups with electromyography equipment (EMG). It measures the number of muscles actually being used. The EMG equipment helps to discriminate these tight muscle patterns. Some individuals who are in the third stage, where the symptoms are locked in for 6 to 12 months, may need further biofeedback treatment or medication or a combination of both. Remember, the sooner you get started with the exercises and the more often you use them, the faster the brain will develop these new skills. Then you can put them to use every day. As my patient Richard described in his story, it is very important to practice these exercises regularly. In the preventative stages, this will take care of most of your overreactions to stresses and hassles in your life. As Richard's story illustrated, symptoms may return if stresses mount up and you do not continue the exercises. Richard had serious injuries for years from the car accident and other stresses, so if you have had serious medical problems or muscle spasms, you need to practice PSR exercises regularly once or twice a day, probably for the rest of your life. In good periods, you can reduce the practice time. When there is more stress, you may need to increase the physical and mental exercises.

The Use of the Second PSR Exercise for Sleep

This second PSR exercise is excellent for helping people fall asleep. After you have practiced the first PSR exercise for 2 weeks and the second for 2 weeks you will be able to use it at bedtime to relax the muscles and calm your mind. I want to describe some of the key factors that help you in having a good sleep cycle.

One of the keys in order to maintain your energy throughout the day is to set a regular sleep time. This means you should pick a regular time to go to sleep, say eleven o'clock at night, and plan to get up at the same time every day. By going to bed at 11:00 and getting up at 6:00 you receive 7 hours of sleep. Most people require from 6 to 8 hours. Very few people can get by with less than 6 hours and very few need more than 8 hours. Pregnant women and people doing extremely hard physical labor or hard workouts (like an Olympic competitor) may need 8 to 10 hours of sleep.

When you go to bed at a regular time your mind sets the sleep cycle to start at that time. You can set your mind's time clock to wake up approximately 7 hours later. If you have irregular hours—that is, going to bed at different times and getting up at different times—you disrupt this sleep cycle and will have poorer sleep. Since many people have a different schedule Friday and Saturday nights, you can stay up an hour or two later, but try to get to bed by 12:00 or 1:00 and get up no later than 8:00 or 9:00. This will give you your 6, 7, or 8 hours of sleep.

Those who are having trouble falling asleep should use the second PSR exercise before going to bed or while in bed. This exercise must often by repeated once or twice to help you fall asleep. It may take 7 to 8 weeks to reset your sleep cycle. You need to develop these PSR skills sufficiently so that your mind can give up thinking about the day's events, worries, problems, or pains and allow and direct your body to go to sleep. That is why the exercise of tensing and relaxing the different muscles is extremely helpful in allowing the body to relax and prepare for sleep. The brain is the major organ in the body. It determines the level of arousal in the body. If the mind is worried or thinking about things, it will tend not to let the person (body) go to sleep.

I do not recommend having alcohol before bedtime. This puts you into a bad cycle whereby if you are worried about sleep you will have another drink or two. The drinks often help you fall asleep, but then 2 to 4 hours after you go to sleep you will often wake up, be restless, and feel dried out from the effects of the alcohol. A drink early in the evening with dinner is fine.

If you are one of those people who wake up in the middle of the night or early morning and need to go to the bathroom, try to keep yourself calm and relaxed. Use a night light to get up and go to the bathroom and go back to bed. Do not turn on regular lights. This wakes you up more. If necessary, you can repeat one or two of the four PSR exercises to go back to sleep. I do not recommend you get up to read or do tasks. This only trains you to get up and work on things or read when you are restless or tired and should be in bed sleeping. Stay in bed and, if necessary, repeat all the PSR exercises (about 40 to 50 minutes). Usually this will help you fall asleep. In rare cases when it does not, it is still better to stay in bed and be relaxed, calm, and resting. You will find that you have enough energy to get through the next day and that night sleep will usually come more easily. Even if you had trouble sleeping the night before, do not sleep more than 8 or 9 hours. You will catch up with the extra hour or so.

This exercise should help most of you who are restless at night fall asleep. Or you can use it in the middle of the night by setting the tape recorder next to your bed. If this awakens your spouse or bedmate, use a small receiver in your ear that hooks into the tape recorder. After you have been practicing it for 2 to 3 weeks, you should be able to do it from memory. Some people find the third PSR exercise helpful for sleep. You can use both two and three if necessary.

If you have more frequent problems with sleep (more than once or twice a month) that are not relieved with the PSR exercises, then you need to get a sleep study done by a sleep expert. Your local physician, hospital, or university medical center will be able to refer you to these individuals.

The Home Practice Chart

I have included a home practice chart (see Table 5-1) that I use at the Stress Regulation Institute. By charting your home exercises for 2 weeks for each of the PSR exercises, you will become aware of the different levels of relaxation you are developing. The numbers (1–10) are keyed to the letter columns below (a, b, c, d). To use the home practice chart:

One, list the number of practices for the first Monday.

Two, list the length of practice sessions, generally between 12 and 15 minutes.

Three, for the first minute, count out your breathing rate so you can see how fast you are breathing at the start of the session and at the end of your practice session (or count for 30 seconds and multiply by 2).

Four, notice any feelings of warmth in the hands, and rate using group a (0 = none, 1 = questionable, 2 = present).

Five, estimate the time it takes to feel some of these warming sensations (listed in group b: 1 =

TABLE 5-1 Home Practice Chart

Name: _____
Week of: _____ to: _____

	Monday	Tuesday	Wednesday	Thursday	Friday	Saturday	Sunday
1. Number of practice sessions							
2. Length of practice sessions							
3. Breathing rate per minute	0 1 2	0 1 2	0 1 2	0 1 2	0 1 2	0 1 2	0 1 2
4. Feelings of warmth in hands (warmth, throbbing, pulsating, fullness, prickle, tingling). (a)	0 1 2 3 4	0 1 2 3 4	0 1 2 3 4	0 1 2 3 4	0 1 2 3 4	0 1 2 3 4	0 1 2 3 4
5. How long does it take to feel warming sensations (approximately)? (b)	0 1 2 3 4	0 1 2 3 4	0 1 2 3 4	0 1 2 3 4	0 1 2 3 4	0 1 2 3 4	0 1 2 3 4
6. Degree of relaxation (c)	0 1 2 3 4	0 1 2 3 4	0 1 2 3 4	0 1 2 3 4	0 1 2 3 4	0 1 2 3 4	0 1 2 3 4
7. How long does it take to feel relaxed? (b)	0 1 2 3 4	0 1 2 3 4	0 1 2 3 4	0 1 2 3 4	0 1 2 3 4	0 1 2 3 4	0 1 2 3 4
8. Describe feelings of stress present today, if any							
9. Ability to control symptoms with techniques (d)	0 1 2	0 1 2	0 1 2	0 1 2	0 1 2	0 1 2	0 1 2
10. Comments or unusual observations. Please use remaining space.							

Code:
(a) 0 = none
1 = questionable
2 = present

(b) 1 = absent
2 = more than 5 minutes
3 = between 3 and 5 minutes
4 = between 1 and 3 minutes

(c) 0 = no change
1 = more relaxed
2 = heaviness
3 = light
4 = detached floating

(d) 0 = none
1 = partially successful
2 = successful

TABLE 5-1 Home Practice Chart (Continued)

Name: _____

Week of: _____ **to:** _____

	Monday	Tuesday	Wednesday	Thursday	Friday	Saturday	Sunday
1. Number of practice sessions							
2. Length of practice sessions							
3. Breathing rate per minute							
4. Feelings of warmth in hands (warmth, throbbing, pulsating, fullness, prickle, tingling). (a)	0 1 2	0 1 2	0 1 2	0 1 2	0 1 2	0 1 2	0 1 2
5. How long does it take to feel warming sensations (approximately)? (b)	0 1 2 3 4	0 1 2 3 4	0 1 2 3 4	0 1 2 3 4	0 1 2 3 4	0 1 2 3 4	0 1 2 3 4
6. Degree of relaxation (c)	0 1 2 3 4	0 1 2 3 4	0 1 2 3 4	0 1 2 3 4	0 1 2 3 4	0 1 2 3 4	0 1 2 3 4
7. How long does it take to feel relaxed? (b)	0 1 2 3 4	0 1 2 3 4	0 1 2 3 4	0 1 2 3 4	0 1 2 3 4	0 1 2 3 4	0 1 2 3 4
8. Describe feelings of stress present today, if any							
9. Ability to control symptoms with techniques (d)	0 1 2	0 1 2	0 1 2	0 1 2	0 1 2	0 1 2	0 1 2
10. Comments or unusual observations. Please use remaining space.							

Code:
(a) 0 = none
    1 = questionable
    2 = present

(b) 1 = absent
    2 = more than 5 minutes
    3 = between 3 and 5 minutes
    4 = between 1 and 3 minutes

(c) 0 = no change
    1 = more relaxed
    2 = heaviness
    3 = light
    4 = detached floating

(d) 0 = none
    1 = partially successful
    2 = successful

absent, 2 = more than 5 minutes, 3 = between 3 and 5 minutes, 4 = between 1 and 3 minutes).

Six, rate your degree of relaxation by using group c (0 = no change, 1 = more relaxed, 2 = heaviness, 3 = a light feeling, 4 = a detached floating feeling).

Seven, rate how long it takes you to relax. Use group b.

Eight, describe your feelings of stress. If you have a long list, then use a separate sheet of paper.

Nine, rate your success at reducing symptoms by using PSR. Use group d: (0 = none, 1 = partially successful, 2 = successful.) If you have a slight headache and you are partially able to relieve your headache, give yourself a rating of 1.

Ten, comment on any observations you made while practicing or after practicing. You can also use the rest of the page or a separate sheet to describe additional observations.

I have included a second Home Practice Chart. Copy or xerox this 7–8 times so you can follow how your home exercises are going during the next 6–8 weeks. You will see your improvement in learning how to relax and develop actual skills that you can use throughout the day to stay calm and relaxed or to reduce symptoms. You can also use this chart for the third and fourth Positive Stress Response exercises.

Remember, as you are doing the exercises you may get drowsy or fall off to sleep. If you have an important meeting, be sure to set an alarm clock for approximately 15 to 20 minutes later just as a backup. As you keep working with these exercises, you will find that you get deeply relaxed but still stay alert. This will help you bring this calm and relaxed state into your daily activities. Your mind will be alert and active while allowing and directing the rest of your body to be calm and relaxed. By charting your home practice of the muscle relaxation exercise, you will be able to use the new skills even more with your breathing checks throughout the day. After 2 weeks you will feel more of the muscles throughout your body relax with just a calm, paced breath or two. Remember to breathe, relax, and smile when you face a hassle, a disappointment, or something exciting in your life.

CHAPTER SIX

STRESS, NUTRITION, AND LONGEVITY

> Our greatest weakness lies in giving up. The most certain way to succeed is always to try just one more time.
>
> —*Thomas Edison*

Sally's Migraine

One of my patients who had severe migraines as often as once every 2 weeks was surprised to learn that many foods can set up or trigger a migraine headache. The classical migraine causes people to see flashing lights, to have other visual sensations, or even to experience hallucinations. Often they have some nausea or vomiting after the "prodromal" (beginning of headache) signals. Anywhere from 5 to 30 minutes later, they experience a pounding and throbbing headache on one side. It usually lasts from 1 to 4 hours. In more severe cases, it can last 2 to 3 days. After seeing a neurologist to rule out any organic problems, such as a brain tumor, the woman came to me for stress management with biofeedback. First, I had her sit down and write out on a chart the course of her headaches each week.

This symptom chart (see Table 6-1) can also be used to monitor other types of pain, such as irritable bowel, Raynaud's, and muscle spasms. On the top half of the chart (numbers 1 through 6) you describe the presence of symptoms, the pain ratings, any disability, and the average use of medications. On the bottom half (numbers 7 through 15) is an evaluation of your home Positive Stress Response (PSR) exercises.

TABLE 6-1 Chief Complaint

Name: _____
Week of: _____ to: _____

	Monday	Tuesday	Wednesday	Thursday	Friday	Saturday	Sunday
1. Are symptoms of diagnosed disorder present today? (a)	Yes No 1 2 3	Yes No 1 2 3	Yes No 1 2 3	Yes No 1 2 3	Yes No 1 2 3	Yes No 1 2 3	Yes No 1 2 3
2. Describe these symptoms if you answered Yes to 1.							
3. How bad is the pain today? (b)	0 1 2 3 4	0 1 2 3 4	0 1 2 3 4	0 1 2 3 4	0 1 2 3 4	0 1 2 3 4	0 1 2 3 4
4. Degree of disability (c)	0 1 2 3 4	0 1 2 3 4	0 1 2 3 4	0 1 2 3 4	0 1 2 3 4	0 1 2 3 4	0 1 2 3 4
5. Duration of pain (hours and/or minutes).							
6. Analgesic drug usage: Daily regulatory medication (record only once) Pain medication (record daily) 1. 2. 3.	Name: 1. 2. 3. 4. 5.	Name: 1. 2. 3. 4. 5.	Name: 1. 2. 3. 4. 5.	Name: 1. 2. 3. 4. 5.	Name: 1. 2. 3. 4. 5.	Name: 1. 2. 3. 4. 5.	Name: 1. 2. 3. 4. 5.
7. Number of practice sessions							
8. Length of practice sessions							
9. Feelings of warmth in hands (warmth, throbbing, pulsating, fullness, prickle, tingling) (d)	0 1 2	0 1 2	0 1 2	0 1 2	0 1 2	0 1 2	0 1 2
10. How long does it take to feel warming sensations (approximately)? (e)	0 1 2 3 4	0 1 2 3 4	0 1 2 3 4	0 1 2 3 4	0 1 2 3 4	0 1 2 3 4	0 1 2 3 4

TABLE 6-1 Chief Complaint (Continued)

Name: _____
Week of: _____ to: _____

	Monday	Tuesday	Wednesday	Thursday	Friday	Saturday	Sunday
11. Degree of relaxation (f)	0 1 2 3 4	0 1 2 3 4	0 1 2 3 4	0 1 2 3 4	0 1 2 3 4	0 1 2 3 4	0 1 2 3 4
12. How long does it take to feel relaxed? (e)	0 1 2 3 4	0 1 2 3 4	0 1 2 3 4	0 1 2 3 4	0 1 2 3 4	0 1 2 3 4	0 1 2 3 4
13. Describe feelings of stress present today, if any.							
14. Ability to control symptoms with techniques (g)	0 1 2	0 1 2	0 1 2	0 1 2	0 1 2	0 1 2	0 1 2
15. Comments or unusual observations. Please use remaining space.							

Code:

(a) 1 = morning
2 = afternoon
3 = evening

(b) 0 = none
1 = slight
2 = moderate
3 = moderately severe
4 = severe

(c) 0 = no interference with activities
1 = interference with activities
2 = had to go to bed
3 = go to emergency room or doctor's office for care
4 = need to be hospitalized

(d) 0 = none
1 = questionable
2 = present

(e) 0 = absent
1 = more than 5 minutes
2 = between 3 and 5 minutes
3 = between 1 and 3 minutes
4 = less than 1 minute

(f) 0 = no change
1 = more relaxed
2 = heaviness
3 = light
4 = detached floating

(g) 0 = none
1 = partially successful
2 = successful

After taking her history and seeing that this 33-year-old woman was not on birth control pills or other medications that can set up a headache, we reviewed some of the other substances that are likely to do so. One of the most common is alcohol. Many alcoholic drinks can trigger a headache. The worst are the scotches and blended whiskeys. The next worst are champagne, red wine, and then, roughly in order, beer, vodka, and white wine. If you are going to have hard liquor, vodka is probably the best because it contains the fewest residues (i.e., it is purer). Vodka can be mixed with orange juice, tomato juice, or tonic water. Some people find that by using a spritzer (white wine mixed half-and-half with club soda) they can drink small amounts without triggering a headache. Next to alcohol, the most common trigger foods are chocolate, peanut butter, strong aged cheeses, aged beef, hot dogs, bacon, ham, nuts, and coffee. If you have coffee with chocolate in it, it is doubly dangerous. Other changes, such as a change in stress levels or barometric pressure (storms), as well as pollen, bright sunlight, or exhaustion can also trigger headaches.

Seasonings such as Worcestershire sauce, A-1 sauce, meat tenderizer, or soy sauce can affect the arteries and trigger a headache. In some cases, other tasty foods like anchovies, olives, salami, liver, and sour cream may have the same effect. Many additives put into foods to preserve them can irritate the arteries and trigger a headache. If you have some chocolate and an alcoholic drink on the same day, they may add up to cause a headache. I can pick up these patterns in charting a patient's headaches for the week. Then I track the amounts and types of food eaten that are possible trigger foods. With Sally, two of the triggers were chocolate and alcohol. After the PSR training, she could have one or the other on a calm day and not get a headache. The same was true when she drank, but if she had both alcohol and chocolate, even the PSR training was not enough to stop the headache. I also did specific biofeedback training on her arteries since this is helpful in treating migraine headaches. In the stepped-care treatment I use PSR training and add an additional eight to ten sessions of specific biofeedback using more elaborate skin temperature biofeedback equipment. A regular thermometer or temperature-sensitive fingerband usually is sufficient for most people to practice with at home. This equipment is further discussed in Chapter Seven. These devices can be ordered through the Stress Regulation Institute in New York City or from a local supplier. I have listed in the Appendix some of the suppliers of these new health products.

Using PSR exercises and a home finger temperature monitor (a Bio-Q fingerband or temperature card) and by reducing her alcohol and chocolate intake, Sally reduced her migraine headaches by 80 percent. Instead of one or two headaches a month, she now has only one or two a year. She was able to do this by practicing the four PSR exercises twice a day. After 3 months she was able to go a full month with no headaches.

The evaluations of the causes of headaches and then charting them is useful in reducing stress-related headaches. With some people, the stress may build up in 1 to 3 hours, while with other people it may take 1 to 3 days. Chart your headaches or other symptoms and see what pattern you identify (see Table 6-2). Then practice the four PSR exercises and use them to reduce your symptoms.

Diet, Health, and Longevity

Nutrition has both positive and negative effects in different populations. The diet and nutritional approach of the Seventh-Day Adventists has had a dramatic effect on increasing their health and longevity. The Chippewa Indians of Minnesota, however, because of their subjugated position in our society, have changed from a relatively healthy diet to a dangerous "cafeteria diet" (heavy in fat and calories). By studying these large groups of diverse people and comparing their rates of heart attacks and strokes, hypertension and cholesterol prob-

TABLE 6-2   Triggers of Migraine Headaches

These substances can trigger migraine headaches and worsen problems like angina, claudication, Raynaud's, diabetes, and other circulation disorders.

Drinks

Scotches and whiskey	White wines
Champagne	Coffee (limit 3 cups per
Red wines (burgundy,	day, check for chocolate
Chianti, etc.)	content)
Beer	Soda with caffeine—Coke,
Vodka	Pepsi, Dr. Pepper, etc.

Foods

Chocolate	Pickled herring
Nuts (peanuts, etc.)	Sour Cream
Cheese (aged or strong	Ham
types)	Raisins
Liver	Broad bean pods
Canned figs	Chinese foods
Aged beef	Anchovies
Hot dogs	Olives
Bacon	Citrus fruits
Salami (cured cold cuts	Avocado
including fermented	Onions
sausage)	

Seasonings

Monosodium glutamate	A-1 steak sauce
(Accent)	Meat tenderizer
Soy sauce	Salt (use as little salt as
Worcestershire sauce	possible)

lems, I have developed a sensible diet that is tasty and yet low in dangerous foods. This diet can help you stay healthy and vital and increase your longevity.

In view of the stresses of life and the importance of nutrition, most people should follow the general guideline that moderation is better. The Seventh-Day Adventists Church, for example, suggests that its members not use tobacco and alcohol. Most are vegetarians and refrain from drinking coffee and other caffeinated drinks.

Thus, scientists find them a very good group to study. As in any group of people, however, not everyone follows the rules 100 percent. About half of them eat no poultry or fish and about 70 percent of them drink no coffee, as compared with the general population where only 10 percent do not drink coffee or other caffeine drinks such as colas and tea.

What is particularly striking about the Seventh-Day Adventists is that they live almost 12 years longer than the average American who does not follow their health practices. Of the ten leading causes of death in the country, particularly coronary heart disease and lung and bowel cancer, they have a low rate. While at a convention in California, I visited the Loma Linda University and Medical School to see some colleagues who were doing biofeedback work there. The medical school and hospital are run on the principles of the Seventh-Day Adventists. We went for lunch and they had all sorts of sandwiches and what seemed to be hamburgers for sale. However, they were all vegetarian dishes made to look like regular lunch meat and hamburger. You could not get coffee, tea, or other caffeine drinks there.

Dr. David Snowden studied a large number of Seventh-Day Adventists and found that the more meat they consumed, the higher the risk of death from heart disease and diabetes. He also found that fried eggs particularly and fried foods in general were associated with an increase in deaths from ovarian cancer. In the eating of animal products some male/female differences caused an increased risk of prostate cancer in men but no increase in breast cancer in women. Dr. Snowden also found, as have some other studies, that coffee drinking was associated with an increase of coronary heart disease in men as well as an increased risk of dying from colon or bladder cancer. He made the point that similar results are found in Seventh-Day Adventists in Norway, Holland, and Japan.

One of the reasons why there may be less bowel cancer is that the Adventists eat a lot of high-fiber foods as well as vegetables and foods rich in vitamin C. These foods are now recommended by the American Cancer Society. Fried food may also be related to an increase in colonic cancers. One of Dr. Snowden's significant findings was that consuming a lot of milk and eggs was related to a higher death rate. On the positive side was an observation that eating green salads was associated with a large reduction in death rates.

Some very helpful dietary suggestions emerge from the study of the Adventists. One that is supported by other studies is that we should cut meat intake and eat only lean meat. It appears that fat is one of the key factors in heart disease. Cut off the fat and throw it away if you are going to eat meat. Or buy the "lean meat" that is now being sold. It has been trimmed of fat or has been grown leaner. The best idea is to eat more fish and poultry and less fatty meat.

The second recommendation is to eat foods with a great deal of fiber in them. Buy whole wheat bread rather than white bread and whole wheat cereals rather than sugared cereals. Fruits such as bananas, apples, oranges, and pears provide bulk and fiber for the bowel. Salads are excellent for being both low in calories and high in fiber. Use a light vinaigrette dressing, not a dressing with lots of calories. I recommend a salad a day, supplementing it with other foods that have fiber.

The third recommendation is to eat fewer courses at each meal and smaller portions of food. It's not healthy to eat a four-, five-, or six-course meal. The calories add up too rapidly. Try to have a main course and a salad. Once or twice a week add an appetizer or dessert. Or try one or two appetizers plus a salad when you eat out, rather than an appetizer, main course, vegetable, and dessert (plus alcohol, coffee, tea, or an after-dinner drink). Remember, moderation is better.

The Powerful Urge to Eat, Drink, and Smoke

If you have had a problem with overeating or being overweight, you probably have noticed that worries or other emotional strains activate your nervous system. Many patients say that when they are thinking or worried about something, there is a tendency to grab a drink, a cigarette, or food. When people talk about hunger pangs they are often talking about emotional and mental states that make them wish to be satisfied. This satisfying action might be to drink alcohol, soda, or coffee, or to grab a cigarette or a pipe to smoke, or to stuff your face with food. When they use these basic feeding actions involving the mouth and tongue, people get a sense of satisfying themselves by pushing away some of the uncomfortable thoughts or feelings or experiences they are going through.

The breathing exercises described in Chapter Three reduce the appetite. Many people use one or two of the PSR exercises for 3 to 4 minutes and then are able to relieve the hunger pangs and not have a snack. You can also use these techniques for drinking and smoking problems. The physical exercise that I will describe in Chapter Seven will also help you control the urge to overeat, overdrink, and smoke too much.

The brain has centers that control eating. While the stomach may be hungry, the brain can slow this hunger, override it, and direct you to wait until the next meal. It is a form of discipline and very important.

Weight Reduction and Three Meals a Day

What counts in weight control is not only the number of calories we take but when we take them and how many we burn off. It is not a good idea to eat after 9:00 or 9:30 in the evening because it is unlikely you will be doing much in the way of physical activity after eating. Unless you exercise the next morning before going to work or before your daily activities, these extra calories are likely to be deposited and stored as fat in your body. That is why it is best to plan three regular meals during the day. Get up and have some food in the morning, preferably something containing fiber, such as bran muffins, whole wheat bread, or some of the healthful cereals that are now available. Adding a banana or other fruits is tasty and provides good nutrition. Fruits are generally low in calories (a banana has about 100 calories).

Aim for about 400 to 600 calories for breakfast. Then

have a moderate-size lunch consisting of 800 to 1000 calories. Dinner should be about 800 to 1000 calories. Women should aim at between 2000 and 2200 calories per day, men for 2600 to 2800 calories. If you have a physically demanding job, then you may require 2500 to 3500 calories. If you need more calories, you should eat a larger breakfast (1000 to 1500 calories). For most people of average weight, 2000 to 2800 calories is the healthy number of calories, given light physical exercise.

If you are gaining weight or not losing weight with this number of calories, then you have to cut down to the 1800 to 2300 range. It is rare that a person who consumes 1500 to 1800 calories per day while doing some moderate exercise cannot maintain a good healthy weight or lose weight. Many people eat 2500 to 3500 calories per day, do not exercise, and slowly gain weight.

If you are having trouble losing weight, try to have just two meals a day, perhaps eating breakfast and lunch and nothing but fluids or fruit for dinner. If you want to drink milk, try low-fat or soy milk. Vegetables are useful as a source of vitamin A. Citrus fruits, cabbage, cantaloupe, strawberries, and tomatoes are high in vitamin C. They also contain unrefined sugars and have a high water content. Olives and avocados provide unsaturated fatty acids that help keep cholesterol down. You can combine this with whole wheat cereals or nuts.

For breakfast there are many tasty foods such as grapefruit, oatmeal with low-fat milk, or whole wheat toast with margarine. Another tasteful snack is sliced bananas with almonds on whole wheat bread. Try using brown rice and mix it with soy milk or low-fat milk.

For lunch or a main meal, prepare a baked potato with margarine, salt lightly with pepper, then add broccoli and salad. You can use lettuce, cabbage, or a combination. Slice half an avocado on it with cottage cheese as another main dish. One whole wheat roll or a piece of whole wheat bread is good for fiber. For dessert you can have a slice of melon or an orange. Also, raisins are tasty light evening snacks. By using lean meat, you can have a 3- to 4-ounce slice of meat to add protein and little fat. Add a salad and a baked potato and you have a satisfying meal of 600 to 700 calories. You can also include two to three eggs per week either in the morning or in the evening. Or cut up one egg and add it to a salad with tuna fish. If your cholesterol is high, just remove half of the yolk of the egg; this will reduce the cholesterol intake by half. If you have very high cholesterol, your physician may tell you no eggs (i.e., no yolks). An excellent light dinner is split pea soup with or without a small serving of ham. You can make a tasty corn chowder with low-fat milk or soy milk. For a low-calorie dessert, there are many ways to use slices of pineapple or other fruits and vegetables.

Fish, once or twice per week, is recommended for a healthy heart and blood vessels. I am including five fish recipes from Metropolitan Life's *Eat Well, Be Well Cookbook*, which has over 100 easy-to-prepare recipes.

SALMON STEAKS WITH BROCCOLI SAUCE

4 salmon steaks
  (1½ pounds, 6
  ounces each)
4 teaspoons margarine
2 tablespoons fresh lemon
  juice
½ cup chicken broth

1 cup broccoli florets
  (about ¼ bunch)
¼ cup chopped onion
  (about ¼ medium)
1 garlic clove, minced
¼ teaspoon salt
⅛ teaspoon pepper

Preheat oven to 375 F. In a shallow baking dish, arrange salmon steaks. Dot evenly with margarine; sprinkle with half the lemon juice. Bake about 20 minutes or until fish flakes easily with a fork. Meanwhile, in a medium saucepan over medium heat in boiling chicken broth, cook broccoli, onion, and garlic about 10 minutes until broccoli is tender. In a blender at medium speed, process mixture with remaining 1 tablespoon lemon juice, salt, and pepper until smooth. Serve sauce over salmon. Makes four servings.

Nutrients per Serving:

425 calories
 40 grams protein
 27 grams fat

4 grams carbohydrates
 65 milligrams cholesterol
415 milligrams sodium

SNAPPER IN LIME VINAIGRETTE

½ cup dry white wine
½ cup water
1 pound snapper fillets
¼ cup vegetable oil
2 tablespoons low-fat plain
  yogurt
1 tablespoon red wine
  vinegar

1 teaspoon fresh lime juice
1 teaspoon Dijon-style
  mustard
½ teaspoon dried basil,
  crushed
¼ teaspoon grated lime peel
⅛ teaspoon pepper

In a large skillet over medium heat, heat wine and water
to boiling. Add fillets and cook covered about 8–10 minutes or until fish flakes easily when tested with a fork.
Remove fillets from skillet and let cool. In a medium
bowl, combine oil, yogurt, vinegar, lime juice, mustard,
basil, lime peel, and pepper; mix well. Cut fillets into
large chunks; add to dressing; gently toss to coat evenly.
Chill 1 hour. Makes four 3-ounce servings.

Nutrients per Servings:

240 calories
 23 grams protein
 15 grams fat

2 grams carbohydrates
60 milligrams cholesterol
120 milligrams sodium

NEW ENGLAND FISH CHOWDER

4 teaspoons vegetable oil
½ cup chopped onion
  (about ½ medium)
¼ teaspoon dried thyme,
  crushed
2 small potatoes, peeled and
  diced (about 10 ounces)
½ cup chopped green
  pepper (about ½ small)

1 cup water
¾ pound flounder fillets, cut
  into 1-inch pieces
¼ pound bay scallops
2 cups skim milk
2½ teaspoons cornstarch
½ teaspoon salt
⅛ teaspoon pepper

In a medium saucepan over medium high heat in hot oil,
cook onions and thyme until onion is soft, about 3 minutes. Add potatoes, green pepper, and water; bring to a
boil. Reduce heat to low; simmer covered about 10 minutes until potatoes are almost tender. Add flounder and
scallops. Cook covered about 8 minutes. In a separate

bowl, combine milk, cornstarch, salt, and pepper; mix well. Stir this mixture into soup; simmer about 5 minutes, stirring occasionally, until fish is tender and soup is slightly thickened. Makes four ½-cup servings.

Nutrients per Serving:

250 calories
  25 grams protein
   6 grams fat

25 grams carbohydrates
55 milligrams cholesterol
480 milligrams sodium

SEAFOOD KABOBS

¼ cup dry white wine
2 tablespoons honey
2 teaspoons Dijon-style
  mustard
  Dash ground red pepper
24 sea scallops (about
  1 pound)

24 cherry tomatoes (about
  1 quart)
2 medium green peppers,
  cut into 24 cubes
12 mushrooms, halved
  (about 6 ounces)

In a small bowl, combine wine, honey, mustard and red pepper. Add scallops; toss to coat well. Cover and refrigerate 1 hour. Drain scallops, reserving marinade. Preheat broiler if manufacturer directs. On four 14-inch skewers, alternately thread scallops, cherry tomatoes, green pepper cubes, and mushrooms. Place kabobs on foil-lined broiler pan. Broil 3 inches from heat source, about 8 minutes, basting with reserved marinade and turning occasionally. Makes four servings.

Nutrients per Servings:

150 calories
  20 grams protein
   1 gram fat

16 grams carbohydrates
40 milligrams cholesterol
380 milligrams sodium

CRAB STUFFED FILLETS AU GRATIN

2 ounces Swiss cheese,
  shredded (about ½ cup)
½ cup frozen crabmeat,
  thawed and drained
  (about 3 ounces)
¼ cup low-fat plain yogurt
2 tablespoons minced
  scallion

2 garlic cloves, minced
¼ teaspoon salt
⅛ teaspoon ground red
  pepper
1 pound sole, cut into
  4 fillets
½ cup dry white wine
½ cup water

In a small bowl, combine half the cheese with the crabmeat, yogurt, scallion, garlic, salt, and red pepper. In the center of each fillet, spoon an equal amount of the crabmeat mixture; roll up jelly-roll fashion and secure with toothpicks. In a large skillet, bring wine and water to a boil; add fillets. Reduce heat to low; simmer, covered, about 8 minutes or until fish flakes easily when tested with a fork. Preheat broiler if manufacturer directs. Gently transfer fillets to a shallow baking dish. Sprinkle with remaining 1 ounce of the cheese. Broil 3 inches from heat source, about 3 minutes, until cheese melts. Makes four servings.

Nutrients per Serving:

180 calories
  28 grams protein
  5 grams fat

4 grams carbohydrates
90 milligrams cholesterol
315 milligrams sodium

Cut up almonds on sole and you have sole amandine, a nutritious, tasty main course. Fruits, vegetables, potatoes, beans, and nuts provide a great deal of protein with moderate to low calories. You can combine dishes and use corn bread or corn with beans and many other combinations to make a nutritious lunch or dinner. Peanut butter on whole wheat provides a great many nutrients with moderate calories and low cholesterol.

One of the key practices is to substitute low-fat cheeses for cheeses high in fat, like cheddar. Use yogurt instead of sour cream. Try to stay away from fatty meats and cheeses and substitute foods such as tuna fish, bean burritos, pizzas in pita bread, and tofu for spreads.

You can also eat healthful snacks like popcorn. If you use unsalted air-popped popcorn, it has approximately 30 calories per cup. If you cook it with salt and oil and add salted butter, it has 155 calories, approximately 14 grams of fat, and 229 milligrams of sodium. The unsalted air-popped corn has only traces of fat and sodium. This is a very low-calorie snack and has moderately high fiber. It also helps your teeth since popcorn massages the gums and helps prevent plaque buildup.

There are other new, more healthful products now being used. A vegetable cooking spray like PAM, for example, has only two calories per serving and no salt, no cholesterol, and low fat. It is made from soy beans so that it does not increase cholesterol. These new products allow you to eat in a more healthful fashion with lower cholesterol and reduced calories. Many companies now are recognizing that it is in their interest as well as the consumer's to produce healthful products by reducing the fat, cholesterol, salt, and sugar. This has been a major change in the last decade; companies are recognizing that moderation is better.

What's Your Healthy Weight?

To help you gauge your weight, look at the average height and weight tables from Metropolitan Life.

Weight at ages 25 to 59 is based on lowest mortality. Weight is given in pounds according to frame (in indoor clothing weighing 5 lbs. for men and 3 lbs. for women; shoes with 1″ heels).

1983 Metropolitan Life Height and Weight Tables

	Men				Women		
Height	Small Frame	Medium Frame	Large Frame	Height	Small Frame	Medium Frame	Large Frame
5'2"	128–134	131–141	138–150	4'10"	102–111	109–121	118–131
5'3"	120–136	133–143	140–153	4'11"	103–113	111–123	120–134
5'4"	132–138	135–145	142–156	5'0"	104–115	113–126	122–137
5'5"	134–140	137–148	144–160	5'1"	106–118	115–129	125–140
5'6"	136–142	139–151	146–164	5'2"	108–121	118–132	128–143
5'7"	138–145	142–154	149–168	5'3"	111–124	121–135	131–147
5'8"	140–148	145–157	152–172	5'4"	114–127	124–138	134–151
5'9"	142–151	148–160	155–176	5'5"	117–130	127–141	137–155
5'10"	144–154	151–163	158–180	5'6"	120–133	130–144	140–159
5'11"	146–157	154–166	161–184	5'7"	123–136	133–147	143–163
6'0"	149–160	157–170	164–188	5'8"	126–139	136–159	146–167
6'1"	152–164	160–174	168–192	5'9"	129–142	139–153	149–170
6'2"	155–168	164–178	168–192	5'10"	132–145	142–156	152–173
6'3"	158–172	167–182	176–202	5'11"	135–148	145–159	155–176
6'4"	162–176	171–187	181–207	6'0"	138–151	148–162	158–179

Remember these are average weights. I and many other specialists think these tables may be 10 percent heavier than is healthy.

To Make an Approximation of Your Frame Size . . .

Extend your arm and bend the forearm upward at a 90-degree angle. Keep fingers straight and turn the inside of your wrist toward your body. If you have a caliper, use it to measure the space between the two prominent bones on either side of your elbow. Without a caliper, place thumb and index finger of your other hand on these two bones. Measure the space between your fingers against a ruler or tape measure. Compare it with these tables that list elbow measurements for medium-framed men and women. Measurements lower than those listed indicate you have a small frame. Higher measurements indicate a large frame.

Height in 1" Heels	Elbow Breadth
Men	
5'2"–5'3"	2½"–2⅞"
5'4"–5'7"	2⅝"–2⅞"
5'8"–5'11"	2¾"–3"
6'0"–6'3"	2¾"–3⅛"
6'4"	2⅞"–3¼"
Women	
4'10"–4'11"	2¼"–2½"
5'0"–5'3"	2¼"–2½"
5'4"–5'7"	2⅜"–2⅝"
5'8"–5'11"	2⅜"–2⅝"
6'0"	2½"–2¾"

Make an approximation of your frame size. Are you overweight?

Obesity

The severity of the obesity problem was reviewed in the "National Health and Nutrition Survey," conducted by the National Center for Health Statistics in 1985. They stated that 44 million people in the United States in the age range 20 to 75 are overweight, and that more than 1.24 million are severely overweight. The 1985 rates of obesity are much higher than those in the first study in 1971. A particularly large increase has been found among blacks. The disorder was also higher among the lower socioeconomic classes. Excessive weight, defined as more than 20 percent above the person's ideal weight, is an independent risk factor for poor health. This means that obesity increases your risk of suffering from hypertension, diabetes, gallbladder disease, and cancer. It is even worse for adolescents because if you are obese as a child, you tend to keep the weight as you grow older. In the years from 1971 to 1985 these two surveys found a 40 percent increase of obesity in children and adolescents. While obese children do not always become obese adults, an estimated 80 percent of them do. Albert Stunkard, M.D., at the Pennsylvania School of Medicine, reported that increases in obesity correlate with the increased percentage of calories eaten as fat. This again points out that fat is one of the keys to reducing your weight and risk of diseases.

In different cultures obesity is sometimes still viewed as a female beauty characteristic. The ideal nude for the famous painter Rubens was a plump or obese woman. While this ideal is fading, it continues to persist. The pattern of fatness has been reversed only recently. Obesity is now in an inverse relationship with social class in the United States. That is, wealthy people tend to stay slimmer than poorer people.

One of the most interesting pieces of information from Dr. Stunkard's survey was that in obese children, the best predictor for developing obesity in adolescents was the amount of time the child spent between the ages of 6 and 11 viewing television. William H. Dietz, Jr., M.D., Ph.D., director of the Clinical and Nutrition Center at Tufts University School of Medicine, feels that if children are watching TV, they are having a larger food intake and they are inactive. One of the best things you can do for your children is to make sure they have a healthy diet, low in fat and moderate in the number of calories. Considering the risk of obesity, you should make sure your children are active with exercise, sports, or physical labor. Consider allowing only 1 or 2 hours of TV per day, especially in the years from 6 to 11 when children's TV habits are developing.

Obesity and the Risk of Hypertension

In his study of obesity at St. Luke's-Roosevelt Hospital in New York City, Theodore B. Van Itallie, M.D., pointed out that the risk of hypertension for overweight Americans, aged 20 to 27 and studied over 5 years, is three times higher than for the nonoverweight. Among overweight Americans aged 20 to 45, the risk jumps to 5.6 times that of the nonoverweight person in this age group. An obese person's risk of hypertension is from three to five times more than that of a person who is not over-weight or obese. This is important because obesity and hypertension are two of the major factors that cause strokes or heart attacks. Dr. Van Itallie, in his report in *Annals of Internal Medicine,* No. 6, December 1985, pointed out that the risk of hypertension, hypercholes-terolemia (high cholesterol), and diabetes is greater in overweight adults aged 20 to 25 than it is in overweight people from 45 to 75. He comments that "being over-weight during early adult life is more dangerous than a similar degree of overweight in later adult life." The earlier you have an obesity problem, the more likely it is to shorten your life.

For diabetics who are overweight, the risk of heart attack, strokes, and amputation is increased approximately three and one-half times. Diabetes can also increase many problems, such as reduced circulation and loss of vitality.

For some people, 5 to 10 extra pounds can be helpful under certain circumstances. Certainly if one has to face surgery, you might want some extra pounds because you can easily lose that weight with surgery. In human history we probably have had a genetic and certainly a cultural tendency until recently to maintain extra weight. The clearest example of this is in the Polynesian culture where kings were excessively obese. They also had slaves and/or a household of servants who took care of them and fed them. Henry VIII in England, Teddy Roosevelt, and Winston Churchill are examples of rich, powerful men who were obese. This is now rare because of the risk factors and the change in cultural view. Recently only the Hunt brothers, in Texas, and a few other celebrities represent the obese powerful rich man.

Overweight and Fat

Because of starvation and the fear of short food supplies, there probably is a tendency to maintain a little extra weight. This has gone to extremes in the United States. The American Heart Association recommends that total fat should not exceed 30 percent of one's daily calorie intake. This 1986 guideline differs from that of 1961, where the recommendation was an intake between 30 and 35 percent of fat in the daily diet. Saturated fat is one of the major contributors to heart disease. It should be less than 10 percent of one's total fat intake. Fat increases the risk of heart attacks and cancer. This is why the American Heart Association has lowered its suggested intake of fats. They also suggest that hamburgers are one of the worst contributors of saturated fat in our diet.

One of the great problems that Americans face is an abundance of food with a high fat content. They are available to everyone, including poor people. This is true particularly of foods such as french fries, hamburgers that are fried, and deep-fat-fried chicken. The American Heart Association recommends that hamburgers be made with lean meat and grilled to further reduce the fat content.

For the last two to three generations, not only have Americans had a surplus of food but the quality of the food has changed. For example, cattle are rarely raised on the open range anymore. After the cattle are a certain age and weight, they are taken into large pens or feeding areas where they are fed corn and other foodstuffs to fatten up. By putting on an extra 100 to 600 pounds of fat, the cattle are worth more money at the market. Unfortunately, many people like the smell and flavor of the fat sizzling on steak. In earlier times, people ate more lean beef. Now we are eating fatter beef. Fat seems to be a high risk not only for obesity but for heart disease by clogging the arteries (arteriosclerotic problems) and for causing certain cancers. These factors—the abundance of food, the change in the way we grow meat, and how we cook and eat it—all create a higher risk for obesity. Obesity increases the risk of heart disease, strokes, and other health problems. The heavier you are, the higher risk you have.

Fast Weight-Loss Fads

The best way to lose weight is to do it slowly and steadily with exercise, diet, and good nutrition. Every year there are one or two new, superfast diets like the Hampton,

Cambridge, and grapefruit diets. Be on the watch for a new fad diet called something like the tomato or potato diet. Both fad diets and surgical techniques have been relatively unhelpful with obesity. They often have serious side effects. For example, a jejunal bypass operation induces weight loss but also results in liver disease in 5 to 10 percent of the patients, as well as kidney stones in approximately 21 percent. Following this operation, people often have persistent cramps and abdominal pain.

Gastric bypass has a high death rate during the operation and a 5 percent increase in stomach ulcers. If a patient has a pouch operation, which reduces the stomach size, the pouch can stretch later. Then the patient can again eat large meals. The most recent surgical approach has been inserting a gastric bubble. The doctor inserts a little bubble that takes up room in the stomach. The patients may receive behavioral and dietary counseling as well. The bubble is removed after 4 to 5 months. Results with the first 100 people were quite impressive. In 6 months, more than 40 lbs. per person were lost. Over a 10-month period, each lost approximately 60 to 70 lbs. Controlled studies were begun in 1986, and it has been estimated now that between 17,000 and 20,000 patients have received the bubble. Except for causing irritation of the stomach lining, initially there were thought to be no serious side effects. Within about a year of the FDA's approval of the bubble for use, however, patients were found to have perforations and ulcers of the stomach as well as intestinal blockage. Late in 1986 physicians received official letters warning them to curtail its use. One patient died and 80 others developed serious medical problems. The letter also recommended that the bubble be used only as a last resort with patients whose lives were threatened by obesity. The letter to physicians also warned that the bubble could suddenly collapse and surgery would be needed to remove it. The rate of the bubble's deflating was approximately 6 percent. In some cases, without emergency surgery, a deflated bubble could cause death.

So while there are new devices, pills, surgery, and many new diets that come out, they are all to be taken with a grain of salt. Eating healthily and exercise constitute the best daily maintenance program. They take time and attention. Like maintenance programs for your car, apartment, or home, they pay off by working better. Establish good eating habits and reduce your stress-induced eating by using PSR training. You should get counseling or medical advice on how to maintain a lower weight if these exercises, menus, and tapes are not sufficient for you to lose or maintain a normal weight.

Smoking

The Federal Trade Commission reports annually to Congress on cigarette and sales promotions. In their 1984 report, they said that domestic cigarette consumption increased approximately 1 percent to 608.4 billion cigarettes sold during the year. This was the first increase after 3 years of declining use. The FTC estimated that magazine ads accounted for approximately 20 percent of the $2.1 billion spent by the cigarette industry during 1984. This was up from the 1983 total of $1.9 billion. This means that approximately $200 million more was spent in 1984 than in 1983. Another way of looking at it is that there was more than a 5 percent increase in advertising for cigarettes. The result was more than $2 billion spent to influence people to smoke cancer-producing cigarettes.

When advertising is increasing and more money is being spent to sell cigarettes, you can see the influence on certain groups. In 1986 the *American Medical Association News* reported that the Chippewa Indians in Northern Minnesota suffered from hypertension and heart disease at a rate higher than any population in the country and higher than any other American Indian group. The results were attributed to the Indians' changing to an urban life-style: higher rates of unemployment, cigarette smoking, alcohol use, and intake of salt, cholesterol, and animal fat. Originally the Indians' diet had been one of rice, wild game, and wild greens. Because the U.S. government gives food to the Indians, the Chippewas switched to using a lot of lard, flour, and salt in their diet. For example, 22 percent of the Chippewas had high blood pressure compared with 15 percent of the general population. Cardiovascular deaths have been reduced in the general population since 1960, but this has not been true of the Chippewa Indians. In 1970 they died at a rate of 200 per 100,000, compared with 270 per 1,000,000 in the general population. By 1980 the death rate in the general population was reduced by 9 percent to 241 per 100,000, while that of the Indians rose 25 percent to 249 per 100,000. Their death rate increased from 200 to 249, while the general population declined from 270 to 241. The Indians had actually gone from a lower rate to a higher rate in only a decade. According to the University of Minnesota study, cigarette smoking was one of the major factors in the hypertension. In their survey of 1984, 78 percent of American Indians in Minneapolis smoked and 88 percent of them had a history of hypertension. The recommendation was that the Indians "return to a more healthy life and ways of their ancestors by exercising more, eating more wholesome foods, and limiting tobacco use to sacred ceremonial purposes." This is good advice for all of us.

In a recent report by the Center on Health Policy at Emory University in Atlanta, tobacco was listed as the leading single factor in premature deaths in the United States. They stated that it causes more than 100 to 1000 unnecessary deaths every day. Other high rates come from alcohol-related deaths from motor vehicles, fire, falls, and drowning. Additional alcohol-related problems are cirrhosis; cancer of the mouth, larynx, and esophagus; and alcohol-related violence. This report emphasizes how much pain, injury, and death are caused by tobacco and alcohol.

Other important information is available on cigarette smoking (this applies to cigar and pipe smoking as well because there are also higher rates of lung, lip, and throat cancer associated with these smoking habits). C. Everett Koop, M.D., the surgeon general of the U.S. Public Health Service, has been very active in pointing out the dangers of smoking both to smokers and to nonsmokers in the same environment. He has stated that smoking is an addiction. Dr. Koop describes consequences related to the use of tobacco, such as colds, respiratory problems, hypertension, heart damage, and cancers. People who breathe in smoke that is in the air around the smoker ("passive smoking") are harmed almost as much as from actual smoking. He says one of the reasons is that the fire or heat of the cigarette prevents some of the harmful chemicals from reaching the smoker's lungs. However, these chemicals get into the air and into the nonsmoker's body.

Dr. Koop wants to work toward a smoke-free society by the year 2000 by having smoking prohibited in all public places, including transportation. It has been estimated that airlines alone spend about $115 million annually to repair aircraft air filters that are damaged by smoking in the passenger cabins. Through the efforts of people like Dr. Koop and the American Medical Association, which is trying to ban cigarette advertising, the number of smokers in this country has been reduced for the first time to less than 30 percent of the population. As recently as 1964 approximately 55 percent of Americans smoked. Physicians are attempting to persuade lawmakers and the general public to take steps that will reduce or stop the smoking habit. Many doctors have stopped and have encouraged their patients to stop as well.

Many doctors are trying to ban advertisements for smoking so that young children are not indoctrinated with the impression that adults smoke and that this is "cool." The ads often try to hook children on smoking, the campaigns trying to make children imitate the Marlboro cowboy or the Virginia Slims woman—"You've come a long way, baby." Ads make smoking appear "adult," as if as an adult you should feel free to harm yourself with hot smoke, tar, and nicotine.

The workplace reveals other interesting information about smoking. Smokers have a 64 percent higher absentee rate than nonsmokers. A recent article in *Management Information Systems Week* pointed out that 78 percent of the people in large corporations do not smoke; 51 percent of the nonsmoking executives used to be smokers. This suggests that if you smoke, it may be a hindrance to your advancement.

One attempt at changing the workplace into a nonsmoking area was made at West Lake Community Hospital in Chicago, with considerable success. They started a policy of nonsmoking. Visitors are not allowed to smoke, and patients, if they can walk, can smoke only with the permission of a physician (physicians did not smoke in the hospital before the nonsmoking policy). Smoking is allowed only in a small section of a cafeteria and in one lobby. After this policy was in effect for 15 months, they found that employee sick days had been reduced by 20 percent.

While cigarette smoking in general has been reduced, there is a disturbing factor. For the first time more high school girls than boys are smoking. Approximately 16 percent of high school boys and 20.5 percent of girls smoke. Irving Rimer of the American Cancer Society suggests this is because the educational programs about smoking in the 1970s were male-oriented. Many famous people have died from lung cancer, such as Dick Powell, Nat King Cole, Edward R. Murrow, and Yul Brynner. Since they were all men, men have paid more attention to the cancer deaths caused by smoking. Mr. Rimer thinks that the cigarette companies began to use the idea of women's equality when promoting tennis tournaments, fashion shows, and rock concerts to persuade women to smoke more. He said, "Women are under the same stresses and strains as men; women have got to learn they can beat these stresses without a cigarette, just as men are doing."

The American Cancer Society also reports that lung cancer has surpassed breast cancer as the most frequent killer of women. In 1976 2200 women died of lung cancer, while in 1985 the estimated number was 40,100. In less than 10 years, therefore, the deaths from lung cancer have almost doubled.

It is not only women who are being affected more by nicotine. An article in the *American Medical Association News* states, "It is unfortunate that the people who suffer the greatest share of health problems are low income and minorities and they are now becoming the heaviest smokers." According to this report, college-educated men, white-collar workers, and high-income earners are less likely to smoke than high school graduates or blue-collar workers, men with low incomes, and women who work outside the home. It further points out that smoking by pregnant women has been linked to adverse effects on the fetus and complications with pregnancy. Children with parents who smoke have a higher frequency of lung problems. Of the 450,000 deaths from cancer in the United States each year, about 30 percent, or 135,000, are due to cigarette smoking. In their proposal to ban tobacco advertising, the AMA has pointed out that physicians who know about the dangers have reduced their smoking, and now only 10 percent of physicians are lighting up versus 30 percent of the general population. This also suggests to me that about 10 percent of physicians, while aware of the dangers, have a nicotine addiction. Why else would people risk the horror of lung cancer and early death?

If, after all the health problems that smoking can cause, you do not reduce or stop smoking, I have one piece of advice: Get a chest x-ray every year. By doing this you may catch a lung cancer in its early stage. If caught early enough, the cancer often can be removed surgically, and you may be saved from an early and painful death. This is what some physicians do who smoke. Rather than deal with their nicotine habit, they see a radiologist and nervously check their chest x-ray for cancer. They'd rather risk death or the removal of a lung than go for treatment for their smoking.

How to Obtain Help for the Smoking Addiction

There are several ways to cut down or to stop smoking. Probably the best one is to join a group that is planning to stop. The annual "smoke-out" encourages the whole country to stop smoking. Many companies have a stop-smoking day. Many physicians run groups and use nicotine gum, hypnosis, or stress management training to help people stop smoking cigarettes. I have found that stress is a major part of smoking. With PSR training, people can feel the "burn" of the hot smoke in their lungs as they smoke cigarettes. Because they are less stressed, they can usually put the cigarettes away and stay off them. Using the stepped-care approach, if the PSR is not sufficient, they join one of the quit-smoking groups such as Smoke Enders, or go for hypnosis or go "cold turkey" with the help or supervision of a family friend, colleague, or physician. The key is to stop smoking. If you stay off cigarettes for about a year, then usually you will stay off. Often the difficult period is right after you stop smoking. That is why stress management is so important. When people stop smoking, their habit or addiction causes them to eat more, and then they go back to smoking because they are eating more. You may gain weight initially, but you can deal with that after you've stopped smoking for a month. Then you can start exercising and reducing your food intake to lose weight.

First, stop smoking. Those are cancer sticks you're smoking!

Alcohol

The next major health change that can help your longevity and vitality is to review your use of alcohol.

One of the new studies from the Kaiser Permanente Health Center in California shows that there is a relationship between higher blood pressure and alcohol use. This relationship is stronger in white men and in persons 55 years and older. There is a slight increase in blood pressure of men who consume more than one to two drinks daily. The study found that with women the increase did not normally show itself until they had three or more drinks a day. This suggests that women tolerate more alcohol before their blood pressure increases. This study also showed that liquor is worse for you than wine or beer.

People who are heavy or problem drinkers often are involved as perpetrators or victims of sexual aggression. Alcohol problems have increased considerably since World War II. However, what has been particularly upsetting is that the number of women who develop alcoholism by age 25 is rising. In other words, alcoholism is not only more prevalent but it is developing in younger women. There also seems to be a difference between men and women in physical arousal with alcohol. As men feel more sexual, their physiological measurements of arousal seem to increase with alcohol. Women say they feel more arousal, yet it does not seem to be true if one monitors the physiological signs. This difference may increase the problem between men and women because alcohol appears to produce a longer latency period with women and decreased orgasmic intensity. I will talk more about the latency period in Chapter Nine.

Alcohol can cause a severe problem called "fetal alcohol syndrome," a disease causing terrible effects on the fetus. Alcohol appears to be one of the more frequent causes of birth defects and mental and physical retardation. Besides hurting the baby, alcohol is deadly to the mother. Women treated for alcoholism were studied for 11 years, from 1967 to 1978; 31 percent of the women died, a mortality rate four times higher than would be expected. It is estimated that their life expectancy was decreased by about 15 years. The positive part of this study showed that among women who stopped drinking, fewer deaths occurred than would be expected if their drinking habit continued.

The number of treatment centers for alcoholism has increased in the United States. Between 1982 and 1983 the number grew from 4223 to 6963. The most common programs usually involve a 30-day treatment period, with follow-up in groups (such as Alcoholics Anonymous) meeting weekly or daily. In addition, the AMA has suggested that a percentage of alcohol ads should describe the adverse consequences of the use of alcohol. This would work the same as with cigarette promotion—a warning would be included in the ads. One of the major concerns is that advertising is influencing children and young adults to drink. In 1984 the University of Michigan did a study, for example, showing that every year since 1973, 90 percent of high school seniors in 135 Michigan high schools said they drank. Sixty-seven percent said they had used alcohol in the past month, and 39 percent said they had had five drinks or more in a row within the last 2 weeks. A surprising 30 percent reported that most or all of their friends got drunk at least once a week. This report is of great concern since many of these people may become alcoholics as they grow older. If you do drink, make sure it is in moderation (no more than one to two drinks of liquor, two to four glasses of wine, or two to three beers per day).

If you or someone you know has a drinking problem, see your doctor or go to a meeting of Alcoholics Anonymous, Al-Anon, Al-Ateen, or Adult Children of Alcoholics. These telephone numbers are in your phone book.

Caffeine and Its Effect on the Nervous System

People who drink a great deal of coffee will be interested in a recent study revealing that when you drink more than eight or nine cups of coffee per day your cholesterol rises, and this increases the rate of heart attacks. These and other studies suggest you should drink fewer than three cups of coffee per day. In general, tea has less than half the caffeine content of coffee, so you should not drink more than three to six cups of tea per day. It seems quite clear from medical evidence that anything above these levels is harmful to your heart, blood pressure, and arteries. Excess alcohol and coffee are an important element in the combination of lack of exercise and poor diet that causes an increase in heart attacks and strokes.

Table 6-3 lists the average amount of caffeine in the most common drinks—coffee, tea, and carbonated beverages. You should also review Table 6-4. It shows the amount of caffeine in prescription and nonprescription drugs. They can add up and cause you to feel jittery and tense.

It may be healthier not to drink any alcohol or caffeine. If you do drink, though, the research shows that moderation is better.

TABLE 6-3   Ranges and Average Caffeine Content of Percolated, Drip, and Instant Coffee and Other Beverages

Beverage	Range	Estimated average per 5 ounces (150 milliliters)
Coffee		
Percolated	97–125	110
Drip	137–153	146
Instant freeze-dried	61–70	66
Tea		
Black, bagged (5 minutes)	39–50	46
Black, bagged (1 minute)	21–33	28
Cocoa	10–17	13
Carbonated beverages (12 ounces)	32–65	

Source: Data from Bunker and McWilliams (1979).

TABLE 6-4   Caffeine Content of Prescription and Nonprescription Preparations

Trade Name	Manufacturer	Caffeine Content (milligrams)
PRESCRIPTION		
ABC compound with codeine	Zenith	40
Amaphen	Trimen	40
Anaquan	Mallard	40
A.P.C.	Burroughs-Wellcome	32
Beta-Phed	MetroMed	32
Buff-A Comp	Mayrand	40
Cafemine TD capsules	Legere	75
Cafergot and P-B	Sandoz	100
Cafetrate-PB suppositories	Schein	100
Compal capsules	Reid-Rowell	30
Di-Gesic	Central	30
Dihydrocodeine compound	Schein	30
Ergocaf	Robinson	100
Ergo Caffein	CMC	100
Ergothein	Wolins	100
Esgic	Forest	40
Ezol	Stewart Jackson	40
Fioricet	Sandoz	40

TABLE 6-4 (Continued)

Trade Name	Manufacturer	Caffeine Content (milligrams)
Fiorinal	Sandoz	40
Florital	Cenci	40
Forbutal	Vangard	40
G-1	Hauck	40
Hyco-Pap	LaSalle	30
Korigesic	Trimen	30
Migralam	A.J. Bart	100
Norgesic	Riker	30
Norgesic Forte	Riker	60
Pacaps	LaSalle	40
Propoxyphene compound 65	Schein	32.4
Repan tablets	Everett	40
SK-65 compound	Smith, Kline, & French	32.4
Soma compound	Wallace	32
Synalgos-DC	Wyeth	30
Two-Dyne	Hyrex	40
Triad	UAD	40
Wigraine	Organon	100

NONPRESCRIPTION

Trade Name	Manufacturer	Caffeine Content (milligrams)
Anacin	Whitehall	32
Appedrine Maximum Strength	Thompson Medical	100
Arthritis Strength BC powder	Block	32
Aqua Ban	Thompson Medical	100
Aqua Ban Plus	Thompson Medical	200
Caffin T-D	Kenyon	250
CP	Western Research	140
CCP Cough and Cold tablets	Medique	64.8
Codexin Extra Strength	Arco	200
Coryban-D	Pfipharmecs	30
DeWitt's Pills	DeWitt	6.5
Dietac	Menley & James	200
Efed II (black)	Alto	200
Enerjets	Chilton	65
Excedrin Extra Strength	Bristol-Myers	65
Goody's Headache Powders	Goody's	32.5
Keep-A-Wake	Stayner	162
Lerton Ovules	Vita Elixir	250
Midol	Glenbrook	32.4
No Doz	Bristol-Myers	100
Periodic	Towne	60
Prolamine	Thompson Medical	140
Revs Caffeine T.D.	Vitarine	250
Sta-Wake Dextabs	Approved	97.2

TABLE 6-4 *(Continued)*

Trade Name	Manufacturer	Caffeine Content (milligrams)
Stay-Alert	Edward J. Moore	250
Stay Awake	Towne	200
Slim Plan Plus	Whiteworth	200
Tirend	Norcliff Thayer	100
Triaminicin	Dorsey	30
Vanquish	Glenbrook	33
Verv Alertness	APC	200
Vivarin	Beecham Products	200

Source: Reprinted with permission by Schwartz (1987).

Cholesterol

In November 1986 the *Journal of the American Medical Association* reported that cholesterol has become important with respect to heart attacks and heart disease. This paper shows that approximately 80 percent of American men have above-normal risk because of higher cholesterol levels. The risk increases when the blood level is above 180 mg. Above 240 mg the risk increases significantly. The general recommendation is to get the cholesterol down in the 200-mg range or below. The healthiest pattern is to be below 180 mg, since this level is associated with the lowest risk of damage to your heart. Other studies show that with a cholesterol over 250 mg, you have an even higher risk for heart attacks and strokes if you smoke.

Cholesterol data from large studies such as the Framingham study, the Pooling Project, and the Israeli prospective study show that at the level of 200 mg of cholesterol there is not a greater increase in coronary heart disease. Above this level, however, the increase rises, until at 250 mg or above the risk is doubled. Above 300 mg, the risk doubles again. So if your cholesterol is above 250 mg, or certainly above the 300-mg range, you need to reduce it.

The other factor medical science has found is that high-density lipoprotein (HDL), which is part of the blood level of cholesterol, can be predictive of heart disease. This blood chemistry measure is a positive predictor because the higher the levels of HDL above 75 mg, the less likely the person is to get heart disease. As will be mentioned later, exercise can help increase the HDL.

Scientists have learned how important the balance of fats is in the blood (HDL to LDL ratio). You want a high HDL level and a low LDL level. That is why I have recommended that fats and saturated fats, which raise the blood levels of cholesterol, should be reduced. Processed foods that use coconut, palm, vegetable shortening or hydrogenated vegetable oils increase your cholesterol. Certain cream replacements use these oils, and they often contain more fats than the same amount of real cream (low-fat milk is better). Losing weight can also help reduce cholesterol.

I recommend that people use unsaturated vegetable oils—oils made from corn, sunflower seeds, soybeans, or olives. These oils tend to be liquid at room temperature and thus can easily be identified.

Cheese is high in fat and increases your cholesterol. It is important not to eat the fat and skin of poultry. White chicken meat or white turkey meat has less fat than duck meat. Fish is highly recommended because fish are composed largely of unsaturated fat, often referred to as fish oils. These unsaturated fats tend to balance the risk of the high-cholesterol content in shrimp and lobster. Moderate to small portions (3 to 5 ounces) of shrimp or lobster contain the healthy elements of the fish fat.

It is important to be attentive to nutrition, because we are finding out more and more that there is a balance of foodstuffs and exercise that are important to health. As recently as 3 years ago, for example, shrimp and lobster, because of the high amount of cholesterol, were basically ruled out of many diets. Now you can have three to four ounces if you do not use heavy sauces of cream, cheese, or butter.

The Importance of Healthy Eating and Drinking

One of the reasons nutrition and what you eat and drink is so important is that smoking, alcohol, caffeine, fats, and calories increase the risk of cardiovascular disease. Cardiovascular disease is any disease that affects the heart and blood vessels. These vessels are the crucial factor in circulating the blood, bringing oxygen and nutrients to all of the cells of the body. Cardiovascular disease is still the leading cause of death in the United States, causing approximately 750,000 deaths per year. Once the heart and blood vessels are damaged, the brain, kidneys, and other vital organs and tissues might also be damaged. I have mentioned some other health problems: hypertension, diabetes, coronary heart disease, or angina, which can lead to heart attacks and strokes. The American Heart Association estimates that 50 percent of all the deaths in the United States result from cardiovascular disease. In 1985 they estimated that more than 43 million Americans were affected by some form of heart or blood vessel disease. High blood pressure affects one in five adults, about 38 million people. Another 1.9 million are affected by strokes and heart attacks. A third of these, 550,000, die from the heart attacks.

Vitamins and Supplements

If you eat a healthful diet composed of vegetables, fruits, whole wheat grains and breads, lean meat, and moderate amounts of dairy products, you should obtain all the minerals and vitamins you need. If you are pregnant or have a restricted diet because of food sensitivities, then your physician may recommend specific vitamins or supplements as necessary.

One of the most beneficial supplements is 250 to 500 mg of vitamin C per day. Vitamin C is thought to be helpful for stress-related problems. Linus Pauling, who has done a great deal of research on vitamin C, suggests you use 1000 mg or more if you have a cold or are undergoing a lot of stress. He also recommends megadoses up to 8000 or 10,000 mg (8 to 10 grams). While this recommendation is controversial, it certainly is clear that some people do better with 250 to 500 mg per day. If you have a cold, you may want to double or triple that amount. Too much vitamin C can result in lethargy, decreased appetite, and even kidney damage.

Another medically useful supplement is vitamin E. Surgeons use it to help with healing wounds. Vitamin E is also recommended for women who have cystic breasts. The dosage ranges from 200 to 400 mg per day. Consult with your physician to determine the proper dose for you.

Many women, after their menopause, need to take, through diet or calcium supplements, 750 or more mg of calcium and approximately 350 units of vitamin D. Check with your doctor, but many doctors now recommend 150 to 2000 mg of calcium daily.

Most physicians recommend that you do not take more than 5,000 IUs of vitamin A and 400 IUs of Vitamin D. Some of the symptoms of overdose of vitamin A are irritability, fever, and bone pain.

Women who have excessive amounts of bleeding during their menstrual periods may need to take pills for iron replacement. One of the other elements that people may be low on is zinc. Check with your doctor, because it is thought that having 15 to 20 mg of zinc every day or every other day may be helpful. The U.S. government recommends that you have about 7.5 to 20 mg per day.

In general, vitamin treatments, hair analysis, and other strange tests are not accepted by the medical profession, and it is "buyer beware." I am suspicious of those that do such tests. It appears to be a conflict of interest when people who treat you sell you vitamins. An increasing number of chiropractors and other practitioners claim to be medical healers or counselors who prescribe vitamins and supplements. In many cases, they have their own name brands. Usually they have prepared them or have them made, and they are often two to ten times more expensive than in a drug or health store. I recommend that you be very cautious and check with your physician. This is a large industry, and the practitioners are interested in selling you their product to make a big profit. They may not have your health, longevity, or well-being in mind.

A recent example of this was the case of Steve McQueen. He gave up on regular medical treatment for his cancer and went to Mexico to get treated with laetril. Within a month or two he died. It is quite possible that with regular medical treatment he could have survived another 6 to 12 months or longer. Beware of great promises and people who sell their own "remedies."

An example of overuse of vitamins was reported by Herbert Schumberger, M.D., a neurologist who had cured four patients of their symptoms. He found that some patients were taking as much as 6 grams (6000 mg) of vitamin B6 (pyridoxine). They would take it for gynecological problems and, from an "orthomolecular psychiatrist/chiropractor," for premenstrual edema, carpal tunnel syndrome, and stress. Others had bought the vitamin B6 at health food stores because they were involved in body building and training. The common symptoms from overdosing of the vitamin B6 were unstable gait, numb feet, general weakness, and numbness and clumsiness of the hands. Dr. Schumberger pointed out that few patients taking less than 2 grams of the pyridoxine had symptoms. However, patients taking more than 1½ or 2 grams for more than 3 months started to get some symptoms.

Another example of this was a woman in New York who began taking a selenium supplement. These tablets, instead of having 150 mg, were not produced correctly and contained much more. After about 2 months, she started losing hair from her scalp and had tinnitus (ringing in the ears), swelling of the fingertips, and discharges from the fingernail bed. Finally she lost a fingernail and had nausea, vomiting, sour-milk breath, and fatigue. Once she stopped taking the tablets, she recovered. It is not true that you can take as many vitamins as you want, and that more is better. You need to be careful and check with your physician before taking large doses of any vitamin.

Other foods, such as ginseng, can also produce high blood pressure, skin problems, amenorrhea, weakness, nervousness, decreased appetite, depression, and diarrhea. When you are thinking about taking supplements be aware that some of them can cause symptoms. Vitamins are chemicals and they need to be carefully monitored.

In regard to the other theories of nutrition and related supplements, I want to call your attention to so-called remedies that masquerade as "homeopathic medicines." The theory that you can use small dosages of chemicals or ingredients labeled in Latin to improve health may be erroneous and dangerous to your health. Harry Kerr, M.D., from the Department of Medicine at the Medical College in Wisconsin, examined some homeopathic medicines that can be purchased over the counter or by mail order. He evaluated the arsenic content and found that the amounts were similar to those stated in the label information in only two of the six examined. The remaining four contained varying amounts of chemicals. In fact, in two of them there was a significant amount of arsenic. Salespeople that he interviewed could not identify arsenic in the ingredients of these preparations and are "therefore incapable of warning the general public of possible dangers on ingestion." Dr. Kerr also pointed out there are often no warning labels.

Not only is the watchword "buyer beware" but remedies (chemicals) can be dangerous. You should not take any compound that is not labeled. One of the benefits of the drug industry is that they have to list all ingredients and are legally responsible to doctors, patients, and pharmacists.

You are best served by having your checkup done by a physician rather than by some nutritionist who is interested in having you visit him or her frequently and buy his or her vitamins. Not only are there theories about nutrition but there is a nutrition industry. The nutrition industry is all too happy to have you spend your money without demonstrating that these supplements or vitamins work.

General Advice

When you are attempting to make a change in your life, it is best to do it one step at a time. If you are smoking two packs of cigarettes a day and drinking five or six cups of coffee a day, do not attempt to give up both at one time. It is an extremely rare person, maybe one in a million, who can accomplish this. If you are that person, fine; this does not pertain to you. For most of us, it is best to choose one habit at a time to change.

If you are smoking too much and drinking too much coffee, try to reduce to five or fewer cigarettes a day and for the next month or two retain this level. At this point, when you have reduced the smoking addiction, address the coffee addiction. The first step is to cut down from five or six cups to four or five cups and then to three or four cups a day. In a month or two try to go to two or three cups a day. After approximately 4 or 5 months, you will have wiped out the most dangerous habit, the cigarette smoking, and have your coffee down to a healthier two or three cups. You will feel calmer and will have reduced the risk of lung cancer as well as the immediate effects of nicotine on the system—irritation of the throat and lungs and constriction of the arteries.

Do not focus on what you have not done; always give yourself credit for what you have done.

Summary

It is important to reduce or stop the high-risk behaviors of smoking, alcohol, and caffeine. Then focus on keeping your weight in a healthy range for your body size. Use the chart of healthy weight on page 114. For calorie intake, women should consume around 2000 calories per day and men about 2500 calories per day. If you are overweight, increase your physical exercise or decrease your calories (or both). If you continue to gain weight, you might have to go down to 1600 to 1800 calories for women and 2200 to 2300 for men. At about 1500 to 1600 calories most people will be able to maintain a lower weight or continue to lose weight. You should not reduce your caloric intake to fewer than 1500 unless you have specific instructions from your physician.

Eat healthful foods. Have a salad and vegetables every day, eat fish at least once or twice a week, and trim all fat from your foods (particularly skin from poultry). Eat lots of grains, vegetables, fruits, and nuts that provide fiber and bulk, using whole wheat cereals and bread.

Life is difficult enough with the everyday stresses and problems. You can use these health and nutrition facts to experience better health. By adding PSR exercises, you can further reduce your risk factors.

CHAPTER SEVEN

THE THIRD POSITIVE STRESS RESPONSE EXERCISE: WARMTH*

The great man is he who does not lose his child's heart.

—*Mencius*

Linda's Raynaud's Disease and Tension

At the beginning of biofeedback training, my expectations were rather narrow. Dr. Grokoest suggested that I learn biofeedback techniques in order to try to prevent further attacks of Raynaud's. My hands were always ice-cold in cool weather, and I was told by my internist that my musculature was taut and tense. He said that he didn't know whether further episodes of carpal tunnel syndrome would be prevented by this training, but at the least I could learn how to keep my hands warm and my body more relaxed. Despite these narrow expectations, over the past year I have been delighted to discover that as a result of the biofeedback (PSR) training, there has been a profound change in my fundamental response to the world around me, and that I am happier and feel better than ever before.

At the biofeedback sessions I learned to profoundly relax my body. I found the process of learning to attain a deeply relaxed state to be quite easy and natural, in spite of the mechanical aspects of the situation. The audiocassettes which instructed me in various methods of relaxation (muscle tension and relaxation, mental

---

*This chapter was jointly written by Keith Sedlacek, M.D., and Robert Kall, M.ED.

144

images, warmth phrases) and the feedback I was getting about the state of relaxation of my body aided me in achieving a feeling previously unknown. I found that it was easier for me to relax using tension and relaxation exercises than the suggested imagery. Then I used the Bio-Q fingerband at home with the warmth exercises. This helped me learn how to warm my fingers when I wanted to. Now I am familiar with the feeling of being very relaxed so that I am no longer dependent on the tapes to help me discover this feeling. However, I still use a tape once a day (and do relaxation exercises without the tape at another time each day) because I find that a tape helps me pace the relaxation exercises nicely.

I am very glad that during each biofeedback session I was encouraged to bring my entire being into what was happening. I was always asked about the thoughts and feelings I was having while I was working with the biofeedback apparatus. I felt that there was a sincere interest in what was happening to me. I found it essential to communicate about what was happening, and I am certain that the biofeedback experience would have been a much less profound one if I had not received such encouragement and directions.

I have discovered that it feels wonderful to be relaxed and warm. When I began biofeedback training, I thought of what I was doing as merely trying to reduce bodily tension. I feel now that the term "stress reduction" is a negative way of expressing the state one attains when one is physically at peace. There is an absence of tension in a relaxed body, but this is not all. There is such a joyful feeling in a relaxed body! During the biofeedback sessions, as my body became more and more relaxed, I experienced very warm, happy, giddy feelings which seemed to sweep through my whole being. Sometimes I would begin to laugh, because my mood became so irrepressibly happy. It felt as though those feelings had always been there, trapped in a tense body. I believe now that our bodies are, by nature, joyful and energetic, and that these feelings disappear when the body is in a state of tension. The process of discovering these joyful feelings seemed easy, natural, unforced.

I feel that the reason that biofeedback training provided me with important insights is that it enabled me, in a manner of speaking, to step outside of my own body into a more relaxed body. From this new relaxed state, I could begin to understand why I had physically responded to the world around me as I had. Also, in this new relaxed state, I could approach situations and tasks with a new nervous system and could relearn responses which had become habitual. The good feelings I attained through biofeedback training guided me toward much self-understanding and change. The primary force motivating these changes was the secure, happy, relaxed feelings I experienced. Experiencing the whole world as less raucous and calmer when I was relaxed helped me to understand that much of the stress around me was disturbing because I was physically tense. When I became tense, I would sense a blocking of the free, flowing, relaxed feelings that I had when my body was relaxed. The desire to maintain the vibrant, alive, responsive feelings became very strong, for I felt that something truly wonderful was happening to me. The satisfactions derived from old habitual reactions to certain situations sometimes felt pale in comparison to the satisfaction of feeling calm, free, and alive, and old habits started to change.

During the course of the biofeedback training, I had a number of very vivid dreams and memories about times long past, when I was around 4 or 5 years old. I was told that I might have recollections about painful experiences in the past. However, the vivid dreams and remembrances concerned warm, happy, vibrant childhood feelings and incidents. A number of times, it was wrenching to come back to reality, so very vivid were these dreams and memories. I felt as though, through these dreams and memories, I was reconnecting to a period before bodily tension had set in, to a time that I could feel more immediate joy because my body had been more relaxed.

When I began biofeedback training, and I was asked about what I found stressful, the only situation that I could think of that made me tense was one in which there was time pressure. I have discovered in the past year that there were many other self-induced causes of stress in my life. I began to understand how there was secondary gain for me in setting things up in my life so that, in a sense, events ran me. When I did so, I was relieving myself of the responsibility of making decisions (and possibly mistakes) about the course of my life. I was brought up to be wary and fearful, not to hurt myself. By creating a whirlwind around me, I was refusing to recognize the choices I was making for myself, the possibility of hurting myself.

Certain episodes during biofeedback sessions revealed some very important things to me about a cause of bodily stress of which I was oblivious. Early in the training, I was responding to a tape which instructed me to tense and relax various muscle groups. I found that once I tensed the area around my eyes, I could not get this area to relax. The area remained so tense that I thought the biofeedback machine was malfunctioning. It was because of these episodes that I began to understand how a childhood sensitivity about a wandering left eye had caused me to continuously tense the area around the eyes in an attempt to keep the left eye constantly focused. I used to expend energy in hiding what I considered to be an ugly part of me, and this resulted in a constant tension. I have found that over time, now that I have gained an awareness of this self-consciousness, the notion that I have something ugly to hide has felt less valid, less compelling. I feel that I am relating more gently, freely, and patiently to those around me because I am not experiencing the strain of constantly trying to control my facial muscles. Even now, facial relaxation feels like a prelude to general body relaxation for me. It is necessary for me to relax my face in order to relax the rest of my body.

As I proceed through daily activities, there are times when I realize that I have lost my calm, centered, steady feeling, and this leads to reflection about what is going on that causes me to lose this tranquil state. I have discovered that certain situations have always been difficult for me and that I was previously often unaware of this discomfort. These new awarenesses, enhanced by discussions with Dr. Sedlacek, have led to some important realizations. I believe that half the battle for self-understanding is learning to recognize when one is being thrown off balance. I believe that biofeedback training has helped to provide me with this type of insight.

Sometimes the simplicity of it all amazes me. A year ago, I saw everyday existence as fraught with bottom-less pits. Now, everything feels easier. My body is always so much calmer that it is hard to believe. At this point, I never reach the degree of nervous tension that used to be a part of my daily existence. And my hands are warmer!

Linda's experience using a combined approach of PSR and biofeedback was very helpful for her Raynaud's dis-ease and muscular tension. She related how the PSR made her more aware of her thoughts, feelings, and physical reactions. As she gained more physiological skills with PSR, she was able to rebalance her emotions and overreactions to other people. Using the second and third PSR exercises enabled her to change her mental and physical approach to life. It has stopped her Raynaud's and has calmed her life.

Let's review how the PSR training works with the arteries and the other organs of the body. Your hands and feet get colder when the peripheral blood flow de-creases. But why do they get colder? And what factors control the amount of blood that flows to your extremi-ties and other organs?

The warmest part of the body is the trunk of your body—the area from your shoulders to your pelvis. Blood flows outward from the trunk to the head and extremi-ties, carrying and distributing the heat it has absorbed at this core. The 98.6 degrees F that we associate with normal body temperature represents core body tempera-ture. The temperature at the surface of the body varies considerably. Finger temperature can range from 96 de-grees to 62 degrees in a room heated to 74 degrees. That's more than a 30-degree spread. The forehead, neck, armpits, knees, and tip of the nose can all vary from each other in temperature. That's why when a ther-mogram is taken of a person, the body shows up in many different colors representing different temperatures.

Hand warming is a passive process. From now on, unless specified, when we refer to the hands and hand warming we also mean the whole peripheral vascular response phenomenon, including the feet and toes. Your hands are naturally warm unless your dinosaur cuts off their blood circulation. When your nervous system is quiet, your fingertips are warm; the blood vessels supplying them are wide open. When you are under stress your fingertips are cold because the arteries have constricted and reduced blood flow.

How Do the Blood Vessels Open and Close?

The blood vessel walls are composed of layers, one of which is muscle. When this muscle layer tenses and contracts, the opening (lumen) of the vessel narrows. The muscles are switched on and off by the sympathetic nervous system. This is the part of the nervous system that mediates the emergency response. It's your dinosaur's prime turf. The system works both hormonally and neurally. When the sympathetic system is activated, the stress hormones are released. Their concentration in the blood increases. Throughout the body these hormones plug into receptors that turn on the emergency reaction, including the tensing of the muscles in the peripheral blood vessel walls. Peripheral circulation decreases and your hands and feet get colder.

With the blood-flow exercises, you have to go past your previous body self-control experience. You will learn

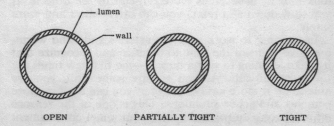

OPEN   PARTIALLY TIGHT   TIGHT

to go even deeper inside yourself to relax the blood vessel wall muscles, which most people have no voluntary control over.

As you are working on the warming exercises, learning to open up the arteries and spreading the warmth through the skin, please remember that this is a new skill. You have had no previous experience with learning to open the arteries. Your only experience is the tendency to race the nervous system and close down the arteries. That is why, in general, cool hands mean an activated nervous system.

Usually, women will run 1 to 2 degrees cooler than men. There are several theories about this difference. One is the difference in physical size and another is that women's arteries are slightly different from men's. The most likely theory is that the difference is due to stress. This stress arousal sign comes from the fact that women are taught to be more reserved and not as physically active as men. This is changing now that young girls are taught to be more assertive and to take part in sports. In colleges we now have equality in men's and women's sports. However, men are still taught to be more active, explosive, and angry while women are taught to be more reserved and polite. This may have an effect on the nervous system, so women are cooler-handed. Women who practice the third PSR may be aware that their hands are a little cooler than men's, but they can learn to adjust just as well as or better than men after some practice.

Having had no previous experience with training the arteries, you need to be willing to try to warm the hands but not to try too hard. This is as if you are driving through a fog. If you try to go faster or try to strain and look into it, it becomes more difficult to see objects. If you slow down and relax, you can drive better and more safely.

In learning to work with the arteries and hand warming, give yourself the time to practice and recognize that it is like learning to ride a bicycle—the first few times are the most difficult. As you acquire some skill, you are able to do it more easily, and then you can do it in more complex and active situations. This is one of the reasons we ask people to begin this in a calm, quiet environment and to take 10 to 20 minutes to practice by themselves without any interruptions. When you are practicing or doing your stress management exercises, you should be left alone unless there is an emergency.

Women hear or are told that with menopause they get hot flashes (flushing). I chaired a symposium on this issue at the Biofeedback Society of America meeting in 1985. There were two papers that presented information on biofeedback and stress management training of hot flashes. The results reported were that about 80 percent of the women could reduce their hot flashes after the stress management training with biofeedback and hand warming. They also felt calmer in general and tolerated the other changes of menopause better.

Conscious blood-flow awareness and control is your key to being able to regulate your nervous system. It enables you to calm the prehistoric panic program of the dinosaur brain so you can combine its strengths with your highest mental and emotional capacities.

Preparation for the Third Positive Stress Response

We used the breathing and muscle exercises first because you are more used to controlling those body behaviors. Sometimes it is better to start where you've had more concrete experience. On the other hand, it's okay if you skipped the first two exercises. Some people do best and are helped most by starting with bloodflow control.

You are going to start with a flexible exercise. You'll be able to use it as you progress in developing your blood-flow control skills. It can take from 5 to 20 minutes to complete. You can speed it up or stretch it out to last longer. Take your time with it the first few times around, then shrink it and do the exercise in 5 to 6 minutes. In Chapter Ten we'll give you a 3- to 4-minute exercise. Eventually, you'll be able to run through the whole exercise in just a few seconds.

The reason you can do it so fast and get useful effects is because of the key phrases you'll learn in Chapter Ten.

First you need to practice this longer warmth exercise. When you do this version of the warmth exercise, use imagery and lots of imagination to make the experience as real as possible. Each time you do the exercise use different imagery, but later on the key phrases will be the same. Eventually you'll condition your body to respond to those key phrases, just as you first learned to print your name. Then you learned to condition yourself to slowly write your name. After lots of practice, you were conditioned to sign your name. Now your signature is second nature to you. You can talk to someone and sign your name, or listen to music as you write checks to pay your monthly bills. This is a conditioned response—you see the check and sign it. The warmth exercise won't be just a conditioned response, just as the ability to play a complicated chord on the piano is not just a conditioned response. Later, the key words will make it easier to maximize your mastery of blood-flow control and use it faster in many situations.

As we've said earlier, people often tend to have one physiological system more vulnerable to stress than the rest of the body systems. If your dinosaur tends to dig its claws particularly tightly into your peripheral vascular system in response to stress, then that system is almost certainly already conditioned. It is conditioned in a negative way to overreact to stress, and to maintain a higher resting level even when stress isn't present. This can be reflected by either cold hands or hands that fluctuate in temperature when room temperature stays the same. Even if your hands are usually above 88 degrees F, if they fluctuate from 88 to 95 to 90 to 93, then they are being activated by your sympathetic nervous system. Blood-flow control involves more than just hand warming. It's also important to maintain temperature stability. Numerous studies have shown that just by thinking unpleasant or stressful thoughts, you decrease hand temperature and peripheral blood flow. If you tend to be someone who is a peripheral vascular overresponder, the temperature and blood-flow changes will be greater for you. Blood-flow control skills will help you to minimize the effects of stressors on your peripheral vascular response. Your dinosaur, your sympathetic nervous system, will be more tightly leashed and controlled. Your old negative conditioned responses to stressors will gradually fade away.

When you use different kinds of imagery to imagine a variety of sensations and body processes, different sensory portions of your brain are activated. If you visualize your hand, then the part of your brain that controls and senses your hand will reflect increased activity. If you think about moving the hand, the motor region of your brain that controls hand movement becomes more active. You don't have to move the hand. You just have to think about it. Focus your mind on your hand and the part of the brain that controls and receives information from your hand becomes more active.

When you use imagery you actually affect the part of the brain that is involved in controlling the part of your body you are focusing on. If you don't try to tense your hand but just imagine it tensing, your hand will tense slightly. It may not be noticeable to you, but it can easily be measured by an electromyograph, a device often used in biofeedback to measure and magnify small changes in muscle tension.

If you imagine or suggest to yourself that your hand feels warm, your brain processes that message. The part of the brain that receives messages from your hand is activated, setting off a circular process. The brain uses the input information and responds by sending out new messages. The more powerful the imagery and the suggestion, the greater their effect will be on the brain's response.

Sophisticated studies have shown that the quality and content of your imagery play important roles in how effective it is in producing actual physiological changes. Imagery is commonly used to increase the hand-warming response. A typical instruction is to imagine yourself lying on the beach. There are two kinds of imagery scripts that can be used. You can use a *stimulus* script: "Imagine the sun beaming down on you. You are lying on the warm sand; occasionally warm breezes waft over you." This script describes *stimuli* that are impinging upon you. The next kind of imagery script is a *response* script:

"Imagine the warm pulsing sensation in your hands as the sun's rays beam on them. You can feel the hot, gritty sand flowing between your toes and draining through your fingers like sand in an hourglass. Warm breezes fan the flush in your tanning skin, caressing you with their gentle touch."

This imagery describes the responses, the sensations you experience as you are stimulated. Use this response-oriented approach rather than the first kind we described. The more complete the response you can imagine and visualize, the more information you are giving to your brain. It's like presenting a case to a jury. If your imagery is complete enough, then you'll persuade your brain to come up with a verdict that causes your body to respond as if it is in the situation you are visualizing. This approach to hand warming is very effective, especially if you are good at imagery. Even if you don't use imagery a lot, you can vividly recreate in your mind a memory of a pleasant, relaxing experience where your hands and feet were warm. By practicing and repeating pleasant, calm scenes, you'll develop your hand-warming skills.

People commonly use the following situations or stimuli to enhance their imagery, recalling them from their own experience:

• Lying on the beach by the ocean, a local river, stream, creek, or lake, or surrounded by tropical palms on a secluded isle.

• Relaxing in your yard, sitting or reclining on a chair, hammock, or blanket.

• Sitting in front of a fireplace, a stove, a heater duct, with your hands and feet close to the heat source.

• Lying in a warm tub of water or under a toasty electric blanket.

• Putting your hands in a bowl of warm spaghetti, rice, or noodles, or your feet in a pan of warm water.

• Touching, caressing, or holding a warm, cuddly, loving body.

• Holding hands with a lover.

- Shadows can also be useful, since they accentuate the difference in temperature. Imagine a tree or an umbrella shading your head while the sun is warming your extremities.

We've listed stimulus situations above. They can help make it easier for you to imagine responses that enhance peripheral blood flow. You could also stage some of those situations with the idea of remembering the warmth sensations that go with them. We suggest that you go to a beach or your favorite summer vacation spot and lock into your memory the response sensations you experience. Or put your hands under warm water. This can help you produce a crisper image.

Some of the sensations that people have included in their imagery are these:

- Feeling tension flowing out, being replaced by relaxation.

- Hands swelling or feeling full or heavy.

- Blood pulsing in hands, fingers, feet.

- Tingly, warm sensations.

- Feeling the blood pushed with great momentum from the heart to the hands and feet.

- A flush or rush of blood.

- Pulse beats (heartbeats).

- Flickering warmth from a fireplace.

- Moist, wet warmth from steam rising from a pot of boiling water or hot soup.

- Warmth associated with friction or rubbing.

So try the warmth exercise by reading through the phrases and repeating them to yourself. The second time you do the warmth exercise, try your favorite mental image with the exercise. Then try a second and a third mental image. If you develop two or three good mental images with the warmth exercise, your skill will develop faster and you'll have a more warming experience.

The warmth training should be done in a quiet room with the temperature at least 72 degrees, preferably between 74 and 76 degrees. This allows your body to feel comfortable in the room. If it is under 72 degrees, you will be losing heat to the room's cooler temperature, and the skin will tend to be cool or lukewarm. On the other hand, if the room is over 80 degrees, then heat is absorbed into the body and your hands will tend to be warmer. Use a room temperature around 74 to 76 degrees because at this temperature you will feel comfortable, and it is your nervous system, not the room temperature, that affects your skin temperature. This is why on a very cold day you will notice that the hands stay cool after you come inside for a few minutes or even for a few hours. If you have chronically cool fingers and cool toes, you have a tendency to tighten down the arteries, and this becomes a locked-in pattern. By using the PSR skill with the warming exercises, you can retrain yourself and have warmer hands and feet.

A comfortable chair that supports your head, arms, and legs so you can deeply relax is a good place to practice. Or you can lie on your back on a rug with a pillow under the back of your knees. The pillow will allow your thighs, hips, and lower back to relax more. You may want to put a thin feather pillow under your neck and head. Your arms should be 6 to 8 inches to each side of your hips. Generally, it is good to turn your palms face up. By putting the palms up, you tend to rotate the shoulders back and flat to the floor. If this is uncomfortable for you at first, then let the hands turn sideways.

The third choice, the one I recommend less strongly because it tends to be associated with sleep, is a bed or a couch. You can use these exercises to fall asleep or go back to sleep, but it is better to practice and learn the skills outside the bed. Then you can learn the skills better and do an extra session before bed or if you wake up during the night.

The Warming Exercise

In beginning a positive warmth response, start by paying close attention to slow, regular-paced breathing. Breathe in for a count of three or four, pause for a count, breathe out for a count of three or four, and then pause for a count. Remember to breathe in a slow, paced manner after each phrase you are repeating. The pause in the parentheses gives you a rough idea of the time between phrases. Ten seconds is about two breath cycles (15 equals three breath cycles). As you practice this exercise for the next few weeks you may find that you'll increase the breath cycle from 5 or 6 seconds to 7 or 8 seconds.

Breathe in a slow, paced manner with your eyes lightly closed. *(Pause about 45 seconds.)*

Repeat each of the phrases two or three times as you read them to yourself.

I am beginning to feel quite relaxed. *(Pause about 10 seconds.)*

I feel very calm and relaxed. *(Pause about 10 seconds.)*

My feet feel heavy and relaxed. *(Pause about 10 seconds.)*

My ankles feel heavy and relaxed. *(Pause about 10 seconds.)*

My knees feel heavy and relaxed. *(Pause about 10 seconds.)*

My hips feel heavy and relaxed. *(Pause about 10 seconds.)*

My feet, my ankles, my knees, and my hips feel heavy, relaxed, and comfortable. *(Pause about 15 seconds.)*

My feet, my ankles, my knees, and my hips all feel heavy, relaxed, and comfortable. *(Pause about 15 seconds.)*

My abdomen and the whole center portion of my body feel heavy and relaxed. (*Pause about 15 seconds.*)

My breathing is slow and regular. My abdomen and the whole center portion of my body feel heavy and relaxed. (*Pause about 15 seconds.*)

My hands feel heavy and relaxed. My hands feel heavy and relaxed. (*Pause about 15 seconds.*)

My arms feel heavy and relaxed. (*Pause about 10 seconds.*)

My shoulders feel heavy and relaxed. (*Pause about 10 seconds.*) My neck feels heavy and relaxed. (*Pause about 10 seconds.*)

My jaw feels heavy and relaxed. (*Pause about 10 seconds.*)

My forehead feels heavy and relaxed. (*Pause about 10 seconds.*)

My face and scalp feel heavy and relaxed. (*Pause about 15 seconds.*)

My neck, my jaw, my face, and my scalp feel heavy, relaxed, and comfortable. (*Pause about 15 seconds.*)

My whole body feels heavy and relaxed. My whole body feels heavy, relaxed, and comfortable. (*Pause about 20 seconds.*)

My breathing is calm, relaxed, and comfortable. (*Pause about 10 seconds.*)

Now I can feel the sun shining down on me, warming the top of my head. The top of my head feels warm and heavy. (*Pause about 15 seconds.*)

Now the relaxing warmth flows down from my head into my right shoulder. My right shoulder feels warm and heavy. (*Pause about 15 seconds.*)

The relaxing warmth is flowing down from my head and into my right shoulder. The relaxing warmth is flowing gently down to my right hand. My right hand feels warm and heavy. (*Pause about 15 seconds.*)

My right hand feels warm and heavy. My right hand feels warm and heavy. *(Pause about 15 seconds.)*

Now the relaxing warmth flows back up to my right arm; my right arm feels warm and heavy. The relaxing warmth spreads up through my right elbow into my right shoulder. My right elbow, my right shoulder feel warm and heavy. *(Pause about 15 seconds.)*

The relaxing warmth flows slowly throughout my whole back. I feel the warmth relaxing my back. My back feels warm and heavy. *(Pause about 10 seconds.)*

The relaxing warmth now flows from my back and neck into my left shoulder. My left shoulder feels warm and heavy. *(Pause about 10 seconds.)*

My breathing is slow and paced. The relaxing warmth flows down to my left hand. My left hand feels warm and heavy. *(Pause about 15 seconds.)*

My left hand feels warm and heavy. The relaxing warmth flows back up to my left arm. My left arm feels warm and heavy. The relaxing warmth spreads up my left elbow into my left shoulder. My left elbow, my left shoulder feel warm and heavy. The relaxing warmth flows to my heart. My heart feels warm and easy. *(Pause about 15 seconds.)*

My heart feels warm and easy. My heartbeat is calm and regular. *(Pause about 15 seconds.)*

My heartbeat is calm and regular. Now the relaxing warmth flows down into my stomach. My stomach feels warm and quiet. My breathing is slow and regular. *(Pause about 15 seconds.)*

Now the relaxing warmth flows down into my right thigh. My right thigh feels warm and heavy. *(Pause about 15 seconds.)*

The relaxing warmth flows down into my right foot. My right foot feels warm and heavy. *(Pause about 15 seconds.)*

Now the relaxing warmth flows slowly up through my right calf to my right knee to my right thigh. My right leg feels warm and heavy. My breathing is slow and regular. *(Pause about 15 seconds.)*

Now the relaxing warmth flows into my left thigh. My left thigh feels warm and heavy. The relaxing warmth flows down into my left foot. My left foot feels warm and heavy. *(Pause about 15 seconds.)*

The relaxing warmth flows slowly up through my left calf, to my left knee, to my left thigh. My left leg feels warm and heavy. *(Pause about 15 seconds.)*

My breathing is slow and regular. *(Pause.)* My breathing is slow and regular. *(Pause about 10 seconds.)*

The relaxing warmth flows up through my abdomen, through my stomach, and into my heart. My heart feels warm and easy. My heart pumps relaxing warmth throughout my entire body. *(Pause.)* My whole body feels very quiet, and very calm. *(Pause.)* My whole body feels very comfortable and very relaxed and very heavy. *(Pause about 15 seconds.)*

My whole body feels very comfortable, very relaxed, and very heavy. My mind is calm. *(Pause.)* My mind is quiet. *(Pause.)* My mind is easy. *(Pause.)* My body is warm. *(Pause.)* My breathing is slow, relaxed, and comfortable. My mind is calm and quiet. I feel an inward quietness. My body is warm and heavy. I am alert in an easy, quiet way. I feel an inward peace. I feel a new sense of well-being. *(Pause about 20 seconds.)*

Enjoy the calm, warm, relaxed feelings. *(Pause about 20 seconds.)*

Now say to yourself, "I feel calm, warm, and energetic." Then count slowly one, two, three, open your eyes, stretch your arms and legs, and slowly get up. Notice and enjoy the warmth and relaxation you feel in different parts of your body. The first few times you do this exercise the feeling of warmth may be very subtle. As you practice more you will feel more warmth in the fingers, toes, lips, or other areas of your body.

People always want to know what a normal skin temperature is and what theirs should be. Studies have shown that there are wide differences in people's average skin temperature. The temperature of the dominant hand is usually more stable than the nondominant (the left hand for most people). The nondominant hand temperature tends to fluctuate more in response to stress. It's also harder to train that hand. That's why, even with the imagery exercise, we start with the easier to train, dominant right hand. The feet are harder to train than the hands, so it may take three or four more weeks to feel the feet warm.

When we use temperature biofeedback, we also start at the easiest site, the dominant (in most cases the right) hand. As skill is acquired, we move to the left hand and then the feet. With biofeedback the same exercise we've described is used, but you get the additional help of the feedback equipment.

You can also use your thermometer for biofeedback. At the Menninger Clinic and many clinics throughout the country, they give each biofeedback student a red-dyed alcohol thermometer costing just a few cents, and they get good results. Using your own version of that, or a wall thermometer, desk thermometer, or thermometer ring, you can add biofeedback to your bloodflow self-regulation program. I use the Bio-Q fingerband. This wraps around the first finger of your dominant hand and uses temperature-sensitive crystals to reveal your skin temperature. You read it as you would a clock.

Twelve o'clock is above the "B" in "Bio-Q." With a little practice, you'll read the Bio-Q at a glance, like a watch. When you are at your warmest, the center will light up. For fun, see what activities in your life light up the Bio-Q. This same "temperature watch face" is available as a ring. A stress temperature card can also be used. You just place your finger on it to give the temperature range. This card is available from the Stress Regulation Institute.

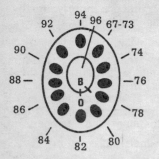

Each spot represents a different 2°F temperature range (except the 67-73° position)

Do the same exercise described in this chapter, but this time tape your thermometer to the fleshy side of your finger or use the fingerband or stress temperature card. Measure the temperature from your dominant hand (right if you are right-handed, left if you are a lefty).

Before you start the exercise, look at your thermometer or Bio-Q fingerband and get a reading. Then begin to do the exercise. After a few minutes, take another look. Has the temperature gone up even a tiny amount? If it has, good. That's a sign you are doing something right. If not, don't worry or start trying too hard, just continue allowing your hands to warm, letting your peripheral blood vessel muscles relax, letting more blood flow into your fingers. At the end of the warmth exercise, check the thermometer to see if you've increased or decreased your temperature. Throughout an exercise, temperature can vary considerably. When your temperature goes up, try to figure out what you did to make it go up. Recall your state of mind, any imagery or calming phrases you might have used. Try them again. Don't give up if they don't work right away. You may get excited over your success and start trying too hard, using good imagery with the wrong mental approach. Keep using the same strategy you've been focusing on and watch to see if your temperature continues to rise.

You may find that it works to take you so far, say to 85 or 86 degrees, but that you plateau there. You may need to experiment further with other strategies to warm your hands up even more to 93, 94, or higher. But remember, it just takes patience and persistence using your cues and response images with the third PSR. You may have to run through these two or three times to get the full effect. As you continue practicing, you'll find special ones that you enjoy and that are particularly effective.

On the other hand, you may find that you start at 87 or 90 degrees and then, after working hard at an exercise, your temperature drops precipitously to 81 degrees or less. That's a common occurrence. Your biofeedback thermometer will keep you honest. You may be working and trying too hard to relax. That often happens with hard-striving, successful individuals. It's a strategy they've found to be effective in attaining and maintaining their success, but it will be their downfall when it comes to relaxation and blood-flow control.

It can be a frustrating battle. People get angry at their feedback equipment. But they are really fighting themselves. Eventually, and it sometimes takes many practice sessions, these superstrivers give up the fight. They stop pushing and, in their frustration, let go of their high-pressure strategy. And lo and behold, much to their consternation and initial bewilderment, their skin temperature begins to rise. Remember, it often takes six to seven bloodflow exercise sessions before you get regular increases. To be fair to yourself, especially if you are a striver or have cold hands, give yourself eight or nine sessions before you expect to see a persistent pattern of warming.

Without the feedback, these cold-handed strivers think they are doing the normal great job, which they do at everything else, with the relaxation. The feedback forces them to reevaluate their strategies and the way they approach them, so they can be successful at relaxation, too.

After you've done the exercise with your eyes closed enough times to warm regularly, do the exercise with them open, watching the thermometer. Most thermometers are only sensitive enough to register changes of 1 or 2 full degrees or more. That's where the expensive electronic clinical thermometers have the big advantage. They can clearly show changes of 1/100th of a degree or less. And unlike the inexpensive thermometers, they give almost instantaneous feedback about tiny temperature changes. Just the same, your home thermometer will give you useful feedback. Several studies have proven that diligent use of inexpensive thermometers can effectively help people learn hand warming.

How Warm Can You Get?

Indoors at constant room temperature of 74 to 76 degrees F, the answer is easy: The warmer the better. Usually the low end of the indoor skin temperature continuum is about room temperature or a few degrees lower. It varies depending on where you set your thermostat. At the upper end of the temperature continuum, people tend to top off at about 95.5 to 97 degrees. It is rare to see someone whose finger temperature is above 97 degrees. If a person has a fever (the core temperature is raised above 98.6), then a finger temperature that high is not unusual. A hot bath, a dip in a hot tub or Jacuzzi, or a few minutes in a sauna will also put the finger temperature up there.

If you average a low temperature, under 86 degrees F, and you can raise your temperature to an average of 88 or 90, that's a big improvement. You may find that after continued practice you can increase it to the mid-90s during the exercise, and then it will drop back while you are working. That's okay. After all, you need to maintain some level of nervous system activation to effectively maintain a productive level of work. In a few weeks you will be able to warm better at work. You'll still react with some cooling, but it will be less drastic and you'll warm more quickly.

After 1 to 2 weeks of practicing the basic blood-flow control exercise, you'll notice physical changes as the muscles relax and the extremities warm. In general, the warmer the hands and feet, the more relaxed and calm you'll feel. Remember, this discussion is based on the consideration that you are practicing in a place that has a normal room temperature. We've already described the cold weather considerations. In hot weather your hands will become very warm since, as explained earlier, the body uses the hands and feet to radiate excess heat. When you are at the beach in 90-degree weather, your hands could very well reach core temperature since the body will be shunting out excess heat through your hands. Obviously, hand warming is not as reliable then. But we don't anticipate that such a high-temperature environment will be the normal one for the readers of this book. When you are exposed to temperatures that high, you often don't need beach imagery, since that's where you already are, or at the pool or in your backyard, relaxing, taking it easy.

In the winter cold, if you have gloves on and you don't expect to be in danger of too long an exposure to the cold, you can use the technique to warm your hands and take the bite out of the air. Many of our patients use hand warming while skiing.

The good thing about this exercise is that the more you practice, the easier it gets and the better it works for you. After some practice you'll find that you don't need to use the thermometer all the time to tell changes in your skin temperature and changes in your nervous system activity. You become more sensitive to the subtle workings inside your body. You can make a simple temperature check by touching your fingertips to your forehead, cheeks, or lips. These are always about the same temperature unless you are outside in the freezing cold. You can tell if the fingertips are warm, cool, or cold by this quick fingertip check.

It is worth taking those few seconds to find out whether your nervous system has increased its activity level and then to decide whether that increased activity is appropriate, given what you are doing at the moment. Wherever you are, whether driving your car, at a business meeting, waiting for a job interview, or sitting at your desk, you can take a few seconds or a few minutes to turn around your temperature trend. As you practice over the next few weeks, you will soon be able to use the abbreviated, key-phrase version of the exercise that is coming up in Chapter Ten. You will also use your own imagery, whatever you have found works best for you.

A quick implementation of your blood-flow relaxation response can take just 10 to 30 seconds. You can do it in almost any situation, even while having a conversation. Just take three or four calm, paced breaths and "warm."

If you have a specific problem, like high blood pressure, migraine headaches, chronic pain, a stubbed toe, phobias, or whatever it might be, try using the PSR warmth exercise. The regular practice of these first three exercises will increase your skills each week. Practicing two or three times a day will help you have these skills ready to use throughout the day. The best times to practice are before breakfast, lunch, or dinner, or just before going to bed.

The functioning of your cardiovascular system (warmth) plays an incredibly important role in the way you perform your tasks. By using the PSR warmth training, you can help your body and mind cope with stresses, including disease and injuries, as well as influencing the overall way you perceive the quality of your life. By taking greater control of the cardiovascular, musculoskeletal, and nervous systems you will be taking greater healthy control over, and responsibility for, all those aspects of your life. You will feel better, more alert, relaxed, and calm. By using these Positive Stress Response exercises, you bring these healthy "conditioned" (learned) responses into play in your everyday life.

CHAPTER EIGHT

STRESS AND PHYSICAL EXERCISE

Exercise strengthens, while inactivity wastes.
—*Hippocrates*

Jack's Angina

While I never really exercised, I have always worked hard at work and never expected to be ill. When I had my annual checkup for a new job, they told me there were some slight irregularities in my EKG, and I would have to have further testing. I had noticed some chest pain at times but had not given it a second thought since it was never a sharp pain or the kind of intense pain that doctors warn you might be part of a heart attack. After my second EKG, they told me I had to have a stress test because the irregularities suggested I might have some "heart problems."

I went to take the stress test, and after only 2 minutes of walking slowly, the doctor told me that I should stop. He told me that my own doctor would talk to me about the results of the test. Meanwhile, he said I should not exercise and that I should stay out of stressful situations. When I returned to my internist, he told me that the stress test had proved positive, and that it appeared there were some difficulties in the arteries to my heart. The pain I had been feeling was angina. He recommended that I start on medication to help keep the arteries open. This would increase the blood supply to the heart, lessening the pain. This was quite a surprise to me since I had never taken any medication, and I was only 39.

He started me with medication twice a day—one in

the morning and one at night. He told me this would slow my heart rate as well. On reviewing with my doctor the times I had pain, I noticed several stressful conditions that triggered my angina. I often had pain when I got into an argument with my boss at work. I am quite high up in the company and rarely had to argue with people. When I did argue, I had some pain in my chest and some trouble breathing for just a minute or two. It also happened when I had an argument with my son about looking at colleges. I wanted him to go to college in the East, and he wanted to look at colleges in the South. My doctor recommended that I try not to argue with people and told me to come back to see him in a month. He also told me there was an operation, a heart bypass, which was a possibility if I had more severe pain. This would require an arteriogram to test the blood flow of the arteries to the heart. This could wait until the next visit. If I was not better then, this test could be done.

To get a second opinion, I flew out for a 4-day evaluation at the Mayo Clinic. They told me the same thing, but they suggested I learn how to handle stresses that triggered my angina. They referred me to an expert in stress and biofeedback, Dr. Sedlacek.

Three weeks later I saw Dr. Sedlacek, who reviewed my history and the information from the Mayo Clinic. He tested me with the biofeedback equipment and a mental stress test. He told me that with the use of medication, biofeedback, and stress management training there was a good likelihood that I would be able to reduce the angina and reduce the medication. I began working on the stress management training with biofeedback, and within the first 2 to 3 weeks, I had less angina as I learned how to relax my muscles. Then I learned how to open my arteries and warm my hands, which took 3 more weeks.

Dr. Sedlacek then worked on teaching me to warm my feet. I had never felt my feet warm up before, but after an additional 3 weeks of practice I could warm them voluntarily.

Dr. Sedlacek, after talking with my doctor, started me on an exercise program of walking half a mile a day. Then I walked a mile a day. Soon, I was walking a mile and a quarter to work each day. Then I bought a stationary bicycle. Dr. Sedlacek slowly built me up to where I was doing 15 to 20 minutes on the bike three times a week. I kept walking to work, and on the weekend I would walk at least 2 miles a day and do my bike. My angina continued to decrease, and I rarely had any attacks for the next month or two.

The Positive Stress Response training also enabled me to talk to my boss and my son without getting angina attacks. By using the breathing, the warmth, and the fourth exercise, I was able to discuss issues or argue without any pain or breathing problems. I no longer go in for treatments every week. I see Dr. Sedlacek every month or two for follow-up visits. I am not having angina attacks and I have been able to cut my medication in half. I feel stronger at work and am able to get a full day's work done. I do two 15-minute Positive Stress Response exercises at home (one in the morning before work and one when I come home from work). After the second Positive Stress Response exercise, I am refreshed and ready to go all evening. I found that these exercises and the physical ones have increased my vitality. They have even affected my sexual relationship with my wife. We are more affectionate with each other. We have sex more frequently and enjoy it more. I also have lost 12 pounds and look better. I have had to take in my pants, but that sure beats having chest pain.

Jack has made a great deal of progress over the 9 months since he found out he had angina. He was overweight and did not exercise. Having developed angina, he needed medication because of the risk of a heart attack. He was trained with the Positive Stress Response, biofeedback, and a graduated exercise plan. The result has been excellent. After seeing him in follow-up, I believe he will continue to do well as long as he practices his exercises. This requires 30 to 45 minutes per day—two Positive Stress Response exercises and a 15- to 20-minute physical exercise program.

Most patients increase their abilities for up to 2 years and then tend to level out. That is why I encourage people to practice the exercises each day for at least 1 to 2 years. Then they can often adjust the amount of exercises depending on how they are doing. After a year, I will have Jack retested on the stress test. If he continues to improve, his doctor and I will evaluate a further reduction of medication or try no medication.

Physical Exercise Reduces Risk Factors

Once people get used to exercising and enjoy it, they find they have more interest in life. They have more energy available for others, sleep better, and handle mental and physical stresses better.

Physical exercise is one of the keys to being healthy and handling stresses. Approximately 20 to 45 minutes of exercise done three or four times a week provides good cardiovascular health and can prevent many common problems like heart attacks and strokes. One of the main causes of death is coronary heart disease. It strikes many men and increasingly more women. In a study of 45,000 former students from the University of Pennsylvania and Harvard University, some specific characteristics were found that related to increased death.

The study reported nine key factors: (1) heavy smoking in early life and continued smoking, (2) increase in blood pressure, (3) increase in body weight, (4) high emotional responses, (5) shortness in height, (6) being an only child, (7) lack of exercise, (8) early parental death, and (9) scarlet fever.

Smoking is probably the worst single health habit you can have. As I have said, it increases your risk for cancer, heart attack, stroke, and other health problems. The second risk factor high on the list was an increase in blood pressure. Reviewing college students from Harvard, researchers found that people who had increased blood pressure were at a higher risk. This has been shown in many other studies as well. In terms of increase in body weight, men who were over 20 percent higher than their recommended weight were at a 78 percent greater risk than men of lighter weight. Those who had gained over 25 pounds (11.5 kilograms) since entering college were at a 60 percent higher risk than those who had gained less. The fourth factor, which they call a "high emotional index," was developed from students' rating themselves on such items as a sensation of the heart beating and a sense of exhaustion (symptoms also related to hypochondriasis). Later in life, these students showed an increased rate of death from coronary heart disease.

The key factors, therefore, are smoking, high blood pressure, obesity, emotions, and lack of physical exercise. While no one can do anything about being short, having scarlet fever, being an only child, or experiencing the early death of a parent, these factors also increase the stress that leads to an early illness or death. What you can do is focus on the risk factors that you can change. You can start to exercise or increase your exercise, reduce your body weight, and cut down on your smoking or give it up completely. You can also use the Positive Stress Response (PSR) exercises to reduce your blood pressure as well as to decrease your negative emotions. By using the four PSR exercises, you will reduce the overreactions of the fight-or-flight response. This helps people be less negative and overly emotional. The chief author of this important study is Dr. F. Paffenbarger, professor of epidemiology at Stanford University School of Medicine in California. Dr. Paffenbarger said that "vigorous exercise associated with lower hypertension . . .may be used as an intervention routine."

Exercise also increases the HDL in your blood. This healthful type of cholesterol is associated with a reduced rate of cardiovascular disease (angina, heart attacks, and strokes). A recent study done by the Federal Centers for Disease Control showed that people who had low or no physical activity had 1.9 times greater risk of heart disease than those with a high level of physical activity. These researchers said that lack of exercise may be a more serious problem than smoking, high blood pressure, or high cholesterol because 59 percent of Americans exercise less than three 20-minute sessions per week. They strongly recommend three or more sessions of exercise for 20 minutes or more to reduce the risk of heart disease.

Introduction to Physical Exercise

How does exercise bring about some of these healthful changes? There are several possibilities. The first is revealed by research done with monkeys, which are similar to man. If you give the monkeys a diet high in fat and calories and exercise one group, the exercised monkeys have fewer heart problems. The nonexercised monkeys had narrowing of their coronary arteries and sudden deaths. After examining the monkeys' arteries, and particularly the arteries that feed the heart, the doctors found that the exercise had helped the blood vessels stay open. The exercised monkeys had less atherosclerosis, larger hearts, and more open arteries. This means that the heart receives more blood than with narrowed arteries. The Pritikin diet and exercise programs show a similar effect on human beings by decreasing fat, cholesterol, and calories and by increasing vigorous exercise. Pritikin claimed a "reopening" of the arteries, better blood flow, and fewer heart attacks. You can get similar results by following the recommendations in this book.

Another benefit from exercise is that you actually do the physical work so that the arteries, heart, and muscles are stronger. I have mentioned that the body needs to be exercised a minimum of 15 to 20 minutes three or four times a week. It is best, however, to exercise 20 to 45 minutes every day.

Exercise helps not only the body but the mind as well. It is a good treatment for mild depressions because it lifts the mood. It is still not clear how this works, but exercise programs are now recommended to treat anxiety and mild depression. Dr. T. Kostrubala has written an excellent book called *The Joy of Running*. He treats patients who have mild depressions with an exercise program and by running with them.

If people have severe anxiety or major depressions, they need medication and physical exercise. For most people, exercise has a beneficial tonic effect on the mind. This helps the mood, so the body runs better. Physical exercise creates a positive habit that supports the healthy functioning of your body and mind.

How Much Exercise Should You Do?

A study of 17,000 Harvard alumni and 6000 longshoremen demonstrated that physical exercise can significantly increase life expectancy. The study found that for those who burned up 2000 or more calories a week in exercise, the death rate was one-fourth to one-third lower than for those who were not active. Burning 2000 calories is equivalent to walking briskly about 24 miles a week. You need to run only 4 to 7 miles every other day, or approximately 12 to 28 miles per week, for good cardiovascular fitness and health.

You can do more than this, but it does not necessarily help you physically or mentally. In fact, people who run more than 50 to 80 miles a week tend to have more injuries. Probably the clearest example of this is the marathon. Instead of running 26 miles in a week, marathoners do it in 1 day. This is an example of overchallenging or punishing your body.

In the Pittsburgh marathon on a warm day in May 1986, there were 3000 runners. Three hundred of them (10%) required rehydration, and others needed additional medical care. Rehydration necessitates putting an intravenous line into the person and putting fluids into the blood because the body has lost so much fluid from running and sweating. They had to take 43 people by ambulance to the local hospital emergency room. Out of these 43, 3 were hospitalized after the marathon. Remember, these were people who were in great shape and had been training for this marathon. The medical director, Freddy Fu, M.D., said they provided one medical person for every five runners. They had 100 physicians, 125 medical students, and 127 registered nurses, plus physical therapists, massage therapists, and other support personnel, including emergency medical service technicians. They actually provided some treatment for over 450 runners during the race. By the final medical station at the 26th mile, more than 1100 needed some form of medical assistance. This shows how people can overdo a good thing.

A particularly important fact from the Harvard study was that you can catch up even if you did not exercise when you were younger. If you start exercising later in life and reduce your smoking, you can greatly improve your health. They also found that the peak usefulness of exercise was burning up to 3500 calories per week. The reduction in death rate leveled off after more than 3500 calories were burned. More vigorous exercises, such as squash or full-court basketball, for 3 or more hours per week resulted in slightly higher death rates than did less strenuous activity. These people were doing more than 3 hours of very vigorous exercise. Like the marathoners, they may have overdone the exercise because they were out to prove something to themselves or impress others.

This study was a very important addition to our medical information. It showed that people who do little or no exercise do the poorest. People who do moderate to vigorous exercise, burning about 2000 to 3500 calories per week, have the maximum benefit. Those people who burn more than 3500 calories may incur a slightly higher risk to their health. It is important to follow this advice of moderate to vigorous exercise. Too little or too much done in a Type A, driven way will not be as healthful for you.

The Hamster's Treadmill: All Animals Need Exercise

Research with rats and other animals shows that if you are going to keep an animal healthy, you must give it some exercise. For example, when you leave a dog at a kennel when you go on vacation, you should look for one that has a dog run, allowing the animal to have some exercise.

Another example is pet hamsters. To exercise a hamster there is usually a running wheel or drum in the cage. This allows the hamster to get in and run in place, amusing the owner and keeping the animal healthier. Pet owners do not like to be charged more for this fancy cage, but it keeps the hamsters alive longer.

The study of the Harvard men and longshoremen, the hamster treadmill, and other studies point out the value of exercise. Exercise not only increases longevity but also increases vitality and enjoyment of life.

The Effect of Technological Change

The development of the wheel enabled people to carry larger loads faster and for longer distances. This technological change helped develop travel, transport, and our society. However, men, women, and children also walked or exercised by driving or pulling wheeled vehicles. When cars become available not just for the rich but for everyone who could spend a few dollars, the need for adults to walk or run decreased dramatically. The availability of automobiles, computers, and other devices means that people do less and less physical work or exercise. Now many adults walk only from their house to the car or from their apartment to the bus, taxi, or subway. They may get as little as 2 to 4 blocks of walking per day. As I have mentioned, they need 3 to 4 miles per day.

With technological changes such as typewriters, computers, telephones, and television, people sit for hours and hours. Even in many blue-collar jobs, the production lines in factories require individuals to stay at one site and sit, stand, and do a task right in front of them, often using only minimal movement. This is quite different from manual labor where people are moving about, hammering, lifting, pulling, shoving, and carrying objects. In the farming and fishing industries, however, even though there are large equipment and labor-saving devices, workers still get a fair amount of physical exercise.

Technological aids have given us many benefits but have significantly decreased our physical activity. Huge buildings concentrate people into smaller areas. After seeing a 30-story apartment building with about 600 apartments facing directly west on the Hudson River, my aunt said to me, "They are living in caves stacked one on top of each other." Her observation, coming after living all her life on farms in Nebraska, was quite true. In New York, Tokyo, Hong Kong, London, and many other areas, people are stacked one upon the other like rats in a cage. Although rats are different from human beings, it is clear from years and years of research that stacking too many rats in cages causes many stress problems, such as bowel problems, irritability, and cancer. It can cause the rats to be hyperaggressive and attack each other. In some cases, overpopulation or living too close together may create infertility in rats. Although this may be a large jump, the analogy certainly seems relevant to human beings.

Many people tend to stay inside, even further limiting their physical activity. Crime as well as the density of population keeps people inside—particularly older people. In general, children like to play and run and be active. Because of crowding, crime, and the availability of TV, however, children too are staying inside for longer periods of time. Increasingly, they have their own TV video games to entertain themselves. For adults, the use of home computers and charge cards encourages the idea that you can bank and shop from your house or apartment and hardly ever need to go outside your home.

The Bottom Line

Another major problem is that many schools, because of tight budgets, have dropped their physical education classes. Former pro football coach George Allen, the chairman of the President's Council on Physical Fitness and Sports, describes the lack of youth fitness as "a disgrace." The President's Council reported in 1986 that in a survey of 19,000 youths aged 6 to 17, 40 percent of boys and 70 percent of girls could not do more than one pullup. A third of school-aged boys and 50 percent of the girls cannot run a mile in less than 10 minutes. George Allen said, "Kids have no endurance, no strength and very little flexibility."

Florida has reviewed its physical education program and decided that every student must take some physical activity and pass a personal fitness course to graduate from high school. This is an excellent idea. Otherwise children grow up lacking exercise, increasing the risk later in life of poor health, large medical bills, and an early death.

The American Health Foundation has prepared workbooks for children from kindergarten through junior high school to teach them good health habits. These are called *Know Your Body* and can be obtained by writing to the foundation at the address in the Appendix. They provide helpful information to children and parents. Encourage your children, grandchildren, nieces, and nephews to exercise. Get them started with a healthful exercise program. Take them along on walks and offer to pay for a sport, gym, or swimming class.

How to Begin

I recommend that you see your physician so he or she can examine you or order a stress test (if needed) to confirm that you can begin an exercise program. If you have any heart disease, chest pain, or other symptoms or medical problems, you must see your physician before beginning any exercise program.

In starting a physical exercise program, one of the first steps is doing some form of exercise regularly. The simplest is beginning to walk a few blocks and then building up to a mile. Try to walk every day. As you build up, gently increase the speed until you can feel comfortable doing a fast pace and feel gently tired afterward. The idea then is to increase to 3 to 4 miles per day or 5 to 6 every other day. Then you will be walking 12 to 28 miles per week. If possible, walking 6 or 7 days a week is even more healthful. If you want to make your walking more vigorous after you are walking 3 to 4 miles per day, you can carry some "heavy hands." They are 1- to 2-pound weights. Or put on a knapsack containing a 1- or 2-pound book on your back. The weight will make you do a little extra work with your cardiovascular system (heart and arteries). Many of my patients walk inside a building or up and down the stairs if they can't go outside.

Muscle stretching, the second Positive Stress Response exercise, and yoga are good starting points for exercise. Another good exercise is using a stationary bike for a few minutes every day. Then build up a minute every week until you do 15 to 25 minutes of pedaling every day or every other day (the minimum). Busy people can ride a stationary bike and read, watch TV, listen to music, or dictate letters at the same time. You can always find 15 to 25 minutes every other day if you want good health and increased vitality and longevity. The next level is to add other activities such as swimming, dancing, volleyball, or working around your home for a half hour.

Another good way to begin exercise is to race-walk or jog. This requires only sneakers, shorts, and a shirt or blouse. You can race-walk or run almost anywhere. Softer surfaces like grass (a golf course or football field) or a cinder or artificial track are easier on the body than concrete or asphalt. Start with 4 or 5 minutes and then build up to 15 to 30 minutes. One of the best books on running is Jim Fixx's *The Complete Book of Running*.

When you are exercising vigorously and you sweat or work out every other day, make sure you do not stay on a low-salt diet unless told to by your physician. If you are sweating you are losing salt, and you need to replace it. This is particularly important for youngsters who may be exercising or playing sports like soccer or basketball 5 or 6 days a week. Remember, the body needs salt and other minerals. If you are exercising vigorously, these salts and minerals need to be replaced. Otherwise you are weakened, or your endurance, strength, and health are hindered.

How Fast Should Your Heart Beat?

Our bodies, particularly our musculoskeletal system and cardiovascular system, need to be exercised. That is why I recommend you use exercise to increase your heart rate by 70 to 80 percent for at least 15 to 20 minutes three times a week. This is the minimum for maintaining a healthy cardiovascular system. A common formula to monitor heart rate to stay in the healthy range when exercising is to subtract your age from 220. Then take 70 to 80 percent of that number. For example, if you are 40 years of age, then subtracting 40 from 220 would give you 180. Taking 70 to 80 percent of 180 would mean that your heart rate should not go over 126 to 144 for a safe exercise level. If you are 60, then you subtract 60 from 220 and get 160. This level would mean you should exercise up to a heart rate of 112 to 128. These are general figures. People who are in good condition may go a little higher. People who are on medication or who have other problems would want to stay well below this heart rate.

Use It or Lose It

Just as you would not leave a car or motorcycle sitting for 5 or 10 years and expect it to run well, you need to "run" your body. Your body needs a healthful maintenance schedule: a sound diet, an adequate amount of sleep, regular vigorous exercise, and a calm nervous system. Otherwise, it is like trying to run your car and never checking your oil or not doing basic maintenance. The car would not last very long.

Many people do little maintenance of their bodies. Often they have the misunderstanding that if they do not exercise, they are somehow maintaining or benefiting their bodies. In fact, it is just the opposite. The body needs to be exercised and is stronger and healthier with exercise. While it is true that "if you do not use it, you lose it," it is even more true that "if you do not use it, you are weakening it" (abusing it).

There are many jokes that people quote, such as "Whenever I feel a need to exercise, I lie down and think about it until it goes away." While there is a certain humor in being slothful and just hanging around, it certainly is not healthful.

How Many Calories Do You Need to Burn?

As I mentioned in Chapter Six, obesity in some societies, because of the patterns of starvation and lack of food, may have had a survival value. People were worried about their next meal. In the United States and most industrial countries, however, starvation is not a problem. Rather, obesity is the problem. It causes shortened lives, furthers physical inactivity, and promotes higher risk of physical damage (heart attacks and strokes).

To get an idea about how many calories you use during a day (24 hours), let's take a person who weighs 180 lbs. In lying down or sleeping or watching TV, the energy used is approximately 80 to 90 calories per hour. So most inactive people need between 1900 and 2200 calories a day. If you are doing some moderate physical exercise like gardening, grocery shopping, mopping floors, a leisurely game of golf, horseback riding, or walking about 2 miles per hour (you are covering 1 mile in 30 minutes), you are burning between 225 and 250 calories per hour. Using a rowing machine or rowing a boat at about 2 miles per hour, swimming at a moderate rate, or bicycling at 7 to 8 miles per hour helps you burn about 325 to 350 calories per hour. This would also be about the same if you were roller skating. If you did some form of vigorous activity, such as dancing or water skiing, you would be using about 400 to 500 calories per hour. Vigorously playing tennis, skating, mountain climbing, or skiing about 10 miles per hour downhill would burn 600 to 700 calories per hour. Playing a hard game of squash or racquetball, bicycling at 13 miles per hour, or jogging about 5 miles per hour would also use around 600 to 700 calories per hour. If you do a very vigorous activity, such as rowing very rapidly at 20 to 22 strokes per minute, you would be using about 900 to 1000 calories per hour. Running from 9 to 10 miles per hour uses up 1000 to 1100 calories per hour.

On an average day, therefore, in sleeping, sitting, and standing, a 180-lb person burns about 80 to 90 calories per hour or from 1900 to 2200 calories in 24 hours. If you do a half hour of vigorous exercise, you will burn off 200 to 400 more calories than if you are sedentary. Thus by exercising you would need to consume 2100 to 2600 calories that day to maintain your weight, while with no exercise you would have to stick to 1900 to 2200 calories.

Simply reducing calories by 200 or 300 a day and exercising for 20 minutes, you would use up a total of 400 to 700 calories a day. If you increase your exercise to 60 minutes, you would use up 600 to 900 additional calories every day.

That is how you can rather comfortably lose 1/2 to 1 pound or more per week. Once your weight is at a proper level, you can have a meal of an additional 200 to

400 calories. This might be an appetizer, an extra serving of the main course, or a wonderful dessert, adding more variety and enjoyment to your daily diet. This is one of the few times in life when you can have your cake (200 or 300 calories) and eat it too.

There are many different ways to exercise. When making rounds to see my patients at St. Luke's Hospital, I would walk up and down stairs. I could make it just as fast as by waiting for the elevator. If you climb a few flights each day and walk briskly whenever you can, you will be adding some useful exercise. My patients who have summer places do gardening or other physical tasks. When on vacation, I recommend they walk 2 to 4 miles and walk up and down stairs. When walking two to five flights of stairs, you are lifting your weight that many feet each time. Since floors are usually 10 feet in height you are going up 30 to 50 feet per trip. This means you burn off more calories while strengthening your heart and other muscles.

Try to do physical tasks around your office or home. These plus an exercise routine three to seven times a week should help you get into that healthy range of burning off 2000 to 3500 calories a week by exercising. The study of Harvard men and longshoremen showed how helpful this can be.

Stretching Exercises

You can do these four new exercises in a chair or, even better, standing.

The first stretching exercise is to raise the hands above the head and stretch the right hand up to the ceiling as far as you can. Then stretch the left hand up, stretching as far toward the ceiling as you can. Then relax the arms. By doing six to eight sets of these reaching-for-the-ceiling exercises, you stretch the upper arms, shoulders, and neck.

For the second exercise, lean the head forward and then gently lean the head backward, repeating this three or four times. The second part of this exercise is to look straight forward and turn your head to the left and look to your left over your shoulder at the room in back of you. Now rotate your head slowly all the way around until you are looking over your right shoulder toward the other corner of the room. In this way you rotate your head 200 to 280 degrees. Keep your head level as you repeat this head-turning two or three more times. On the second or third rotation, you will notice a gentle stretching of the neck and shoulder muscles.

In the third exercise, lean your head forward toward your chest and rotate your head to the right (clockwise), rolling your head slowly 360 degrees in a full circle. Do this two or three times, and then do the same in the opposite direction. Go left (counterclockwise), making as wide a circle with your head as possible. Imagine you have a pencil taped to the top of your head, and you want to roll your head around and draw as big a circle as you can. Often you will feel areas of tight muscles because instead of smooth big circles, there will be tight areas and your head will not go out as far as you roll it around.

Each day as you exercise, notice where the tight areas are and loosen them up with these exercises. This series of three exercises is helpful for the neck and shoulder muscles. I have used these exercises and recommend them for my patients with muscle contraction headaches and those who often have muscle spasms in the neck and shoulder region. The reaching for the sky and the neck and shoulder exercises should be done every 2 to 3 hours if you are at a desk or sitting for 6 to 8 hours a day. For headache patients or people with muscle spasms, I recommend that they do these exercises in the morning when they get up. It is also good to do them before bedtime. Often muscles will tighten up at night and be tight when you wake up. Along with the Positive Stress Response exercises each day, you can get additional benefit from these miniexercises for the head, neck, and shoulders.

These three exercises and the PSR exercises are also good to do on plane flights. My patients and I have found you can travel longer with less jet lag by using these exercises every 2 hours. Many of my patients tell me they now experience little or no jet lag.

A good exercise for the back and shoulders is to start

by standing up straight or sitting straight up in your chair (although sitting is not quite as good). Put both hands straight above your head toward the ceiling and lean your hands back—way back. Look up and back at your hands and gently lean backward from the middle of your back. Think of a bow shooting an arrow. Instead of having a straight back, you will be gently leaning back. Your upper back and arms would be like the top half of the bow prepared to shoot an arrow. Take two or three slow, paced breaths while stretching upward and back. Then if you are sitting, just lean forward and put your head and face over the desk so your upper back and shoulders are now a reversed bow, bowing forward—out over the desk. If you are standing, lean forward and just hang from the waist. Your head can hang down toward the knees and floor as far as is comfortable for you. Let your arms and hands dangle in front of you. This exercise will help you limber up if you can gently reach down toward your ankles and touch your calves, ankles, or toes. Just stretch gently, do not force yourself. Breathe two or three slow, paced breaths.

Then straighten up and lean back into the "bow" position by leaning up and back. Stretch the hands up and back over your head. Look up and back at your hands, over the top of your head. Breathe two or three slow, paced breaths and then relax. Then bend forward again toward your feet or forward on the desk. Repeat this exercise two or three times with two or three slow, paced breaths at each bowed position. After doing this exercise for a week or two, you will find it stretches the middle and upper back, shoulders, neck, and scalp. By doing this once or twice a day, you will keep your spine more supple and your muscles more relaxed.

After using these exercises and the Positive Stress Response exercises, I find my patients have fewer headaches and muscle spasms, and they are able to concentrate more, make fewer errors, and type more accurately. At the Stress Regulation Institute, we have found that people learn typing and computer skills more quickly with the PSR training. By combining the PSR with biofeedback, physical exercise, and specific educational training, we speed up the efficiency and the production as well as the health of an individual.

Why So Much Back, Shoulder, Neck, and Face Pain?

Over the years I have wondered why tension and pain in the head, neck, shoulders, and back seem to be so prevalent. These key areas are often overactivated by the fight-or-flight response. The jaw tenses and the shoulders raise slightly and the lower back seems to brace for fight or flight. This is worsened, however, by sitting too much, not standing or exercising, and particularly by rarely reaching up above the shoulders or head. Most people have been trained from their school years to sit in a tense position and work on what is in front of them at their desk, bench, or video display. This static position is particularly hard on the neck, shoulders, and back.

Not only has this static position become a common one in school and at work, but there are also hardly any sports or daily activities that encourage us to extend our hands up above our shoulders and head. In baseball, for example, other than throwing, everything else is in the lower range. In fact, the strike zone is defined as the area below the shoulders down to the knees. Except for passing and catching the ball above the shoulders, football is in the middle range (chest) or lower.

Soccer is played basically with the feet from the waist down. Hockey is played even lower down on the ice. The puck rarely bounces higher than the knees, so players are always leaning forward and down. This is also true for field hockey. Tennis is usually played at mid-waist level or lower. Rarely are there smashes above the head. The serve is the one part of tennis where you do stretch up. You serve only every other game, and hit mostly ground strokes, so about a tenth or less of tennis is played above the shoulders.

There are a few sports where there is more activity above the shoulders. Much of basketball is played above the waist because you are rebounding, shooting, or defending with your arms up in the air. The only sport that is better in this respect is volleyball, where for more than half the time, you are playing at shoulder level or higher. These two are excellent sports for maintaining your height and the upward flexibility of the shoulders, neck, and back.

People who develop a humped spine as they get older shrink at the neck and shoulder area as well as in the lower back. This is all too frequent because of the stress of sitting and of not reaching up. At work or at home, you can check this for yourself. As you go through the day, you will see you do almost everything around the waist level.

A good exercise as you are cleaning your house is to look up at paintings that are usually set at eye level or lower. Reach up to clean the dust on top of your pictures, and clean above the mirror and above the sink in the bathroom. Try to develop little exercises at work and home of reaching up—use the stretching exercises (and devise new ones for yourself).

Add Variety in Your Exercises

You can make exercise more fun by adding different types like dancing, golf, bowling, or bicycling. If you have not been athletic, take some lessons in squash, handball, tennis, or skiing. Or take up an outside activity like gardening or volunteer work in a park. Any physical activity for 30 to 60 minutes will use up another 200 to 600 calories per hour.

You should include not only the exercise but some new activity that you always wanted to try out. Team up with a buddy to take dancing lessons. Bring your children, grandchildren, friends, or spouse. Physical exercise is good for them too.

Take up race-walking or light jogging. There are also many health clubs that offer not only swimming, jogging, and weight lifting but also yoga, stretching classes, and aerobic exercise. YMCAs often have excellent facilities at a reasonable price. Equipment such as "rebounders" are available. They use a spring system 6 to 8 inches above the floor, so you "rebound." They cost anywhere from $30 to $150. A rebounder is gentle on the system and can be used at home to jog, jump, or dance for 15 to 25 minutes 3 to 7 days a week. Or buy a jump rope and jump at home for exercise. You can carry it with you on trips. You may want to rotate your exercise by swimming every day or every other day. Swimming is one of the best exercises, since you use almost all of the muscles and it's difficult to suffer a muscle pull or injury. There are other sports, such as tennis, squash, and basketball, which are more vigorous and provide a game atmosphere of competition along with the physical exercise. Golf is a slower game but you do get to walk several miles.

Listen to your body and do exercises that do not hurt you. Some aerobics classes are vigorous, and instructors should first observe you to see if you need special instruction. In aerobics classes, pick something at a beginning level. More and more, people are recommending the softer exercises, not just running or jumping in place. Too much bouncing up and down on a hardwood floor or outdoor jogging on concrete is hard on the body. Try to pick softer surfaces that cushion your jogging or this type of vigorous jumping. Start slowly and then build up the speed and the intensity of the exercise program. Some people do pushups or jumping jacks at home or use video exercise tapes on their VCR. Jane Fonda, Richard Simmons, and others have produced video exercise tapes. You can make it more fun if you add music to the stretching and exercise routines. Try using a home computer that has exercise programs and children's exercise games. Other people have put lap pools in their homes or swimming tanks so that you can swim against a jet current. These can be as small as 6 feet by 12 feet. When you use one of these exercise programs and raise your heart rate, your heart, arteries, blood pressure, and strength improve dramatically.

Try to pick an exercise routine that will fit into your schedule once a day, or at least three to four times a week for 15 to 30 minutes. If you can set aside an hour on Saturday or Sunday, this will top off your exercising. All my patients who have started exercising notice within 2 to 4 weeks that they are feeling better and looking better. In 1 or 2 weeks after starting an exercise program you will get over some of the sore muscles and the achy feelings and feel new strength and vigor in your body.

One way of evaluating fatigue is to observe closely the first 3 or 4 minutes of your exercise program. You will usually find that after these 3 or 4 minutes you will feel better. At this point you can decide whether to continue or stop. If you are tired or exhausted, stop. If you feel okay, go on for another 3 or 4 minutes and then check again. Continue to do your full 15- to 30-minute routine if you still feel all right. Using this tiredness check, you may find that some of the fatigue that you were feeling was actually fatigue of the mind.

I expect your experience will be like mine—about 95 percent of the time you will enjoy the exercise and your mind will benefit from it. You will also think more clearly and be calmer. This tiredness check, along with the PSR exercises, will help your brain recognize the difference between mental fatigue and physical fatigue. With the PSR techniques plus physical exercise you will be better able to evaluate your energy levels and use your energy when and where you want to. You will find that your mind works better when your body gets its maintenance exercise. A regular exercise program increases your strength, well-being, and longevity.

CHAPTER NINE

STRESS AND SEX

Whoever loves and is loved is protected from
the blows of fate.

—*De Musset*

Wendy's First Childbirth Experience

When I became pregnant with my first child, I was in
the middle of a course of biofeedback training for
treatment of Raynaud's disease. Dr. Sedlacek and I
decided that I would continue this training through the
pregnancy, not just for the Raynaud's (which often
eases during pregnancy, as the volume of blood flowing
through the body increases) but to enhance the relaxation and breathing techniques I would learn in my
childbirth preparation class.

I was then a full-time graduate student; I was also
working part-time. It was important to me to remain
as calm and relaxed as possible; I thought the biofeedback training would help me and the baby get through
the pregnancy.

Anxiety is common during pregnancy. Like many
women, I found myself worrying about my baby, my
readiness to be a parent, combining career and family—
everything! After doing some reading, I also began to
worry about worrying: Anxiety *can* make a pregnancy
harder all around.

I was enjoying the feelings of well-being I was getting from the biofeedback experience. I knew I had
already learned to relax more deeply than I'd been
able to before—I could see how much better on the
biofeedback equipment I used, and, more importantly,
I could feel it in my body. In the first trimester, I used
my newly acquired skills to reduce the morning sickness I suffered from all day. As my pregnancy pro-

gressed and I kept practicing the biofeedback exercises, I felt increasingly better and less anxious.

My baby had been carefully planned to arrive at the beginning of my summer vacation. My husband and I had chosen a free-standing birthing center staffed by midwives for prenatal care and birth. I was healthy, and it never occurred to us that anything might go awry with our perfectly laid plans.

BUT—early in the 33rd week (7 weeks before the due date) I felt a little queasy and crampy, as if I was getting a stomach virus. I went to a late lunch meeting and ran some errands before heading for home. Once there, I sat down to study for the next morning's midterm exam. At some point I became aware that the cramping had become regular, and that I was passing what could be amniotic fluid. I couldn't be in labor yet, I thought, it's just too early. But I called my midwives and headed back into the city. They pronounced me in active labor and several centimeters dilated—my baby was coming, midterm exam or no.

The backup obstetrician we'd chosen asked that I meet her at the hospital immediately. Suddenly our idyllic out-of-hospital birth became a high-tech delivery, with lots of attendant noise, lights, and important-looking specialists hovering around. My husband had brought with him to the hospital the small GSR biofeedback unit I'd used for home practice. I sat with that on a table to my left and a fetal monitor screen to my right. That way I could watch both my own and the baby's progress through the longest, strongest contractions, and could monitor my overall relaxation.

Labor was short and not difficult for me—even with the fears and added stress of the very unexpected prematurity. A tiny but sturdy little boy arrived on the scene not long after I'd been admitted to the hospital. Later, several of the staff of the neonatal intensive care unit where my son spent his first days asked me if I'd beem given oxygen during his birth—they'd been impressed by how well oxygenated he was and how well he'd done. My continued biofeedback practice made nursing him a soothing, calming experience for us both when he was a baby.

Dov is now a healthy, happy 5-year-old. He has

always been calm, with a sweet temperament, and his nursery school teachers recently described him as the "mellowest" child in the class. He can (when he so decides) take a deep breath and calm himself down, and he recently surprised us by using his own pre-schooler's version of relaxing and imagining to ski down a tough new slope.

Since my son's birth, I've worked with other women expecting their first babies, and most of them have felt as positive as I about the use of biofeedback training during their pregnancies.

As I write this, I am halfway through the third trimester of my second pregnancy. Is this going to be a "biofeedback baby"? I wouldn't have it any other way.

The PSR Childbirth Program

In March of 1987 Wendy, who is now a psychologist, and I presented a paper at the Biofeedback Society of America meeting on PSR training with biofeedback for first pregnancies. In the study reported on, all the women received Lamaze courses. We trained 38 women, all of whom were having their first child. The first 13 received 10 hours of general information on childbirth and on how to prepare for the delivery. The second group of 13 received 10 hours of training with general relaxation. The third group, 12 women, received PSR training with home biofeedback equipment for 10 sessions of 1 hour each. While this program was open to women of any age in New York from 21 to 40, we got a large number of women who were 35 or older. This indicates that older women may have more anxiety and stress about giving birth for the first time.

With good care and proper monitoring techniques (such as amniocentesis, or a sampling of the placental blood in the fetus), many of the risk factors for older women can be reduced. They still have anxiety, since most women in our society give birth earlier in life. Women can have children up to the age of 45 or 50, but after 40 there is a large increase of certain birth defects, such as Down's syndrome.

What we found was that those women who received the PSR training with biofeedback, home exercises, and audiocassettes were able to deliver more easily and quickly. We believe they were better prepared because of PSR and physiological training. We also found that 6 weeks after the birth, more of the PSR-trained women continued to breast-feed their babies. This suggests a better mother-child relationship. Before there were Lamaze classes, women had less than optimal training for childbirth. I believe that PSR and biofeedback will supplement Lamaze classes because we can train the physiological processes better. Doctors will be pleased because the women are more relaxed, use less medication, deliver more quickly, and have healthier babies. The mothers seem happier with their deliveries and their babies as well.

Sex Drive

Sex in animals is basically done to procreate. The drive to procreate is different in human beings. Unlike many animals, we don't rut once a year in the spring to produce young; we are capable of conceiving young every month. Society has channeled this primary drive to produce children to further the tribe, city, state, or country. More children means more workers and soldiers for society, thus more power. This tradition continues strongly with the Catholic Church, which has argued that sex is solely for procreation. The Orthodox Jewish faith follows the biblical instruction not to masturbate or waste one's seed.

Our thoughts about sex often include dreams of children or of being pregnant or having a family. Most of us grew up in a family, so there is a powerful societal drive as well as a primitive animal urge to procreate and/or have sex. Some of these primitive feelings are often described as lust. Even President Carter, who is a very religious man, was honest enough to admit he had "lust in his heart" when he looked at certain pictures of women.

Sexual activity has also received a tremendous amount of publicity in films and romance novels. The great screen romances have been important to our society, but X-rated movies and porno films often make a great deal of money and sometimes influence our sexual ideas.

Each of us has to be concerned with sex, not only for enjoyment but to procreate—to produce new human beings. Many of my patients have mentioned that they wanted to have a child. Planning their careers and when to have children is often stressful for them. It is particularly stressful in women who have difficulty bearing children. This is why I described our research with childbirth. We also found that women who learn the PSR were more easily able to become pregnant. This may be because, with general relaxation, they handle stress better and/or because they are getting better blood flow to the vagina wall and into the uterus. This may provide a more healthy environment for the egg to be fertilized, develop, and grow.

There is probably no stronger urge, other than starvation or thirst, than the sexual drive. Be aware of both levels—the animal and the intellectual brain. Depending on your upbringing, age, and sexual experience, you will be operating on at least these two levels—the primitive procreation drive and the more recent sexual freedom and enjoyment level.

Precautions

The old adage that you should know the person you're going to bed with is more true today than ever before. Medical data show that the more sexual contacts you have, the more diseases and disorders you are exposed to. For example, it has been shown that if you are involved with someone who is a bisexual or a homosexual, or has used drugs intravenously, you risk contracting AIDS. Since this is a fatal disease, be certain you know the habits of the person you are sleeping with. You may want your partner to be tested for the AIDS virus.

It has also been shown that the more different sexual contacts you have over a lifetime, the more likely you are to develop hepatitis B. Promiscuity is responsible for most of the apparent infections as well as the unapparent infections (these are hard to recognize when they are mild, or mild to severe). This is true for heterosexuals as well as homosexuals.

A condom provides some of the best protection against contracting sexually transmitted diseases.

Physiology Does Not Lie

One of the key physiological differences in men and women is their approach to, and enjoyment of, sexual pleasure. In general, men are more easily activated or turned on by visual stimulus and erotic thoughts. It is a common experience for young men to be aroused at a movie, or even in a classroom situation, and to start to get an erection.

Women are likely to be raised to think of sex as love. They do not have the same intense early experiences as men of being turned on by a physical display. They may have some lubrication of the vagina or feelings in their breasts or other sexual feelings of warmth and excitement, but these are not displayed as prominently.

The underlying sexual difference physiologically between men and women is that men tend to get an erection and ejaculate rather quickly. In 1 to 3 minutes, men may get an erection, ejaculate, and be done with sex for the evening. Often they don't mean to ignore the woman's feelings, but it is their physiologically comfortable speed.

An additional difference in the physiological arousal is that while making love women usually prefer and enjoy fondling, caressing, and romantic talk for several minutes. They often need 5 to 10 minutes to get to the first level of excitement and then move to the second level leading to orgasm. In some cases, it may take 10 to 20 minutes to have an orgasm.

This underlying physiological speed of sexual arousal is very important. A woman can have satisfying sexual experiences without orgasm but may need several minutes to be prepared for orgasm. Men may come to orgasm in

30 to 60 seconds. Thus, in romantic novels the sexual activity is often described from a female perspective. It will almost always include a longer seduction or lovemaking period. This physiological difference is something that men often become aware of as they have sexual experiences with women and adjust to the woman's timing. Women also learn to tell their man what they like to have done to them and what they like to do. They must also be aware of the time difference for arousal and explain this to their lover (if he doesn't already know).

This is why men in particular should use the PSR exercises to slow down and relax to extend lovemaking and the preliminaries of caressing, talking, and petting leading to the act of intercourse. The woman should consider not exciting the man too rapidly toward ejaculation. A woman can let the man pleasure her for a few minutes, while the man can use the PSR skills to remain calmer in the first stage of sexual play. Some have suggested that men think about such odd things as the names of key players on baseball teams and go through all the names of all nine men and backup pitchers as a kind of mental delay tactic to slow their speedy sexual response. I recommend that men practice the slow, paced breathing and enjoy the pleasant conversation and lovemaking.

Mental and emotional patterns are important in sexual activity as well. If a person is rushed or irritable or angry, it is difficult to relax and enjoy being loving to another human being. In the sexual act, it takes time to let go of the rest of the world and of problems or worries in order to focus on the other individual. In many cases, I have recommended that individuals or couples practice their PSR exercises before sex so they have a more relaxed physical and mental attitude. Then they can devote the lovemaking and attention to each other.

Most people, as they practice the exercises, find that within 5 to 15 minutes they feel calm, relaxed, peaceful, and even serene. It is easier for them to mentally let go, then, of the worries or problems of the day or the anticipated events of the next day. They gain better physiological skills and adjust to the other person's mood and sensitivities. This practice allows the mind and body to be more in touch and to communicate with each other.

Especially when they do the third PSR exercise, most

people feel warm, relaxed, serene, and sensual. People report that they have these pleasant feelings when they are falling asleep or starting to wake up in the morning. They may feel like a cat just lying in bed, comfortable and calm. They may also have had erotic thoughts or fantasies, or they may get an erection or think of their loved ones. Women feel very sensual and often are surprised that they have some lubrication in the vagina or have sensual thoughts about their lover and loved ones.

Do not be surprised if you notice some of these additional feelings that go with being calm, relaxed, and peaceful. There is a gentle energy flow and excitement as you think about people you love. This can be a mental or physical love, a love for a pet or a child or a lover or a good friend.

Male Impotence

Dr. William Masters, one of the pioneers in the study of sexual problems, has pointed out that impotence can result from "drugs, alcohol, stress and anxiety about sexual performance."

It has been estimated that over 10 million men suffer from impotence. Eighty to ninety percent of the problem has been attributed to psychological difficulties. More recent research has pointed out that as much as 25 to 30 percent of impotence can be caused by aging and problems such as vascular disease and the effects of alcohol, smoking, and diabetes. Some of these problems can be treated with the PSR training as well as additional biofeedback retraining to monitor penile erection. Some medications make it difficult to get or maintain an erection, including, particularly, medications for blood pressure and headaches. If you are taking any medications, check with your doctor.

Vitamins in general are not helpful for sexual problems. The only proven medication is a chemical called yohimbine. It can be helpful for selected patients. This drug should be used only after you have been examined and studied by an expert in sexual problems. The most effective preparation has the trade name of Yocon. Do not buy this chemical over the counter or through newspaper ads; it should be prescribed by your physician. Imitations of this drug or the wrong dosage can be of no use and can cause even further problems.

For selected medical patients, penile implants are now available and may be helpful. Make sure you get a second opinion before having surgery.

Vaginismus

PSR along with biofeedback has been used successfully to reduce the pain caused by vaginismus. This is a medical condition in which the muscles tighten or go into spasm, and it is painful or almost impossible to have intercourse. The traditional medical treatment has been to insert graduated vaginal dilators (slightly enlarged metal probes) to help expand the vagina, but this is rarely fully satisfactory. After learning to use the PSR, most women are able to relax the vaginal muscles. An additional method, if this does not fully relieve the vaginismus, is to use biofeedback and have the woman self-insert a small probe that monitors and records the amount of muscle activity. The woman tenses and relaxes her vaginal muscles. This strengthens the muscles in a controlled fashion, and the woman gains control. She learns how strong the muscles are and understands why she clamps down out of fear, anger, or panic. In many cases the muscles are strong enough, but the woman is not able to regulate the specific tension and relaxation patterns. By using biofeedback equipment, she sees exactly the different levels of muscle tensing and relaxing. The equipment not only trains the muscles but trains the woman to relax. Sometimes I counsel these women because there may be other psychological worries or fears that have caused such strong vaginal spasms. In most cases the PSR training and the biofeedback retraining are enough.

Sexual Therapy

Dr. Masters and his main collaborator, Virginia Johnson, run the Masters and Johnson Institute in St. Louis. Since 1958 they have been treating sexual dysfunctions and doing clinical research on sexual patterns. Their first book, *Human Sexual Response,* was one of the major reports on research and treatment of sexual problems. In 1986 they brought out a book called *Masters and Johnson on Sex and Human Loving.* They say that as many as half the people in the country, at one time or another, have some sexual distress ranging from lack of interest to not being able to function sexually.

Masters and Johnson have helped develop a short-term treatment of 15 to 20 sessions for sexual problems. Their books have pointed out many of the positive effects of treatment. Most medical centers have competent sexual therapists to consult if problems are not corrected by the PSR training. Useful publications are available from the Impotence Information Center and the American Association of Sex Educators, Counselors, and Therapists (AASECT) (see Appendix).

Men who are older or who have difficulty maintaining an erection can also add PSR to the biofeedback training. A small, expandable band (strain gauge) registers the expansion of the penis. The changing size of the penis is fed back to the man by the feedback device so he can practice and train voluntarily to increase the size of the penis and maintain his erection. The device is particularly useful for problems of early ejaculation because one can practice increasing the size and duration of the erection. After doing this several times and practicing with a home unit, a man can transfer this ability to intercourse. He can practice getting an erection, maintaining it for a minute or two, then relaxing and enjoying sexual play. Then he can work on strengthening the erection for another 2 to 3 minutes and practice maintaining it for intercourse. Not only does this give him a voluntary skill in maintaining an erection, but it helps him get over the fear of losing an erection because he can bring it back when he wants. The training also can slow early ejaculation problems by doubling or tripling the length of time the erection is maintained. This allows a man to move into the time frame where the woman is more likely to fully enjoy the sex. These are ways of using the stepped-care approach with sexual problems.

We are learning that the brain is a dominant organ, even in sexual activity. The body needs to be healthy and relaxed to enjoy sex, and this depends on our brain. Men who have had a stroke on the right hemisphere have more major sexual dysfunction after their stroke than men who have had left hemisphere strokes. This suggests that the more spatial and creative half of our brain—the right side for right-handed people—has a large part to play in maintaining sexual function. This research suggests that we need both halves of our intellectual brain functioning well to maintain good sexual functioning.

One of the major skills you'll learn with the four PSR exercises is to balance the intellectual and animal brain. This inner body feedback of mind/spirit/body will help you be more sensual and sexual.

Nicotine has a vasoconstricting effect (that is, it tightens the arteries), so smoking might cause or worsen impotence. In a Canadian study of 170 impotent patients, those who smoked were observed. In every category, from light to moderate to heavy tobacco use, impotent patients smoked more than would be expected from the general population. One way of studying this effect was measuring the penile blood pressure. It was lower in patients who smoked than in those who did not. Twenty-one percent of impotent patients with a history of smoking showed abnormally low penile blood pressures, compared with only 8.8 percent of the nonsmokers. Abnormally low penile blood pressure can make it difficult to get an erection or to retain an erection.

Dr. William Masters has classified sexual dysfunctions as not only sexual problems but also dissatisfactions and disorders. He points out that in 30 years of treating couples and individuals, approximately 80 percent of them could see a beneficial effect after retraining their physiology and obtaining a better understanding of their sexual relationships. Dr. Masters trains people with special techniques such as slow massage and other "sensate focus" techniques. He made the key point that a sexual dysfunction is part of the relationship, not just a dysfunction.

Sexual therapy tries to make the relationship secure so that sex can be enjoyable and sensual. This means that the relationship between the two partners must be one of full communication. For this reason, Dr. Masters talks about using "I" words, rather than words like "we're," "you are," or "let's do this." He tries to get people stating what they want: "I feel frustrated" or "I feel hurt." Try to start your communication with the pronoun "I," to express your needs, desires, or concerns. This will help you and your partner have more positive, open communication. By decreasing negative or confusing statements, anger and frustrations decrease and sexuality becomes a more sensual and full experience.

In addition to communication, it is important to understand the stages of intercourse. The lubrication of the vagina for the female and erection for the male are a key part of the first stage of sexual arousal-play. This is followed by the second stage, the mounting stage. The third stage is the thrusting stage, and the fourth is ejaculation. Unless these four stages take less than 30 or 40 seconds, the woman plays an active role. The vagina relaxes as the penis is inserted in the mounting phase, and then in 30 to 45 seconds it slightly tightens down to grip the penis.

An important fact of erection for the male and lubrication for the female is that it ebbs and flows. After a minute or two men may lose 10 to 25 percent of their erection (ebb). Then a few minutes later the penis will engorge and enlarge again (flow). If the man is worried or anxious when he feels this ebb phase, he may get frightened. This can create a negative reaction, and he may lose his erection. Knowing this physiological fact, a man can go with the ebb and flow and enjoy a longer intercourse. That is why the Masters and Johnson approach of using "sensate focus" has men and women exploring each other's bodies but not touching the breasts or genitals. They are taught to feel the sensual experience of the other partner's body, the temperature of the body, the texture of the skin, the pleasant feelings, and then using the "I" language to describe what each person wants.

Dr. Masters said that when he and his partner first started in 1955, only 10 percent of their patients had organic problems and sexual dysfunctions. In the last 10 years this number has increased to 18 to 20 percent. He believes this is because there are more complete work-ups and tests available now than could be done in the 1950s. There is also more use of the antihypertensive medications and other drugs that interfere with or block erections and ejaculation. There are 40 million male diabetics who may have some erectile problems. Dr. Masters says this does not mean that the behavioral approach to their sexual retraining will not work. In fact, he says that over half of these men, approximately 20 million, can recover full function with "sensate focus" training and retraining.

I agree with him that men and woman should first get retraining or PSR training before they resort to some of the surgical techniques that have become available over the last few years. As Dr. Masters said, impotence is usually a mental reaction involving fear and negative responses. The basic need is for security in the relationship.

Dr. Masters also pointed out that women should not be passive in the sexual relationship. They should be active and not demanding. One of the worst things a woman can do to get the man into an observing role is to say things such as "Any luck yet?" or "I have never refused him." Dr. Masters' key point is that both parties are responsible for their own sexual pleasures. Sexual pleasure is not something that one partner does to the other partner. It is a cooperative adventure in enjoying the four stages of sex and their relationship.

Masters and Johnson point out that the whole idea of being sexual has to do with your thinking about being a sexual being. You need to be responsible for your own sensuality and sexual pleasure. Think about giving and getting sex and making the other person comfortable and excited. Men, particularly, should talk about sex and be more romantic. This does not mean that you have to be flattering and obsequious, but that you learn what your partner likes and that you both talk to each other about what you like and dislike. Be positive. If you are nega-tive, the other person will be more sensitive and take it as a criticism rather than as a way of learning what you like. It also means that you should spend time together regularly, not just having sex; otherwise, you can cause a heightened arousal worrying about having sex tonight (or in the morning or afternoon). So have fun in all aspects of your life, and have sex as a sort of dessert after the meal of the day.

In any relationship, you need to pay attention to its quality. This takes time and attention. People often forget that while they work at their job and devote time to other activities, they do not often think about developing and maintaining their relationships. One of the other major points Masters and Johnson make is that people have to realize that at different times of the day and night, they may have different feelings about having sex. You need not have 100 percent desire to have sex. You and your partner can talk to each other and get comfortable until both of you are interested in having sex.

Lust and Love

Besides the animal nature and lustful feelings and the release that comes from a sexual encounter, there also can develop a feeling of mutual love and respect. This is a blending of the mind, body, and emotions, a combination of the physical feeling of lust and the emotional feeling of caring and tenderness for another person. A mature person can learn to treat another person as special, as deserving of affection, care, and love.

The stresses and overreactions involved in lust and love retrigger primitive emotional-mental patterns. You can falsely anticipate that a little upset or argument can be life-threatening. If you feel that your life or well-being is threatened, then you will defend with the fight-or-flight response and may physically strike out or withdraw or freeze. When you apply the PSR training to sexual situations, you will move to a more mature viewpoint of lust and love. It allows you to see that the other person can also be angry, frightened, or worried. In a calmer state, you can accept unkind words or a defensive or offensive statement that might come in the heat of the battle or from a withdrawn, defensive position. Using this analogy of seeing people as defending or attacking or freezing in place will be helpful in dealing with them sexually as well as in discussing other important topics, such as money and power (dominance/submission).

It may be difficult for some women to develop an adventurous attitude toward making love and visually stimulating her partner. An encouraging and understanding man can help his partner to accept herself as being physically attractive and desirable to him. A man can express verbally to a woman how desirable she is to him. He can give his partner a gift of lingerie for her to wear while they are alone, or bring flowers or another gift.

For men it is important to remember that verbal and physical expressions of affection can make a woman feel wanted and aroused. Although it is important for lovemaking to satisfy our physical desires, it is also important for a woman to feel emotional closeness. Women often complain that the only time their partner touches them is when they are making love. Cuddling and hugging at other times creates feelings of emotional closeness with your partner that can carry over to your sexual encounters. Train yourself by holding hands for 10 minutes a day or by hugging at least once a day. Another way to feel emotionally close to your partner is to create a special and romantic mood just for the two of you. Dine alone by candlelight, take a walk or shower together, prepare a favorite meal just for your partner, buy a special gift, and make love by candlelight to music you both enjoy.

Remember, when lovemaking is warm and fulfilling for both partners, the pleasures of sexuality can help you over some of life's rough spots.

If you are having sexual difficulties, see your physician or call a sex therapist. You can overcome reduced desire and other sexual problems (see Appendix for a list of qualified sex therapists' organizations).

Surgery and Its Effect on Sexuality

While all surgery is stressful because of people's worry about surviving, surgery on any sexual area is even more stressful. All patients have fantasies about what will be done to their bodies, as well as concerns about their capacity to function sexually after surgery. Two major examples are breast and prostate surgery, which involve male and female sexual functioning. These examples point out that special meaning and thoughts occur concerning the genitals or other sexual areas for individuals. Think of the words "buttocks, vagina, breast, skin, penis, uterus, clitoris," and you will see that everyone has strong emotions and thoughts connected to these areas as well as their functioning.

You should always ask your physician about any side effect of surgery and get a second consultation before any surgery. Sometimes there are alternate surgical techniques that have fewer side effects and a quicker recovery. Do not be concerned about hurting your physician's feelings. Ask him or her any and all questions that you have. Make a list of them and have your spouse or a close friend go with you to review all of the points. In the Appendix I have listed the address of the American Cancer Society, which offers courses, pamphlets, and other information about surgery. This may be a valuable resource for you or a loved one who is facing or who has had surgery.

It is also important to know that there is reconstructive surgery that can remake or reshape a breast. This is often better physically and psychologically than being fitted with a special bra, as was done in the past for breast cancer. Most women feel better after this cosmetic surgery since their "new breast" looks and feels similar to their original breast.

The psychological involvement in genital and sexual reproductive organs is quite intense. That is why many programs, such as the one at Pennsylvania Hospital Center in Philadelphia, run by my brother, Thomas Sedlacek, M.D., Director of Oncology, provide support and counseling for women before and after their operations. If your doctor does not discuss feelings, fears, questions, concerns, or fantasies about your operation or its outcome, then you should consult with another physician. If your physician is not comfortable or does not have the time to talk with you after your operation, you may want to get some sexual counseling or treatment from another experienced physician or counselor (see Appendix). As Dr. Masters has said, many sexual dysfunctions, including those caused by surgery, can be eased or corrected by counseling or sexual therapy.

Summary

Not only are stress and mental factors some possible causes of sexual problems, but physical problems can prevent one from having full satisfaction. Some of the key impediments are drugs (including alcohol), smoking, diabetes, high cholesterol, and high blood pressure. Many of them can now be treated.

Remember that women require a longer time to become aroused and have an orgasm, while a man may have an orgasm rather quickly. He should slow down to match the woman's speed. He can talk more and add kissing or fondling of the breasts, vagina, or clitoris to the lovemaking. Both men and woman should expect an ebb and flow of erection and lubrication during the sexual stages of play, mounting, thrusting, and ejaculation.

An additional factor is the "superman and superwoman" fantasy. People work so hard in trying to be aggressive and advancing their careers that they have little energy or interest left over to enjoy sex with their lover.

So use the PSR training to take the edge off the day's problems and refresh yourself for your personal relationships. The inner calm and balancing of the animal and intellectual brain will help you be more sensitive, sensual, sexual, and satisfied.

THE FOURTH POSITIVE STRESS RESPONSE EXERCISE: THE SUMMARY EXERCISE

> Advice is like snow; the softer it falls, the longer it dwells upon, and the deeper it sinks into the mind.
>
> —*Samuel Taylor Coleridge*

Nancy's Audition

I am an actress-singer, and I came to biofeedback in my search for a cure for two problems: migraine headaches and insomnia. I had suffered from migraines for a number of years (and, in fact, they were not as intense or as frequent as they once had been), but the insomnia—at least in its extreme form—was a more recent development. The experience that caused me to feel that some kind of action was necessary was a night in which I did not sleep at all because of a very important audition the next day. The audition was, even in retrospect, potentially one of the most important of my career. Although I got through it and sang respectably, I did not get the job, but actually I was primarily upset about the extent and level of my anxiety. In a business where performances and auditions are a regular part of the daily routine, it is obviously disastrous to let oneself get this upset about any single challenge. Shortly after this, a friend who also suffered from migraines told me of the help biofeedback had given her in that area. Since both insomnia and migraines are stress-related, it seemed to me that this was certainly worth trying.

Both the migraines and the insomnia have all but disappeared since I began biofeedback. I still have a migraine every 2 or 3 months, but of considerably less intensity than before. Insomnia is similarly infrequent, and never has it been for the entire night.

I came to biofeedback already knowing that I was a "Type A," and also that I possessed the typical migraine personality characteristics. What I didn't realize was that I had accepted these as a given and had assumed that there was little, if anything, I could do about it. This, for me, has been the incredible value of the biofeedback treatments. I feel that in my case, the actual physical responses in the sessions have been less important than the implications of the approach that the physical monitoring taught me: that reactiom to stress is everything, not the stress itself. Therefore, I do not have to be the helpless victim of the stresses that are thrown at me, because I can learn to monitor my reactions. With the insomnia problem, for example, I was compounding the situation by becoming hysterical over the insomnia and whipping myself into a frenzy of frustration and helpless rage at the unfairness of life—all of which not only extended the insomnia but also guaranteed total physical exhaustion! A further extension of this was my growing awareness of the importance of how I perceive certain "facts": incredible tension was resulting from my identification of some auditions not just as a threat (and they need not even be seen as that) but as somehow almost life-threatening. The awareness that I was the one giving these challenges this cosmic importance was all that was needed for this exaggerated view to begin to moderate.

Furthermore, I have always been a doer, a person who could marshal an enormous concentration of will and take action against problems and challenges. That there are areas in which this kind of assaultive response does not work was something I already knew (certain corrections in vocal technique, for example), but I had not been able to devise any alternative. Again, the physical technique of biofeedback gave me a new tool that had applications beyond physical symptoms: the amazing extent to which awareness and identification of a problem or pattern of behavior—and mental acknowledgment (without excessive self-criticism) that this was inappropriate—could actually lead to significant changes in habitual reactions.

For me, I certainly see my biofeedback homework exercises as an ongoing way of life. All of my Type A instincts are there beneath the surface, ready to overreact to everything with too much speed and intensity. Every week there is at least one incident where I observe the old out-of-proportion response to minor frustrations: Most especially, I still suffer from a tendency to wage a constant battle against the tyranny of the clock. But that too is getting better.

This patient points out how our attitude affects our ability to sleep and be refreshed. The stress of demanding too much of oneself and one's schedule can trigger fatigue and headaches. She points out how anticipation can race the nervous system, causing too much excitement or overscheduling of one's day. By using the Positive Stress Response (PSR) exercises you can continue to learn how to be calm and more effective. Becoming aware of your particular stress patterns, you can use PSR to readjust physically and mentally. Be aware of how you overreact and then use your new skills to rebalance your reactions. Be creative and let your mind direct you to new solutions.

To add to your ability, I will describe the fourth PSR exercise after reviewing the key aspects of the first three PSR exercises.

The first exercise focused on breathing and relaxation. This calm, paced breathing is an important part of calming the nervous system and letting the brain think while keeping the rest of the body more relaxed.

The second exercise allowed you to practice your breathing while tensing and then relaxing specific muscle groups. I asked you to pay particular attention to the feelings that go along with the tension of the muscles and then the feeling associated with relaxing your muscles. This exercise outlines for the brain the ability to be active in one part of the body and relaxed in the other parts. While there are general patterns that spread to different muscle groups, try to isolate the tension and keep it from spreading to the rest of your body and your nervous system.

The third PSR exercise, warmth, had you start with a new exercise that allowed you to open up the arteries by relaxing the smooth muscles in the walls of the arteries. This helps you relax all of the internal organs, since most of them are made of smooth muscles. Learning to warm the hands and the feet gives you a calm, warm feeling throughout your body.

Since you have practiced these exercises, I now want to combine them into a shorter exercise that you can do in 5 to 6 minutes. Be sure you have practiced each of the first three PSR exercises for 2 weeks. If you have not practiced all of the exercises for 6 or 7 weeks, your skills are not well enough developed to shorten them into a summary exercise.

The Fourth Positive Stress Response Exercise

Begin by getting into a relaxed position in a comfortable chair that supports your head and legs, or by lying on your back flat on the floor with your knees up or a pillow under the knees.

Step 1: Start with the slow, paced breathing for about 40 to 60 seconds.

Step 2: I want you to repeat each of the phrases I give you out loud to yourself in a slow, paced manner, and then repeat them two or three times quietly to yourself. Feel down into your right arm. Feel the length, width, and breadth of your right arm and say out loud to yourself in a slow, paced manner:

"My right arm is warm and heavy."

Repeat this phrase to yourself three or four times with a slow, calm breathing pattern (15—20 seconds).

Step 3: Let the warmth and relaxation spread across the shoulders and chest to the left arm and down into the left arm. Let the warmth and relaxation completely fill the left arm. Let the warmth flow down to the elbow, wrist, hand, and fingers. Imagine the length, width, and breadth of the left arm filling with warmth and relaxation. Say out loud to yourself:

"My left arm is warm and heavy."

Repeat this phrase to yourself three or four times with a slow, calm, breathing pattern (15—20 seconds).

Step 4: Now picture in your mind the whole upper half of the body—the face and scalp, down the neck to the shoulders, to the hands and arms, down the chest and back to the waist—as relaxed and warm. Picture the whole upper half of your body relaxing and warming as you use the key phrase for the upper body, which you say out loud to yourself:

"My arms are warm and heavy."

Repeat this phrase to yourself three or four times with a slow, calm breathing pattern (15—20 seconds).

Step 5: Now, as you relax the upper half of the body, let the warmth and relaxation spread down into the right hip and down into the right knee, calf, and down to the toes. Allow that warmth and relaxation to fill the whole right leg, the whole length, width, and breadth of the right leg. Say out loud to yourself:

"My right leg is warm and heavy."

Repeat this phrase three or four times with a slow, calm breathing pattern (15—20 seconds).

Step 6: Allow the warmth and relaxation to spread across the hips to the left leg and down the left leg to the knee and the calf, the ankle, and into the foot and toes. Let the whole left leg fill with warmth and relaxation. Say out loud to yourself:

"My left leg is warm and heavy."

Repeat this phrase three or four times to yourself with a slow, calm breathing pattern (15—20 seconds).

Step 7: Picture the whole lower half of your body as relaxing and warming from the inside out. Now relax the whole lower half of the body, from the waist down to the hips, down to the knees, the calves, the ankles, feet, and into the toes. Say out loud to yourself:

"My legs are warm and heavy."

Repeat this phrase three or four times with a slow, calm breathing pattern (15—20 seconds).

Step 8: Now feel the warmth and relaxation from the head and scalp spread down to the shoulders and to the arms, to the chest, down the back to the waist, down the waist to the hips, knees, calves, ankles, feet, and toes. Let your whole body relax and warm from the inside out. Let the muscles be loose, limp, and relaxed. Your breathing is slow and paced. Say out loud to yourself:

"My arms and legs are warm and heavy, comfortably warm and heavy."

Repeat this phrase three or four times with a slow, calm breathing pattern (20—25 seconds).

Step 9: Now take about 40 to 60 seconds and enjoy these warm, relaxed feelings as you breathe in a slow, paced manner.

Step 10: Say to yourself: "I am relaxed, energetic, and calm." Now count to yourself, one, two, three, and then let your eyes drift open. Stretch, feeling relaxed and calm as you look around the room.

This exercise takes about 6 to 7 minutes to go through the first time. As you practice for the next week, you will begin to memorize it. Then for the second week, you can try it with your eyes open if you wish. By the third week, have it memorized and be able to do it with your eyes open. When you have memorized the fourth PSR, it will take only 4 to 5 minutes. You can also use your Bio-Q band, temperature card, or thermometer to monitor your finger and hand warming. Later you may wish to practice with foot warming. Foot warming will take an additional 3 to 6 weeks of practice.

If you find that distracting thoughts, ideas, or worries come into your mind, continue to repeat these phrases five or six times. An additional technique, if you have interrupting thoughts or ideas, is to say to yourself the word "one, one," and repeat this as fast as you like for a minute or two. This usually helps your mind to focus on the physical and mental exercises that you are doing, rather than on other thoughts.

When you do this exercise remember to use your favorite imagery that was described with the third exercise.

If you imagined yourself lying on the beach, then use your *stimulus* script, such as, "Imagine the sun beaming down on you. You are lying on the warm sand. Occasionally, warm breezes waft over you."

This script describes *stimuli* that are impinging upon you. Also use your *response* script: "Imagine the warm, pulsing sensation in your hands as the sun's rays beam down on you. You can feel the warm, rough sand between your toes and your fingers. Warm breezes fan your tanning skin, caressing you with their gentle touch."

This imagery describes the responses and sensations you experience as you are stimulated. I prefer the response-oriented approach rather than the first kind we described. However, you can use both. The more complete the response you can imagine and visualize, the more information you are giving your brain. If you can recreate in your mind the vivid memory of a pleasant, relaxing experience where your hands and feet were warm, add that to these exercises.

These are commonly used situations or stimuli to enhance relaxation and warming:

- Lying on the beach by the ocean, a local river, stream, creek, or lake, or surrounded by tropical palms on a secluded isle.

- Relaxing in your yard, sitting or reclining on a chair, hammock, or blanket.

- Sitting in front of a fireplace or stove with your hands and feet close to the heat source.

- Lying in a warm tub of water or under a toasty electric blanket.

- Putting your hands or feet in a hot tub or bath.

- Touching, caressing, or holding a warm, cuddly, loving body.

- Holding hands with your lover.

You could also stage some of those situations with the idea of remembering the warm sensations that go with them. Try to remember or visit a favorite beach or summer vacation spot and lock into your memory the response sensations you experience.

Some of the sensations that people have described including in their imagery are these:

- Feeling tension flowing out, being replaced by relaxation.

- Hands swelling, or feeling full or heavy.

- Blood pulsing in hands, fingers, feet.

- A tingly, warm sensation.

- Feeling the blood pushed with great momentum from the heart to the hands and feet.

- Feeling of warm viscous fluid, the thickness of honey, filling the fingers, hands, toes, and feet.

- A flush or rush of blood.

- Pulse beats (heartbeats).

- Flickering warmth from a fireplace.

- Moist, wet warmth from steam rising from a pot of boiling water or hot soup.

- Warmth associated with friction or rubbing.

The fourth PSR exercise is an important one because we are combining and shortening the first three exercises. I want you to do this exercise again using your favorite imagery. You can also use the word "relaxed" instead of "heavy." Try each word for a week and see which one works better for you. Some people find that using both words works best.

Let's do this exercise once more using the word "relaxed." Start by sitting comfortably for about 30 seconds. Adjust your posture to a comfortable position. Sit or lie quietly, with your eyes closed.

First, focus on your breathing, inhaling slowly and calmly to a count of one, two, three, four, pause for a count of one, and then exhale, breathing out for a count of four. Pause for a count and then repeat for about 30 or 40 seconds.

Then, focus your mind on your right arm. Slowly repeat to yourself two or three times (15 seconds), the key phrase:

"My right arm is warm and relaxed."

Use response imagery to visualize your right arm relaxed and warm. Embellish the key phrase with both situational and response imagery, keeping the focus on your right arm. Then allow the warm, relaxed feeling to flow, move, or spread across your chest and upper back to your left arm. Use imagery enhancement to focus on your left arm from the shoulder down to the fingertips, and use the key phrase:

"My left arm is warm and relaxed."

Repeat the phrase to yourself three times. Continue your paced, even breathing (15 seconds).

Create a picture in your mind of your whole upper body relaxed, from the waist up to your neck and face, shoulders, back, and arms. Use the key phrase:

"My arms are warm and relaxed."

Repeat this phrase three times, quietly, to yourself, and let the whole upper half of your body become relaxed and warm (15 seconds). Again, combine stimulus and response imagery to enhance the effects.

Next, move your mental focus down to your right leg, from the hip down to the toes. Imagine the whole leg relaxed and warm. Use the key phrase:

"My right leg is warm and relaxed."

Repeat the phrase slowly to yourself three times (15 seconds). Allow the warmth to move across your hip and lower back to your left leg. Imagine the whole leg relaxed and warm. Use the key phrase:

"My left leg is warm and relaxed."

Again, repeat the phrase to yourself three times (15 seconds).

Picture in your mind the whole lower half of your body relaxed and comfortable, with full peripheral vascular circulation. You can even take a look at the illustrations of the hand and foot vascular systems when relaxed and form an image of your arteries wide open with a good feeling of warmth. Then, use the key phrase:

"My legs are warm and relaxed."

Repeat it to yourself three times, allowing the lower half of your body to relax even more each time you repeat the phrase (15 seconds).

Finally, picture your whole body, from head to toe, being relaxed, with all of your extremities warm, relaxed, calm, and comfortable. Amplify the mental picture with your stimulus and response imagery. Then use the key phrase:

"My arms and legs are warm and relaxed, comfortably warm and relaxed."

Repeat this phrase three times, letting the whole body relax and warm as deeply as possible (20 seconds).

Experience the deep level of relaxation. Focus on the open condition of your vascular system and the relaxed state of your muscles (10 seconds). Say to yourself: "I feel relaxed, energetic, and calm." Then, count one, two, three, and gently let your eyes open. Stretch and yawn, and then proceed with your daily activities.

This exercise is a general one that you can use as a framework to develop and further your own personalized blood-flow control strategy. As mentioned earlier, you can vary the length of this exercise from a very quick body imagery scan, taking just a few seconds, to a whole lengthy practice exercise lasting from 5 to 7 minutes. Many people enjoy repeating this exercise two or three times, and taking 15 to 20 minutes to relax and refresh themselves.

I've also found that some people often resist using the lengthy version of this exercise. They come to session after session apologizing or making excuses for why they haven't done it. It requires a major change in your attitude about how you take care of yourself. You have to make a conscious decision that you deserve a 5- to

20-minute rest period, a minivacation each day, perhaps even twice a day. It's valuable and good for you.

First, while you are actually performing the exercise, you are quieting your nervous system, reducing its activity level, giving your body and mind a rest. It restabilizes you at a calmer, more peaceful level of activity. This can be a useful and effective way to break the daily tension buildup pattern. For this reason alone, the 20-minute exercise is worth doing. But there's another important value.

This is the practice effect. As I've said before, if you want to learn to play the piano, you've got to practice long and hard. The same is true for tennis and any other activity that requires some degree of skill. An important part of learning to play the piano is practicing your scales and chords, so that when you actually incorporate them in a composition, your fingers move faster than they would normally be able to if you had to think through every single note that you are touching. You develop a response capability. That specific behavior becomes a trained response that you can get your body to reproduce without having to think through each step. You do the same thing each time you sign your name or play a sport.

You learned initially by trial and error and lots of practice. And that's what you'll be doing with this short warming exercise. The 20-minute session gives you a lot of practice. The key phrases are the cues that you use to set off that reflexive response. Each time you practice the third exercise, you are more deeply embedding this response in your nervous system so that when you need it you can call upon it quickly. You can then turn it on right away with the fourth PSR exercise. That's what will eventually enable you to use the breathing check (two or three paced breaths) so effectively. After 8 weeks of practice, a few key phrases will produce effects almost as powerful as if you did the long, 20-minute version of this exercise. But that takes practice. The more practice time you invest in developing this trained response, the more potent a self-control tool it will be when you really need it.

You also have to decide when to do your exercises. Sometimes, when you are feeling uptight, the time is obvious. You do it when you need it to relieve yourself, to feel better. But it would be more advantageous and healthier if you could figure out times to do the exercise before you develop discomfort. It would be better if you could prevent the onset of problems.

One common approach is for people to use their coffee breaks at work or at home for a relaxation break. If you are at work and there's an empty office where you can do the 20-minute exercise without interruptions from ringing phones or co-workers, that's great. But if necessary, you can go to the bathroom, go into the stall, close the door, and do the exercise there. A surprisingly large number of patients have reported that this works very well. Many people even use their bathroom at home as a place to get away from it all. My patients use it before a concert, a meeting, or even in the dentist chair. You can help assist your dentist to do better work on you by being relaxed.

Your goal is to learn how to relax yourself while you are wide awake and alert, to keep your mind sharp, crisp, and clear without overactivating the rest of your body.

Many people don't find the coffee break to be the best part of the day for doing the exercise. Their daily stress pattern may call for a different timing. One way to find out the best times to break up daily stress buildup is to keep a record of your stress levels and/or any stress-related symptoms you may have throughout the day.

Usually you'll find that there is a gradual buildup to a stress peak at a certain hour. The buildup can take 2 or 3 hours or just 15 minutes. Common peaks are found when the kids or a spouse are due home, near the end of the workday, before, during, and after dinner, near bedtime, and at awakening. But everyone's pattern is different, and yours may not fit any of those I've listed. This list might help you, but a few weeks of charting might yield a surprising discovery. Charts are designed so you can also list your activities, medications, and foods. Sometimes you will find a connection you never before realized existed. I've included the practice chart in Chapter Five, and you should use it again with the fourth PSR exercise.

Now I'm going to give you an even shorter version of the fourth exercise.

After 2 to 3 weeks, you will be able to use this fourth exercise in meetings with your eyes open. You will find it is invaluable. After practicing for another 2 weeks you can shorten it to the basic ten steps, taking as little as 1 or 2 minutes.

The Short Fourth PSR Exercise

Step 1: Breathe in a slow, paced manner for 20 to 40 seconds. Then repeat each of these key phrases to yourself in your mind as you feel into your body.

Step 2: "My right arm is warm and heavy." (Repeat once or twice with one or two slow, paced breaths.)

Step 3: "My left arm is warm and heavy." (Repeat once or twice with one or two slow, paced breaths.)

Step 4: "My arms are warm and heavy." (Repeat once or twice with one or two slow, paced breaths.)

Step 5: "My right leg is warm and heavy." (Repeat once or twice with one or two slow, paced breaths.)

Step 6: "My left leg is warm and heavy." (Repeat once or twice with one or two slow, paced breaths.)

Step 7: "My legs are warm and heavy." (Repeat once or twice with one or two slow, paced breaths.)

Step 8: "My arms and legs are warm and heavy, comfortably warm and heavy." (Repeat once or twice.)

Step 9: Breathe for 20 to 40 seconds in a slow, paced manner and enjoy those relaxed warm feelings.

Step 10: Say to yourself: "I feel calm, warm, and alert." Then count one, two, three, stretch your arms and legs, and open your eyes with a relaxed, calm feeling.

As you do this shorter exercise, use the key phrases as I've listed them above. Remember to keep breathing in a slow, paced manner during the ten steps. You can shorten them by repeating them one or two times instead of three or four times. This will compress the exercise to 1, 2, or 3 minutes. After a month you will be able to use the key phrases once or twice and get almost the same benefit as you did in 5 to 7 minutes.

This exercise is excellent when you are riding in an elevator, sitting in a car, or waiting for someone. It is also useful before a meeting or during a meeting. If you have only 20 to 40 seconds, you can use the slow, paced breathing to relax so you can be in a calm, alert state.

I mentioned in Chapter Nine that when they do the third and fourth exercises some people feel sexual and sensual and relaxed. You may feel energized, calm, or even euphoric. By working together, the mind and body become more efficient, and you may experience many different sensations when practicing. You may feel "light" or "heavy" or experience a floating or drifting feeling. Some people also feel a turning sensation or a feeling of opening like a beautiful flower. You also may feel a light tingling in the fingers or toes as the arteries open up, and you feel your pulse or a gentle warm throbbing as you notice the circulation in the fingers, abdomen, or neck. These are signs that you are increasing the circulation and deepening the relaxation. At first these sensations may appear more noticeable or feel stronger. As your skills become more developed, many of these sensations become more gentle or fade into the background and you will hardly notice them.

You also may notice that you have little daydreams or other thoughts or ideas. Many people have told me that after the first 8 to 10 weeks of practice, they find that they experience creative images that are helpful to them in their work. One artist told me recently that she had just painted a landscape and it was the most beautiful piece she had ever done. She felt more creative and found she was painting better. Use the PSR to relax and become more efficient; you will also find creative uses that will fulfill more of your potential in other areas of your life. In many ways the PSR training allows people to be more creative and intuitive. Do not be surprised if you are increasingly observant of yourself and others and can use the latent potential that has been hidden or pushed under by the tensions and stresses of everyday life.

Be sure to try this fourth PSR exercise any time you are in a stressful situation or preparing for one. You will see how the previous three PSR exercises channel into this shorter version. You will feel calmer, more alert, energetic, sensual, flexible, and creative in handling stress.

CHAPTER ELEVEN

STRESS AND THE FUTURE

The great secret of happiness is to be on good
terms with oneself.

—Fontenelle

Jane's Virus

I entered the biofeedback (PSR) training program in
November of 1986. At that time I felt as if 1 had no
control over my physical health. I had suffered since
childhood from various ailments, culminating with the
diagnosis of Epstein-Barr virus in the spring of 1984.
The virus was so debilitating that I was unable to work
for 7 months and was basically bedridden. My recu-
peration was very slow, and I began to believe that I
would never get completely better. Every day when I
woke up I felt fatigued, depressed, and unable to cope
with the daily demands of my life.

During the first month of training and practice I
began learning how my body was functioning. When
practicing muscle relaxation techniques, I found that
when I was not consciously trying to relax my muscles,
I would hold my body in a very rigid fashion. I was so
used to tensing that when I first started letting go of
that tension it felt unnatural and a little bit scary. It felt
as if some sort of protective shell was being removed.
With continued practice, however, I noticed that when
I relaxed my muscles the migraine headaches and neck
pains from which I was in almost constant pain would
disappear. It took another 2 months of practice before
I was able to release the tension in my head and neck
without the use of the biofeedback (PSR) tapes.

During that 2-month period I was learning something that was essential to my being able to make practical use of what I had been working on during the daily sessions. I realized that if I was able to focus directly on what was happening at a particular moment (as I did when I listened to the tapes), then my mind would stop racing. This in turn would allow me to look at myself to see whether I was tensing my muscles and to relax them if I was. Every day when I left my apartment I made a habit of concentrating on the walk up the hill to get to the bus stop. I tried to keep my focus on that walk and not let my mind race ahead to what I was going to encounter when I got to work. Most often I found that when I started up the hill I rounded my shoulders and brought them up toward my neck. I also took a deep breath and held it. In the beginning I felt that I couldn't make it up the hill without gearing up like this. When I made a consistent daily effort to relax and breathe as I took that walk, however, I found that it wasn't necessary to expend all of the energy I had been using just to walk up the incline. By the end of that 2-month period I possessed the mental ability to prevent the buildup of tension that had led to so much of my sickness.

As I continued to master the focusing-in process, it became easier and easier to deal with stressful situations and to think about how to react instead of just reacting. The process of experiencing a situation, stopping to think about how to respond, and then responding had the effect of slowing time down. It didn't really, but it was just that I could get much more accomplished because I no longer had to use all my energy to fend off stressful situations. Now I had an active effect on the stress.

After 7 months of training I have complete good health for the first time in 27 years. I understand now that sickness was my way of reacting to stress, and that it is not an inherent, uncontrollable part of my biological makeup as I had always assumed.

This patient reported that she had poor energy and several ailments that were diagnosed as Epstein-Barr virus in the spring of 1984. This virus is also called chronic Epstein-Barr virus or chronic mononucleosis. It has been studied at the Harvard Medical School, and they prefer to call it "chronic mono syndrome." They say the syndrome is characterized by symptoms of fatigue, low-grade fever, sore throat, aching muscles and joints, headaches, sharp shooting pains in different parts of the body, and sometimes depression as well as difficulty in concentrating. This syndrome usually occurs in young adulthood but may occur even in children. It affects women about twice as often as men, and it may follow an episode of infectious mononucleosis or a cold. Often people feel as if they have a flu that continues for several weeks or months. Then they may have a few good weeks or months and then feel sick again. Laboratory tests are rarely positive. Sometimes there is an increased sedimentation rate or abnormal levels of antibodies to the Epstein-Barr virus. Many researchers and physicians question the reliability of the blood antibodies in this syndrome.

The cause of this chronic mono is unknown. However, one theory is that these viruses are constantly in the body. The virus can be activated by stress, other infection, or fatigue, and can then cause worse fatigue, pain, or other symptoms. Another theory is that there is a specific new type of virus that stress may trigger, leading to these symptoms. This is speculation, however, and physicians are studying different viruses and following many patients to understand this syndrome and see if they can determine what causes it. They also are trying different treatments to evaluate possible relief for their patients. One medication, amitriptyline (trade name Elavil), has been helpful in low dosages from 10 to 40 mg. Anthony Komaroff, M.D., chief of general medicine at Harvard Medical School, has been following many of these patients. He and his staff hope to find some new answers as to what causes this and how best to treat it.

In Jane's case, for 2½ years she had been unable to cope with the daily energy requirements of her life. Within 7 months she was able to reverse this syndrome. I believe this is because as people use the PSR they reduce the muscle tension and improve the strength of their immune system. This causes the virus to go into remission—that is, to go back "asleep." A sleeping virus is in the system but does not cause the devastation that many of these people experience. Jane relates how, by using the PSR exercises, she can relax the muscles and not waste her mental and physical energy. This led her mind to see that she could then use these techniques in other situations to better handle the stresses of her everyday tasks.

She is now functioning normally and feels for the first time in years that she is healthy. She has been able to work part time without being sick and is looking forward to full-time work. She also is considering going into a different field of work since she is now more energetic and optimistic. As she told me, she and her husband now enjoy their time together. She can do more things, and he is pleased that they now have a fuller relationship. She was a partial invalid. Now they look forward to taking a 2-week vacation. They went on their first successful 4-day vacation 2 months ago. Her husband is happy and pleased to have his wife back.

People who looked fatigued, washed out, or in pain before PSR training become bright-eyed, energetic, and much happier in dealing with the tasks of life. Their relationships with their spouses, friends, and family improve dramatically. By retraining the mental and physical connections of their nervous systems, people can fine-tune these nervous systems. A healthy nervous system is the key to handling the stresses of life, including viruses.

Future Stresses

Stress will continue to increase because technology continues to change the world and people are forced to make more choices and decisions, both individually and as a society. Some of the key stresses worldwide are local wars, the threat of nuclear global war, and pollution of the environment. On a personal level, the challenge of changing male and female roles, the lack of the local extended family, urbanization, and new viruses (AIDS) increase stress and affect our health and well-being. Another reason for increased stresses is that there are limited resources and more people are expecting more goods and services. There is intense competition among nations. Many countries—the United States, Britain, Germany, Japan, Korea, and others—are competing in exporting foodstuffs, computers, and other technology, as well as in one of the oldest items of economic exchange—weapons. The vast amount of debt accumulated by certain countries has put in doubt some of the international funding of debtor countries like Brazil and Mexico. Countries with billions of dollars of debt threaten the financial stability of banks, other countries, and perhaps the worldwide economic system.

Some of the individual choices people face are the following: Should you try to influence the sex of a child by some of the new techniques available? Should you adopt, use artificial insemination, or engage a surrogate mother? Should you abort a child who has a disease or disorder? Should you work for love or money, or can you create or find a job that has a fair share of both? Should you take early retirement or work until 65 or longer?

The speed of change continues. Now many TV commercials are 15 seconds or 30 seconds rather than the traditional 60 seconds. At commercial breaks you see one, two, three, or four different commercial ads—each one accelerated with music and fast images. These all give a sense of time speeding up, and this grabs our attention and speeds up our nervous systems. There are 24-hour TV stations on cable or from a satellite dish. More and more input is going into our nervous systems 24 hours a day. These and other factors continue to increase the challenge and stresses on individuals and countries. Therefore, we will need Positive Stress Response (PSR) management skills to develop the abilities that are potentially available in the human nervous system.

We have made rapid changes over the centuries because of the tremendous capacity of our brains and bodies to adapt and adjust to new stresses. For example, we have cured many infectious diseases and can now treat many diseases and disorders with medication and surgery. However, nature continues to change and challenge mankind. Diseases such as AIDS and a contaminated blood supply now haunt us. A negative part of human nature compels some people to use over-the-counter drugs to avoid the struggles and challenges of life. The Russians have a severe alcoholism problem, and alcoholism is also a major problem in the United States. In addition, we have an increasing problem with the use of illicit drugs that affect people's minds, mood, and behavior. Prescription drugs are often overused or abused, as seen in the testimony of Betty Ford, Liza Minelli, and others. The most recent epidemic is with crack, a form of potent cocaine that is extremely addictive. Violent robberies are committed in order to buy this drug.

These problems have faced us before. After the Civil War there was a great deal of morphine addiction among men who had been wounded in the war. More recently, there was concern about soldiers returning from Vietnam because of their use of strong marijuana and opium. Worry about this addiction problem proved overblown, because most soldiers stopped their drug use when they were returned to more normal social conditions. Stronger action against the importation of cocaine and heroin is necessary. Drug smuggling has become a huge business and threatens our country's stability and lawfulness.

One of the ways to combat these stresses of modern life is to train to increase your coping ability. This is one reason for using the PSR exercises. They will help your brain and body work better together to deal with future changes. I have mentioned some of these skills in the patients' stories. As you practice the exercises, you will find that your mind will use the exercises in your own particular situations. You don't have to rehearse every situation that might come up in the future. The mind has the ability to take these PSR skills and project them into new situations. These skills are similar to learning to spell. You don't have to run through every letter in the alphabet in order to spell new words. Once you know the general rules of spelling, you can spell new words quite accurately the first time. Similarly, the skills of mind and body can be used in new situations. One of the first examples of this was Ed's story in Chapter Two. His creative thinking in a moment of panic demonstrates how he used his skills in a situation he had never run into before.

Increase Your Coping Ability

There are three ways people can help themselves to cope better: (1) Be aware of the importance of nutrition and exercise (wellness programs). (2) Use technology to help solve some of these problems. (3) Retrain your nervous system through PSR training.

Fitness and Wellness Programs

The use of fitness and wellness programs by large corporations is evidence of their value. These corporations include Johnson & Johnson, Prudential, and Blue Cross and Blue Shield. One of the largest is the Johnson & Johnson program called "Live for Life." Started in 1979, this work-site program included exercise, reduction of smoking, lowering of cholesterol, and weight control. The *Journal of the American Medical Association* in December 1986 reported on over 8000 members of the Live for Life program compared with a control group of about 3000 nonmembers over a 5-year period. What they reported was that people who joined the Live for Life program had a higher smoking cessation rate than non-Live for Life employees (23 percent compared with 17 percent). Members also reduced their risk for coronary heart disease (32 percent versus 13 percent for the nonmembers). In addition Live for Life members reduced their weight and other risk factors such as cholesterol. Many more of the members also increased their physical activity (20 percent of the Live for Life women versus 7 percent of the nonmembers). Twenty-nine percent of the men increased their exercise versus 19 percent of the non-Live for Life members. A review of the 5-year follow-up of this program clearly showed that the Live for Life program supported more healthful life-styles. The annual inpatient cost increase for the Live for Life members was approximately $43 versus $76 for the nonmembers. This meant that over $1 million was saved for this study period. This is one example of how an exercise program and attention to diet and smoking can help people reduce their risk factors and increase their vitality and health.

Another example of how well these programs can help was recently demonstrated by Blue Shield of California. They started their wellness program in the spring of 1986. One year later, 70 percent of the company's 1600 employees were participating. They have already seen a marked decrease in sick days and physician visits, resulting in an annual saving of $140 per employee. The saving is equal to eight times the current employee cost of the program. Other health risks also have been reduced, such as weight problems, cigarette smoking, and excessive drinking. This program was developed by a group of doctors led by James Fries, M.D., from Stanford University Medical School. Blue Shield has been impressed with this program and has offered it to other Blue Shield and Blue Cross plans under the name of "Health Trac." They also will be offering the program to other organizations.

Large reductions in direct medical health care costs can result from these programs. For example, one study showed that medical care costs increased by 35 percent in one company without a fitness program but only by 1 percent at Canadian Life, which had a fitness program. The people who adhered to the fitness program at Canadian Life showed a 5 percent reduction in medical care costs the year following the beginning of the program. Prudential showed a 45.7 percent reduction in the actual major medical costs. Even more interesting, the higher the level of fitness the person achieved, the lower the medical costs. At AT&T Dorthea Johnson, M.D., estimated that they would save $2.6 million per year through their TLC program (Tender Loving Care).

These reports are important because they also make recommendations for prescreening people for the fitness programs. They recommend a review of the family medical history, a physical examination, and laboratory tests to classify the patients as either healthy or at a high risk, or already suffering a disease. The last two categories would need to be more closely followed medically for engaging in physical vigorous exercise. They also pointed out that the program should be designed to make the changes necessary for each employee as well as for the organization. Some of the programs suggested were exercise, nutrition, weight control, smoking cessation, stress management, women's health, and home and auto safety.

These fitness programs are bringing about a change in the medical field's interest in preventive medicine. No one is better able than you to take care of your diet and exercise program and health. Physicians like myself, who are involved in retraining people, encourage these forms of self-regulation because no one else is going to get as much benefit as you are. While your friends, family, and society will benefit, you're going to be the primary beneficiary. So it's in your interest to exercise and acquire PSR skills.

There is an additional benefit that has been talked about in meditation and religious groups. Good healthy habits and feelings—"good vibes"—can spread to the rest of society. This effect is seen by religions supporting certain healthy habits. They have tried to do good work for others in terms of charity and volunteer work. Many of our first hospitals were formed out of this intent to take care of people and help them. This altruistic spirit can be furthered by using the PSR for your benefit and the benefit of society.

Technological Change

A good example of how technology helps us and also stresses us is the use of computers and video terminals. You can track how much time people spend at the computer and how much work they produce by monitoring each keystroke they strike on the computer keyboard. Thus, telephone operators can be monitored to see how fast they answer calls and how many calls per hour they handle daily. While this measures the number of calls or how many keystrokes are made, it does not say whether the customer or complaint was answered successfully— just how quickly it was handled. Technology can speed things up, but it does not always improve service. Faster does not automatically mean better.

One of the increasing causes of certain symptoms is the increased use of computers and computer games. This has been discussed in a book called *Health Hazards of*

VDTs. There were about 15 million VDTs (video display terminals) in the United States as of 1987, and this number continues to grow. It is estimated that by 1990 the number will increase to 79 million, and it may be 100 million by the year 2000. In some of the first studies in Sweden in 1970, the effects of VDTs on stress were focused on visual fatigue and eye complaints. In addition to ionizing radiation emitted by VDTs, other concerns are the possibly harmful levels of ultraviolet infrared microwaves and very low frequency electromagnetic radiation. This may be related to complaints of facial dermatitis (rashes) associated with VDT work. Other common symptoms are eyestrain, irritation, headaches, and neck, shoulder, back, and wrist pain.

One of these reports suggests that stress is a major factor because the musculoskeletal tension reflects other stresses associated with VDTs in the workplace. Other signs are psychosomatic nervous disorders, disturbed sleep, coronary artery and heart disease, gastrointestinal upset, and endocrine imbalances. In one survey of Southern New England Telephone, three-fourths of employees reported dizziness, headaches, and muscle aches when they were assigned to tasks and were monitored on the VDT. Employees knew they were being monitored for each keystroke. Because of the fast pacing and the fact of being observed, people developed headaches, dizziness, or muscle aches.

In a March 1987 *New York Times* article by Harley Shakin, "When the Computer Runs the Office," the cost of stress-related symptoms was estimated at $15 to $75 billion a year. He reported that almost one-third of the monitored workers lost time from work for health-related reasons due to stress. Only one out of five of the workers not monitored lost time from work because of health reasons related to stress. The American Telephone and Telegraph Company announced in 1987 that they had banned all pregnant women from their semiconductor production lines. This was in response to a Massachusetts study showing there was a higher incidence of miscarriage with women who work at producing computer chips. These women work in so-called clean rooms where the chips are fabricated. While a tentative conclusion, this study suggests there is a slightly higher risk with some of the new technologies.

How Technology Helps

The miniaturization of electronic components will probably allow us to carry small packs of 1 to 3 pounds of monitoring equipment throughout the day. This equipment can show skin temperature, as Dr. R. Freedman from Detroit has done in his studies of treatment of Raynaud's patients. It is also possible to monitor blood pressure, heart rate, muscle activity, and other important physiological functions. This is currently being done for astronauts and for cardiac patients in hospitals. This equipment enables us to discover when stress is affecting an individual and when particular stresses affect blood pressure, muscle activity, or the bowel during the day and night.

The miniature equipment will also allow us to intervene earlier and start treating people who are at risk. Before "halter monitoring," for example, physicians thought that when they saw a skipped beat or two on an EKG this might be an indication of heart disease. A halter monitor is a small tape recorder in a 3- to 4-pound pack that people can wear 24 hours a day to monitor their EKG (heart rhythm). After monitoring thousands of people for 24 hours, it was made clear that almost everybody's heart skipped a beat occasionally, particularly when they were exposed to different stressful conditions. After evaluating these data, physicians now recommend that there is little reason to be concerned unless you have a "run" of more than three or four skipped beats per minute. In a similar way, since 1986 it has been possible to monitor blood pressure for 24 hours a day so we can see it fluctuate as people function in their actual jobs. Taking your blood pressure once is only monitoring 1 of approximately 1400 possible readings during 24 hours. Through 24-hour monitoring, we can learn a lot more about what is a healthy blood pressure, which people are at risk, and how many people need treatment.

For example, there are some patients who, perhaps because they feel more comfortable in a hospital or office, have slightly lower blood pressure readings there. These people are probably undertreated (medication or PSR or biofeedback). Conversely, there are other patients whose blood pressure is artificially high in a doctor's office or hospital. They are probably being overtreated with medication because of the stress-related higher blood pressure occurring only in the office or hospital. They may be told to take it easy or use more medication when they are relatively healthy. This is why many people are now having their bood pressure reevaluated by the 24-hour monitoring. Technology continues to make available more information about how the body and brain work. It helps physicians make better decisions on who and when to treat and how aggressively to treat them.

I have mentioned earlier some of the work done in Washington on stepped care of hypertension. At the Stress Regulation Institute, I train groups of people in a similar way, helping to retrain their nervous systems to reduce their blood pressure and medications. These programs continue to grow, and there are many other centers that are running similar programs across the country. The Menninger Foundation is one of these centers, and I have listed it and other programs in the Appendix. If you or someone you know has blood pressure problems, this is a viable and healthy addition to the standard medical treatment.

PSR training can be used for children, Type A behavior, a healthier immune system, and to reduce the pain and cost of other illness.

PSR for Schoolchildren

One way to change the future well-being of people is to implement stress management and PSR training with children when they begin school. A good time to start school-aged children is when they begin to read and write. Later they can use their computers for physiological feedback to help them learn in a calm, alert, and relaxed way. Some of this work has already been done by members of the Biofeedback Society of America. Elizabeth Stroebel has produced tapes and exercises for children to train them with simple physiological feedback and relaxation.

A good example of how the PSR training can be used has been shown by Mrs. Stroebel with her husband's

(Charles Stroebel, M.D., Ph.D.) "Quieting Response" to help children reduce stress. Going to school is an imposition for many children, particularly the males. This is why Dr. Stroebel has said that in addition to teaching the three Rs of reading, writing, and arithmetic, schools also teach a fourth R—relaxation. His book and Mrs. Stroebel's address are listed in the Appendix.

Elizabeth Stroebel in Connecticut and Loretta Engelhardt in South Dakota have developed school programs that are available on some computers, so you can do this training at home. These skills are now also being taught to adults in colleges and in corporations. Having taught stress management and PSR to various groups and to individuals and their families, I have seen tremendous benefits for them all.

Type A Personality

Another example of behavioral intervention that uses some of the techniques of PSR training is the work of Meyer Friedman, M.D., at the Mount Sinai Hospital in San Francisco. Dr. Friedman is the coauthor of the book *Type A Behavior and Your Heart*. His group studied 1013 post–myocardial infarction (heart attack) patients. They observed whether Type A behavior could be altered.

Over 862 patients were assigned to a control group receiving group cardiac counseling. The experimental group of 592 received both the cardiac counseling and Type A behavior counseling. The remaining 151 patients served as a comparison group. They did not receive counseling of any kind. At the end of 4½ years there was a large reduction of Type A behavior for the people in the group receiving Type A counseling and cardiac counseling. That is, 35 percent reduced their Type A behavior compared with 10 percent of the people who received only cardiac counseling. The illness rate with cardiac problems was 12.9 percent in the Type A counseling group, whereas it was 21 percent in the group that received only cardiac counseling and 28 percent in the group who received no counseling. Even after 1 year there was a large reduction in cardiac deaths in the group that received the Type A counseling training. This trend continued throughout the folowing 3½ years. Dr. Friedman said that this was the first time that anyone had shown a reduction in cardiac illness (as well a death from heart attack) by directly altering Type A behavior.

This result points out that counseling can be helpful not only in changing your behavior but in reducing the risk of a second heart attack. The counseling was just that. It did not include the physiological retraining that I have outlined in the PSR exercises. By combining counseling and PSR exercises you can experience better health and fewer cardiovascular problems (angina, heart attacks, and strokes).

Using PSR with Your Immune System

The work on improving the immune system using biofeedback and PSR is rapidly advancing. In the field of immunology, many people are not only using relaxation techniques but are strengthening the training by physiological biofeedback, mental imagery, and meditation. PSR training for the immune system combines these techniques. Dr. Steve Locke is one of the leaders in this field. He coauthored *The Healer Within*, which describes his observations over 10 years at Boston's Beth Israel Hospital. He has been investigating how stress affects the nervous system and influences the strength of the immune system. The immune system is the body's main defense against diseases. Dr. Locke evaluated 114 presumably healthy students who volunteered to fill out questionnaires designed to measure the stress of life changes. About 2 weeks later, the questionnaires were readministered and a blood specimen was drawn to evaluate the natural killer cell activity. This is one measure of the immune system's strength. Most subjects reported few psychological symptoms and faced stresses well. These people were called "good copers." They had higher killer cell activity than those who experienced a high level of symptoms and stress and who were designated as "poor copers." Dr.

Locke believes that these results "suggest that symptoms such as anxiety and depression may negatively affect immunity." He suggested that there is a link between the nervous system and the killer cells that can help us understand and give a theoretical basis as to how stress affects our immune system.

Another researcher doing related work is Marvin Stein, M.D., chief of psychiatry at Mt. Sinai in New York. He is interested in the interplay between psychosocial factors of disease. According to Dr. Stein, "There is no question that coping plays a role—so do social supports." He demonstrated that there is impaired immune function when people are in a state of bereavement. These examples show how the mind and body are constantly being affected by outside stressors. The attitude that the mind holds toward the world and toward the person's own body can affect the number of killer cells that help defeat an invasion of bacteria, viruses, or cancerous cells. This can be the difference between staying well and becoming slightly ill or very ill. Dr. Bruce Sarlin and I with colleagues at Presbyterian Hospital have used the PSR training with medical students at Columbia's medical school. We were able to show that PSR increased the strength of their immune system during exams. We worked with 30 students and plan to train 90 more next year. The PSR training can increase your ability to mobilize killer cells to strengthen your immune system. This will help defend you against illnesses and tolerate and handle stresses better without getting sick.

We are now able to monitor not only the blood flow to the periphery of the body, as we do now in biofeedback, but the actual blood flow *in* the brain. By using advanced scanning equipment, we can monitor blood flow in the brain by observing the amount of glucose used for different parts of the brain. This improves the diagnosis and treatment of many diseases, including depression, schizophrenia, and thyroid problems. Next, we might be able to understand complex intellectual functioning. The brain has locations devoted almost exclusively to specific functions. For example, there is a motor cortex strip that handles all of our motor coordination, including what is called the "motor homunculus." The frontal lobes have certain centers that contribute to intelectual functioning and memory. In the occipital lobes there are centers devoted almost exclusively to vision. Thus, by studying the brain we can observe normal, healthy, and perhaps genius functioning. It might be possible to use this new equipment to retain the brain's pattern of thinking, emotions, and physiological functions. We may be able to support healthy functioning by retraining, just as we are now retraining the nervous system with biofeedback and PSR. One of the goals of medical science is not only to explore but to develop new understanding of how the brain and body work. Then we can use this new research to develop treatments to cure diseases or moderate the ravages of diseases such as heart attacks, strokes, and paralysis.

One example of this is the improved treatment of strokes. We can retrain stroke patients with biofeedback by monitoring specific muscle groups and retraining them to achieve better results than are achieved with regular physical therapy. With this retraining we can help more people with strokes to recover more hand and foot strength and dexterity.

A Right-Left Mind-Body Exercise

You can experience retraining by doing some physical movements using your nondominant hand, the left hand for 90 percent of us. Try doing tasks during the day to train the opposite side of the brain. It will help you in case you have a stroke on the dominant side of the brain. When reading this book, for example, you may want to try just for 10 minutes using your left hand to turn the pages. Lift more weights with your left hand. If you are driving a car, experiment with using the left hand a little more and relaxing the right hand slightly.

Another interesting experience is to take 5 minutes to practice printing your name with your left hand. Try it once with your left hand, and then print your first name with your right hand. Then go back and print your first name with your left hand three or four more times. By printing with your right hand and then going back to the left, you can compare the two. You will improve your skills by practicing three or four times. Then you can practice more by adding your last name. This week try writing your first name, and next week try writing your last name. In 3 or 4 weeks, you will have had a valuable experience in retraining yourself. This is helpful not only in retraining both sides of the brain but also in understanding the power of retraining your nervous system step by step. It takes 4 or 5 minutes each day, but it will be worth the time.

Individual and Societal Costs of Stress-Related Problems

I recommend providing PSR training for all high-risk groups. Minorities, particularly blacks, have twice the number of heart attacks that whites do. This may be due to their diet, but it may also have to do with their stresses. It is not only blacks who suffer, but most blue-collar workers. A study at DuPont found that from 1963 to 1982 there was a 38 percent reduction in the rate of fatal heart attacks among the large chemical companies' white-collar workers. There was only an 18 percent reduction, however, among the blue-collar workers. In general, blue-collar people are not as attentive to altering their life-styles. This was shown in several studies where they tended to eat, drink, and smoke more than white-collar workrs. This puts them at a higher risk for heart attacks and strokes.

Another example of diverse health versus wellness cost is the study by Michael Alderman, M.D., at the Montefiore Medical Center in New York. He estimated that if only 20 percent of individuals with hypertension were able to stop their medications, this would save $600 million per year. That is for just 20 percent of the people with high blood pressure. The amount spent on headaches, low back pain, and other pain syndromes could be reduced at least $5 to $6 billion. We could have much better health and more money to spend on other problems in our society if we could improve our health and reduce these medical costs.

How PSR Can Help

The PSR training can help you in dealing with medical problems or in avoiding serious medical symptoms or illness. One of the frightening prospects as we look at the future is the steady increase in costs for medical care. The same technology that is bringing about a great improvement in dealing with health problems also is quite expensive. Computers, CAT scanners, and sophisticated equipment to monitor babies all require tremendous amounts of money. The expense of kidney dialysis is in the billions; the cost for kidney and heart transplants can be even higher. Society will probably not choose to spend billions of dollars more for a heart transplant program. It is much better to do PSR training, physical exercise programs, and changes in diet to prevent the heart diseases and severe heart attacks that lead to a possibility of a heart transplant. I agree with the estimates that $20 to $25 billion per year may be saved by using stress management techniques like PSR.

If people do not take care of their health, it is quite clear that in the next decade there will be other forms of rationing of health care. This is already being done in many countries such as Sweden, France, and Britain. Unlike in the United States, elective surgery requires a wait of 1 to 3 years, or it may never be done. Certain countries have also instituted strict requirements for kidney dialysis and transplants because of the cost. As economists continue to stress the bottom line, cost becomes a larger factor in what the federal government, corporations, and private insurers will pay for.

The federal government and private companies are already suggesting putting people into new types of insurance plans, such as HMOs, where you no longer have a choice of whom your doctor will be. With many of these plans a doctor may have to choose the most inexpensive treatment, not the one that is best for you. With some of the criteria and plans for saving costs being pushed, you may get average care rather than the best care—the cheapest care rather than good care. These are real concerns and there are now several lawsuits concerning this "cost containment" issue at HMO. People are living longer, and if they do not take good care of themselves, they will have greater health costs after the age of 60 or 65.

Wellness programs, exercise, nonsmoking, and stress management practices may be required for health coverage or less expensive health coverage. The bottom line is that using PSR will save you money and it will also keep you healthier and give you more energy and longevity.

The Future of PSR

With PSR training children may be able to develop intellectual skills and integrate their animal wishes and drives. This will help produce a new generation of people who are less likely to become dependent upon drugs, to be negative, or to be depressed in their approach toward life. They'll be able to further integrate their minds, bodies, and emotions into healthy patterns that will help them enjoy the challenges of life.

It will also reduce the pretense of keeping up with the Joneses, jealousy, and other negative attitudes. If we train our children not to be on the attack or on the defensive in their lives (fight, flight, or freeze), they can take the middle ground with the PSR training. They can integrate their feelings and thoughts and see that other people also have similar feelings and thoughts. They can communicate with and understand the other person's emotions or overreactions. A calmer, healthier society will develop from these positive attributes, which are respected, admired, and useful in the world.

Even with PSR training you will be stressed, and symptoms might flare up once in a while. These flare-ups will be an opportunity for you to learn to use your skills more. Almost always they signal a problem or help explain the history of the symptom. You will usually come to understand these patterns and further reduce your symptoms.

You must remember, however, that you always will have response to stresses. If the phone rings, you are going to respond. Whether you jump in the air or turn to reach for the phone and say "Damn it, I'm busy now" will largely depend upon your use of the PSR and the number of stresses you are experiencing that day. By dampening or reducing the overreactions, you can pick up the phone and talk calmly and have an enjoyable phone call. If something is upsetting, you will do better by being calm, relaxed, and thoughtful. Remind yourself, "There is no emergency. Breathe and relax." You'll find you can negotiate better over the phone or in person. You can use a forceful tone or manner when needed but with the PSR you won't go on in a bad mood for hours or days.

Remember, you can now cope better by observing your tension and stress patterns because your mind and body will be reacting more calmly in identifying these stresses. Continue to keep learning from any stress reaction or overreaction. If you are an unusual person and your symptoms are not reduced, consult with your physician or go in for a physical checkup. You probably have a medical problem that requires medical consultation and treatment. You may need the addition of biofeedback or a more lengthy course of stress management training. Programs are now available throughout the country. Listed in the Appendix are organizations like the Behavioral Medicine Society and the Biofeedback Society of America, which have physicians and other health personnel who are well versed in treating major stress problems.

Also in the Appendix, I list some of the key articles reviewing the PSR training that is usually used as the first step to treat the problems we have discussed. These articles, many of them published in *Behavioral Medicine* and *Biofeedback and Self-Regulation*, discuss the use of some kind of biofeedback training and treatment which usually involve the PSR training.

We have billions of brain cells that allow us to monitor our bodies' reactions in the background, almost below the conscious level. You can consciously, preconsciously, and unconsciously attend to daily activities and be creative and active while remaining calm. Anchor the day with two good 15- to 20-minute PSR exercises. If it is a particularly busy day, then try to get one full exercise in and use the summary exercise. It can be done in as little time as 2, 3, or 4 minutes. You can also practice the fourth exercise after 4 to 5 weeks. Having memorized it, you can do this with your eyes open while you are waiting for an elevator or at a stoplight or on a bus or subway. There are many times during the day when you will be able to put in the fourth PSR exercise in 2 or 3 minutes.

The best times to do these exercises are in the morning before breakfast, before lunch, after work, in the middle of the evening, or just before bedtime. By having two solid anchor exercises each day, and using the short breathing checks and the fourth exercise several times during the day, you will discover a calmer and more energetic, creative you. Remember to breathe. Even one or two slow, paced breaths can calm you after you've learned PSR. In your private life you will be more sensitive, sensual, sexual, and satisfied. The PSR can lead you to be more successful in your daily life and to focus on the continuing challenges that appear each day. Remember, stress provides both an opportunity and a challenge to adapt and change (endure or triumph).

Summary

In terms of the future stresses of the world, the self-regulation and self-control idea of one's own mind and body is important. The other problems in the world are larger systems that respond to your nervous system. There is the level of you, your family, and friends, then your workplace and your town or city. After these, consider the state, the country, and the whole world as an interlocking system. Because of the nuclear threat, we are one world. A war in the Middle East affects all of us and poses a threat to all of us. In a similar way, the increased use of fossil fuels—causing acid rain, which destroys forests, leading to an increase in the earth's temperature, flooding, or other disasters—is a concern to all of us. The use of gases that are reducing the ozone level can lead to millions of skin cancers. That is why it is so important to try to have personal self-regulation, and then to see how it can spread to your town, your city or state, your country, and the world.

Some of these events take 10 to 30 years to develop. If we observe the possible changes, then truly "an ounce of prevention is worth a pound of cure." The Russians have found this with Chernobyl. Even a year after the accident they were still trying to handle the atomic radiation and high temperatures that exist in the ruined shell of that atomic reactor. An ounce more of prevention would have saved lives and millions, perhaps billions, of dollars. Let us hope we do not have to wait until tremendous disasters overtake us before we take proper action that will help each of us live in a healthy environment.

For those of you who are pessimistic, try to recall that a decade ago people were pessimistic about people taking up running and exercising. Now it has become a healthful life-style. This has produced a whole new industry of exercise clubs, fitness trainers, and wellness counselors in schools and corporations. A healthy "health industry" has been created. Another example of this is the federal government's response to public opinion on such issues as smoking. With the AMA and the American Cancer Society leading the way, smokers are now being put on the defensive. They are being told this is a danger, and if they wish to get lung cancer by smoking it is their business and they have to do it in selected areas. Only a decade ago people on planes were subjected to pipe and cigar smoke. I hope that soon they will not be subjected to any cigarette smoke. There are several national programs influencing people to exercise, eat a healthful diet, and use stress management. There have been programs in Massachusetts and Arizona trying to persuade whole communities of 40,000 to 50,000 people to lose weight, exercise, eat better, and learn to use stress management.

Your mind is an incredible organ. It thinks as well as running the physical and emotional functions of the whole body. By using your PSR skills you can strengthen this unique ability that the human being has to observe its own thinking and influence its pattern of reacting—the mental, physical, and emotional spheres. With PSR training you can be aware of any particular negative patterns and add a neutral and positive thought (feeling or expectation). This feeds back into the mental, emotional, and physical spheres, becoming another biofeedback loop where, by positive thinking, you affect your emotions and your physical reactions. In this way you can then read just your mental, physical, and emotional patterns by changing or influencing any one or all of these three factors. Thus, you can change your thinking with positive thinking (PSR thinking), your emotional reactions by being aware of your overreactions, and your physical reactions with the use of PSR.

These self-regulation techniques can be applied in many ways. One of the most important ways to change stress overreactions is to train children to use physiological feedback and stress management (PSR) early in their lives. You can use PSR for yourself and then encourage your loved ones and friends to develop the PSR skills. Then you can enjoy the stresses of life rather than suffer from them. When faced with a stressful situation, smile to yourself, take a breathing check of three to four slow, calm, paced breaths, and say to yourself, "Relax. There is no emergency. I can figure this out." Remember, a slow, calm, paced breathing pattern is about 8 to 10 breaths per minute. Stress never stops, but now you can deal with it better. Your mind, influencing the body with the skills of PSR, can create new patterns of reacting to and dealing with stress. You will be surprised how inventive and creative your mind can be when it is calm and using the PSR skills.

Calmer, healthier, more energetic people who do not overreact can better deal with their personal relationships and the larger problems in our ever-changing world.

APPENDIX

Suggested Reading

Basmajian, J. (Ed.). *Biofeedback: Principles and Practice for Clinicians* (2nd ed.). Baltimore: Williams and Wilkins, 1983.

Benson, H. *The Relaxation Response*. New York: Avon, 1976.

Berglass, S. *The Success Syndrome*. New York: Plenum, 1986.

Bryce, B. *The Love Muscle*. New York: New American Library, 1983.

Comfort, A. *The Joy of Sex: A Gourmet Guide to Lovemaking*. New York: Crown, 1972.

Cousins, N. *Anatomy of an Illness as Perceived by the Patient*. New York: Norton, 1979.

Culligan, M., & Sedlacek, K. *How to Avoid Stress before it Kills You*. New York: Gramercy, 1980.

Dement, W. *Some Must Watch while Some Must Sleep*. San Francisco: Freeman, 1982.

Eliot, R. *Stress and the Major Cardiovascular Disorders*. Mount Kisco, NY: Futura, 1979.

Field, T., McCabe, P., & Schneiderman, N. *Stress and Coping*. Hillsdale, NJ: Erlbaum, 1985.

Friedmam, M., & Rosenman, A. *Type A Behavior and Your Heart*. Greenwich, CT: Fawcett, 1974.

Jacobson, E. *You Must Relax, Progressive Relaxation*. Chicago: University of Chicago Press, 1938.

Kostrubala, T. *The Joy of Running*. Philadelphia: Lippincott, 1976.

Locke, S., & Culligan D. *The Healer Within*. New York: Mentor, 1987.

Luthe, W. (Ed.). *Autogenic Therapy* (Vols. 1–6). New York: Grune and Stratton, 1969.

Maddi, S., & Kobasa, S. *The Hardy Executive*. Chicago: Dorsey Professional Books, 1986.

Masters, W., & Johnson, V. *Human Sexual Response*. Boston: Little, Brown, 1966.

Masters, W., & Johnson, V. *Masters and Johnson on Sex and Human Loving*. Boston: Little, Brown, 1987.

McGuigan, F., Sime, W., & Wallace, J. (Eds.). *Stress and Tension Control 2*. New York: Plenum, 1984.

Met Life's Eat Well, Be Well Cookbook. New York: Simon & Schuster, Fireside Book Division, 1986.

Pearce, B. G. (Ed.). *Health Hazards of VDTs*. New York: Wiley, 1984.

Pelletier, K. *Mind as Healer, Mind as Slayer*. New York: Delacorte, 1977.

Sarno, J. *Mind over Back Pain*. New York: Berkley, 1986.

Schwartz, M., *Biofeedback—A Practitioner's Guide*. New York: Guilford Press, 1987.

Selye, H., *Stress Without Distress*. New York: Lippincott, 1974.

Stroebel, C. *Q R: The Quieting Reflex*. New York: Berkley, 1982.

Stress-Related Articles

HYPERTENSION

Blackwell, B., Bloomfield, S., Gartside, P., Robinson, A., Hanenson, I., Magenheim, H., Nidich, S., & Ziegler, R. Transcendental Meditation in Hypertension. *Lancet*, 1976, *January*, 223–226.

Blanchard, E. Andrasik, F., Acerra, M., Pallmeyer, T., Gerardi, R., Halpern, M., & Musso, A. Preliminary results from a controlled evaluation of thermal biofeedback as a treatment for essential hypertension. *Biofeedback and Self-Regulation*, 1984, *9*, 471–493.

Cohen, J., & Sedlacek, K. Attention and autonomic self-regulation. *Psychosomatic Medicine*, 1983, *45*, 243–257.

Engel, B. T., & Bleeker, E. R. Application of operant conditioning techniques to the control of the cardiac arrhythmias. In P. A. Obrist et al. (Eds.), *Cardiovascular Psychophysiology: Current Issues in Response Mechanisms, Biofeedback, and Methodology*. Chicago: Aldine, 1974, pp. 456–476.

Glasgow, M. S., Engel, B. T., & Gaarder, K. R. Behavioral treatment of high blood pressure. II. Acute and sustained effects of relaxation and systolic blood pressure biofeedback. *Psychosomatic Medicine.* 1982, *44*, 155–170.

Kristt, D. A., & Engel, B. T. Learned control of blood pressure in patients with high blood pressure. *Circulation,* 1975, *51*, 370–378.

Patel, C. Randomised controlled trials of yoga, and biofeedback in management of hypertension. *Lancet,* 1975, *July,* 93–95.

Patel, C. Biofeedback-aided relaxation and meditation in the management of hypertension. *Biofeedback and Self-Regulation,* 1977, *2,* 1–41.

Pickering, T. G., & Miller, N. E. Learned voluntary control of heart rate and rhythm in two subjects with premature ventricular contractions. *British Heart Journal,* 1977, *39,* 152–159.

Stone, R. A., & DeLeo, J. Psychotherapeutic control of hypertension. *New England Journal of Medicine,* 1976, *294,* 80–84.

Weiss, T., & Engel, B. T. Operant conditioning of heart rate in patients with premature ventricular contractions. *Psychosomatic Medicine* 1971, 33, 301–321.

HEADACHES

Adler, C. S., & Adler, S. M. Biofeedback and psychosomatic disorders. In J. V. Basmajian (Ed.). *Biofeedback: Principles and Practice for Clinicians* (2nd ed.) Baltimore: Williams and Wilkins, 1983.

Blanchard, E. B., Jaccard, J., Andrasik, R., Guarnier, K., & Jurish, S. E. Reduction in headache patients' medical expenses associated with biofeedback and relaxation treatments, *Biofeedback and Self-Regulation,* 1985, *10,* 63–68.

Budzynski, T. Biofeedback in the treatment of muscle-contraction (tension) headache. *Biofeedback and Self-Regulation,* 1978, *4,* 409–434.

Diamond, S., et al. The value of biofeedback in the treatment of chronic headache: A 5-year retrospective study. *Headache,* 1979, *19,* 90–96.

RAYNAUD'S DISEASE

Freedman, R., Lynn, S., Iannai, P., & Hale, P. Biofeedback treatment of Raynaud's disease and phenomena. *Biofeedback and Self-Regulation,* 1981, *6,* 355–364.

Mittelman, B., & Wolff, H. G., Affective states and skin temperatures: Experimental study of subjects with "cold hands" and Raynaud's syndrome. *Psychosomatic Medicine,* 1939, *1,* 271–292.

Raynaud, M. *New Researches on the Nature and Treatment of Local Asphyxia of the Extremities* (Barlox, Trans.). Selected Monographs. London: New Sydenham Society, 1888.

Sedlacek, K. Biofeedback for Raynaud's disease, *Psychosomatics,* 1979, *20,* 537–541.

Sedlacek, K. Biofeedback treatment of primary Raynaud's disease. In J. V. Basmajian (Ed.), *Biofeedback: Principles and Practice for Clinicians* (2nd ed.). Baltimore: Williams and Wilkins, 1983.

Surwit, R. S. Raynaud's disease. In L. Birk (Ed.), *Biofeedback and Behavioral Medicine.* New York: Grune and Stratton, 1973.

Taub, E. Self regulation of human tissue temperature. In J. E. Schwartz, & J. Beatty (Eds.), *Biofeedback: Theory and Research.* New York: Academic Press, 1977.

Taub, E., & Stroebel, C. F. Task Force Study Section Report: *Use of Biofeedback in the Treatment of Vasoconstrictive Syndromes.* Prepared for the Biofeedback Society of America, U.C.M.C. c 268, 4301 Owens Street, Wheat Ridge, CO 80033, May 1978.

STROKES

Benjamin, J. V., Kukulka, C. G., & Narayan, M. G. Biofeedback treatment of footdrop after stroke compared with standard rehabilitation technique: Effects on voluntary control and strength. *Archives of Physical Medicine and Rehabilitation,* 1975, *56,* 231–236.

Brundy, J., Korein, J., & Grynbaum, B. B. EMG feedback therapy: Review of 114 patients. *Archives of Physical Medicine and Rehabilitation,* 1976, *57,* 55–61.

Middaugh, S. J. EMG feedback as a muscle re-education technique: A controlled study. *Physical Therapy*, 1978, *58*, 15–22.

Wolf, S. L., Baker, M. P., & Kelly, J. L. EMG biofeedback in stroke: A 1-year follow-up on the effect of patient characteristics. *Archives of Physical Medicine and Rehabilitation*, 1980, *61*, 351–355.

BOWEL FUNCTION

Engel, B. T., Nikoomanesh, P., & Schuster, M. M. Operant conditioning of rectosphincter responses in the treatment of fecal incontinence. *New England Journal of Medicine*, 1978, *290*, 646–649.

Schneider, C. *Biofeedback treatment of irritable bowel syndrome*. Paper presented at the annual meeting of the Biofeedback Society of America, Denver, CO, March 1983.

Whitehead, W. E., Burgio, K. L., & Engel, B. T. Biofeedback treatment of fecal incontinence in geriatric patients. *Journal of the American Geriatric Society*, *33*, 320–324.

SEXUAL FUNCTIONING

Kegel, A. H. Sexual functions of the pubococcygeus muscle. *Western Journal of Surgery*, 1952, *50*, (10), 521–529.

Sedlacek, K., & Heczey, M. A specific biofeedback treatment for dysmenorrhea. *Biofeedback and Self-Regulation*, 1977, *12*, 294.

DIABETES

Rosenbaum, L. Biofeedback-assisted stress management for insulin-treated diabetes mellitus. *Biofeedback and Self-Regulation*, 1983, *8*, 519–533.

LOW BACK PAIN AND BRUXISM

Nigl, A. J., & Fischer-Williams, M. Treatment of low back strain with electromyographic biofeedback and relaxation training. *Pychosomatics*, 1981, *21*, 429–499.

Sofberg, W. K., & Rugh, J. D. The use of biofeedback drives in the treatment of bruxism. *Journal of the Southern California Dental Association*, 1972, *40*, 852–853.

CANCER

Burish, T., Shartner, C., & Lyles, J. Effectiveness of multiple-site EMG biofeedback and relaxation training in reducing the aversiveness of cancer chemotherapy. *Biofeedback and Self-Regulation*, 1981, *6*, 523–535.

Case, C., Schendler, C, Baught, T, et al. (Eds.). *The Breast Cancer Report: A Guide to Medical Care, Emotional Support, Educational Programs and Resources* (2nd ed.). NIH Publication No. 80-1691, Bethesda, MD, 1984.

TINNITUS

Grossman, M. Treatment of subjective tinnitus with biofeedback. *ENT Journal* 1976, *55*, 22–30.

House, J. W. Treatment of severe tinnitus with biofeedback training. *Laryngoscope*, 1978, *88*, 406–412.

ARTHRITIS

Achterberg, J., McGraw, P., & Lawlis, G. F. Rheumatoid arthritis: A study of relaxation and temperature biofeedback training as an adjunctive therapy. *Biofeedback and Self-Regulation*, 1981, *6*, 207–223.

STRESS

Glass, D. C., Krakoff, L. R., Contrada, R., Holton, W. F., Kehoe, K., Mannucci, E. G., Collins, C., Snow, B., & Elting, E. Effect of harassment and competition upon cardiovascular and plasma catecholamine response in type A and type B individuals. *Psychophysiology*, 1980, *17*, 118, 121.

AIRSICKNESS

Levy, R., Jones, D., & Carlson, E. Biofeedback rehabilitation of airsick aircrew. *Aviation, Space and Environmental Medicine*, 1981, *February*, 1981, 118–121.

Organizations

Alcoholics Anonymous, General Services Board of AA, 468 Park Avenue South, New York, NY 10016.

American Association of Sex Educators, Counselors and Therapists (AASECT), 11 Dupont Circle, NW, Suite 220, Washington, DC; (202) 462-1171.

American Cancer Society, 4 West 35 Street, New York, NY 10001.

Ameican Health Foundation, 320 East 43 Street, New York, NY 10007; (212) 953-1900.

American Heart Association, NYC Affiliate, Department C, 205 East 42 Street, New York, NY 10017.

Arthritis Foundation, 1314 Spring Street, NW, Atlanta, GA 30309; (404) 872-7100.

Impotence Information Center, Department USA, P.O. Box 9, Minneapolis, MN 55040; 1-800-843-4315.

National Council on Alcoholism, 12 West 21 Street, New York, NY 10010; (212) 206-6770. There are local branches throughout the United States.

YMCA of USA, 101 North Wacker Drive, Chicago, IL 60606; 1-800-USA YMCA

Audiocassettes and Biofeedback Information

Behavioral Medicine Society, P.O. Box 4119, Lynchburg, VA 24502-0119.

Biofeedback Society of America, 10200 West 44th Avenue, Suite 304, Wheat Ridge, CO 80033.

Futurehealth, Inc., P.O. Box 947, Bensalem, PA 19020, (215) 639-2430.

Menninger Foundation, Biofeedback and Psychophysiology Center, Box 829, Topeka, KS 66601-0829.

Sensory Environment Engineers (SEE), Attention: Sandy Ballard, P.O. Box 8309, Newport Beach, CA 92660.

Stress Regulation Institute, 239 East 79 Street, New York, NY 10021, (212) 288-9309. Four audiocassettes, eight sides, one with music, are available which complement this book.

Elizabeth Stroebel, 119 Forest Drive, Wethersfield, CT 06019.

INDEX